TRANSPORTATION ENGINEERING (THEORY & PRACTICE)

AUTHOR (S)

Dr. Raji A. K
Professor & Head (Retd.), Dept. of Civil Engineering, NSS College of Engineering, Palakkad - 678 008, Kerala.

Dr. K. K. Babu
Professor (Retd.), Dept. of Civil Engineering, NSS College of Engineering, Palakkad - 678 008, & Former Director, Sreepathy Institute of Management and Technology, Palakkad, Kerala.

REVIEWER

Dr. Mridula
Associate Professor, Dept. of Civil Engineering, College of Engineering Roorkee, Roorkee- 247667, Uttarakhand.

KHANNA BOOK PUBLISHING CO. (P) Ltd.
4C/4344, Ansari Road, Darya Ganj, New Delhi, India

All India Council for Technical Education
Nelson Mandela Marg, Vasant Kunj, New Delhi, India

Dear Readers,

To prevent the piracy, this book is secured with HIGH SECURITY HOLOGRAM on the front title cover. In case you don't find the hologram on the front cover title, please write us to at contact@khannabooks.com or whatsapp us at +91-99109 09320 and avail special gift voucher for yourself.

Specimen of Hologram on front Cover title:

Moreover, there is a SPECIAL DISCOUNT COUPON for you with EVERY HOLOGRAM.

How to avail this SPECIAL DISCOUNT:

Step 1: Scratch the hologram

Step 2: Under the scratch area, your "coupon code" is available

Step 3: Logon to www.khannabooks.com

Step 4: Use your "coupon code" in the shopping cart and get your copy at a special discount

Step 5: Enjoy your reading!

ISBN: 978-93-5538-677-9

Book Code: DIP465EN

Transportation Engineering (Theory and Practice)

by Dr. Raji A.K. and Dr. K.K. Babu

First Edition: 2026

Originally Published by:

All India Council for Technical Education, Ministry of Education, GOI

Exclusively Published & Distributed by:

Khanna Book Publishing Co. (P) Ltd.

4C/4344, Ansari Road, Daryaganj,
New Delhi (INDIA)

Visit us at: **www.khannabooks.com**

Write us at: **contact@khannabooks.com**

To view complete list of books, Please scan the QR Code:

KPH

Printed in Bharat.

प्रो. टी. जी. सीताराम
अध्यक्ष
Prof. T. G. Sitharam
Chairman

सत्यमेव जयते

आज़ादी का अमृत महोत्सव

अखिल भारतीय तकनीकी शिक्षा परिषद्
(भारत सरकार का एक सांविधिक निकाय)
(शिक्षा मंत्रालय, भारत सरकार)
नेल्सन मंडेला मार्ग, वसंत कुंज, नई दिल्ली–110070
दूरभाष : 011–26131498
ई–मेल : chairman@aicte-india.org

ALL INDIA COUNCIL FOR TECHNICAL EDUCATION
(A STATUTORY BODY OF THE GOVT. OF INDIA)
(Ministry of Education, Govt. of India)
Nelson Mandela Marg, Vasant Kunj, New Delhi-110070
Phone : 011-26131498
E-mail : chairman@aicte-india.org

FOREWORD

Engineers are the backbone of any modern society. They are the ones responsible for the marvels as well as the improved quality of life across the world. Engineers have driven humanity towards greater heights in a more evolved and unprecedented manner.

The All India Council for Technical Education (AICTE), have spared no efforts towards the strengthening of the technical education in the country. AICTE is always committed towards promoting quality Technical Education to make India a modern developed nation emphasizing on the overall welfare of mankind.

An array of initiatives has been taken by AICTE in last decade which have been accelerated now by the National Education Policy (NEP) 2020. The implementation of NEP under the visionary leadership of Hon'ble Prime Minister of India envisages the provision for education in regional languages to all, thereby ensuring that every graduate becomes competent enough and is in a position to contribute towards the national growth and development through innovation & entrepreneurship.

One of the spheres where AICTE had been relentlessly working since past couple of years is providing high quality original technical contents at Under Graduate & Diploma level prepared and translated by eminent educators in various Indian languages to its aspirants. For students pursuing 2nd year of their Engineering education, AICTE has identified 87 books, which shall be translated into 12 Indian languages - Hindi, Tamil, Gujarati, Odia, Bengali, Kannada, Urdu, Punjabi, Telugu, Marathi, Assamese & Malayalam. In addition to the English medium, books in different Indian Languages are going to support the students to understand the concepts in their respective mother tongue.

On behalf of AICTE, I express sincere gratitude to all distinguished authors, reviewers and translators from the renowned institutions of high repute for their admirable contribution in a record span of time.

AICTE is confident that these outcomes based original contents shall help aspirants to master the subject with comprehension and greater ease.

(Prof. T. G. Sitharam)

ACKNOWLEDGEMENT

The authors are grateful to the authorities of AICTE, particularly Prof. T. G. Sitharam, Chairman; Prof. M. P. Poonia, Vice-Chairman; Prof. Rajive Kumar, Member-Secretary; and Dr. Amit Kumar Srivastava, Director, Faculty Development Cell; for their planning to publish the book on "Transportation Engineering (Theory & Practice)". The valuable contributions of the reviewer of the book, **Dr. Mridula,** Associate Professor, Department of Civil Engineering, College of Engineering Roorkee, Roorkee-247667, Uttarakhand, in making it student-friendly and giving it a better shape in an artistic manner, are sincerely acknowledged. The prompt response and the subtle comments made by her during the process of review are greatly appreciated and gratefully acknowledged.

The authors are thankful to Ms. Aswathy E (their former student), and Rahul, Vignesh, and Lakshmi (children of the first author) for diligently preparing the figures and QR codes used in the text. The authors wish to express their gratitude to their family for their active support, constant inspiration, and perseverance.

This book is an outcome of various suggestions by AICTE members, experts, and authors who shared their opinions and thoughts to develop further engineering education in our country. Acknowledgements are due to the contributors and different workers in this field whose published books, review articles, papers, photographs, footnotes, references, and other valuable information enriched us at the time of writing the book.

Dr. Raji A. K,

Dr. K. K. Babu

PREFACE

This textbook on "Transportation Engineering (Theory & Practice)" is primarily intended for second-year Diploma course under the AICTE curriculum. The contents are organised to give comprehensive coverage of highway engineering and railway engineering. Meanwhile, the development of transportation infrastructure in our nation is surging ahead. The vehicle population, in both urban and rural areas, has been increasing at an alarming rate in recent years. The government has also realised the necessity of implementing major projects in the transport sector, comprising all modes, to cater to the increasing travel demand. Hence, it is imperative to equip professionals with knowledge of the latest as well as conventional practices in transportation engineering.

Furthermore, it should be noted that the contents of the book are designed and presented in line with the principles of implementation of outcome-based education, as suggested by the AICTE. Thus, at least five unit outcomes are specifically defined at the start of every unit, and their mapping with the specified course outcomes is given for the beneficiaries of the book, in order to attain the final programme outcomes specified by the AICTE for the *Diploma level course. The contents*, comprising of five units, are presented lucidly, and they cover the entire syllabus exactly as per the AICTE Model Curriculum. It includes a wide range of topics, of which the first three units are dedicated to highway engineering and the remaining two units are for railways. In the highway engineering section, it starts with an overview, followed by geometric design of highways, materials, and construction of highways. Whereas in the railway engineering section, it covers topics like basics of railway engineering as well as the geometrics, construction, and maintenance of railways. In every unit, numerous multiple-choice questions with answers, short and long-answer questions, including numerical problems and practical exercises that are pertinent to the contents of the unit, are added. It should be noted that several sections include dynamic QR codes for supplementary reading, which can be scanned for useful supporting information. At the end of the unit, apart from Practical, Unit Summary, and Exercises, there is also a special section called "KNOW MORE" that has been thoughtfully created to offer readers access to additional information pertinent to the unit. This section mostly includes several "activities" for the students to familiarise themselves with the topics they have studied, as well as some "interesting facts" relating to the contents of the unit to create inquisitiveness and curiosity in them. There is a separate list of "references and suggested readings" in each unit, in addition to the "references for further learning" given at the end of the book. Figures and explanations are extensively provided to give a grounding in the principles of transportation engineering. Wherever required, a number of illustrative numerical problems are given for a better understanding of the topic. The vast experience gained by the authors in teaching, research, and consultancy has enabled them to include the latest developments and specifications in different areas of transportation engineering. Though the book primarily addresses the needs of diploma level students in Civil Engineering, it will be equally useful for under-graduate students and practising engineers.

It is genuinely hoped that the book will inspire students to study and discuss the concepts and principles of transportation engineering, which will undoubtedly help them to create a strong foundation in the subject. Working on the various topics covered in the book was, in fact, a great pleasure. Any constructive criticism and suggestions from the users of the book that will help improve it in the subsequent versions, are greatly appreciated. The comments may be mailed to rajiudayakumar@gmail.com. Dedicating this book to the teachers and students makes the authors incredibly happy.

Dr. Raji A. K,
Dr. K. K. Babu

OUTCOME BASED EDUCATION

For the implementation of an outcome-based education the first requirement is to develop an outcome based curriculum and incorporate an outcome based assessment in the education system. By going through outcome-based assessments, evaluators will be able to evaluate whether the students have achieved the outlined standard, specific and measurable outcomes. With the proper incorporation of outcome based education there will be a definite commitment to achieve a minimum standard for all learners without giving up at any level. At the end of the programme running with the aid of outcome-based education, a student will be able to arrive at the following outcomes:

Programme Outcomes (POs) are statements that describe what students are expected to know and be able to do upon graduating from the program. These relate to the skills, knowledge, analytical ability attitude and behaviour that students acquire through the program. The POs essentially indicate what the students can do from subject-wise knowledge acquired by them during the program. As such, POs define the professional profile of an engineering diploma graduate.

National Board of Accreditation (NBA) has defined the following seven POs for an Engineering diploma graduate:

PO1. Basic and Discipline specific knowledge: Apply knowledge of basic mathematics, science and engineering fundamentals and engineering specialization to solve the engineering problems.

PO2. Problem analysis: Identify and analyses well-defined engineering problems using codified standard methods.

PO3. Design/ development of solutions: Design solutions for well-defined technical problems and assist with the design of systems components or processes to meet specified needs.

PO4. Engineering Tools, Experimentation and Testing: Apply modern engineering tools and appropriate technique to conduct standard tests and measurements.

PO5. Engineering practices for society, sustainability and environment: Apply appropriate technology in context of society, sustainability, environment and ethical practices.

PO6. Project Management: Use engineering management principles individually, as a team member or a leader to manage projects and effectively communicate about well-defined engineering activities.

PO7. Life-long learning: Ability to analyse individual needs and engage in updating in the context of technological changes.

SYLLABUS

Transportation Engineering: Theory & Practice

(The syllabus for theory is exactly as per the AICTE Model Curriculum)

IV Sem.	CEPC208	Transportation Engineering	2L+0T+0P	2 credits
IV Sem.	CEPC218	Transportation Engineering Lab	0L+0T+2P	1 credit

COURSE OBJECTIVES:

Following are the objectives of this course:

1. To identify the types of roads as per IRC recommendations.
2. To understand the geometrical design features of different highways.
3. To perform different tests on road materials.
4. To identify the components of railway tracks.

PROPOSED COURSE CONTENT:

Unit I: Overview of Highway Engineering:

- Role of transportation in the development of nation, Scope and Importance of roads in India and its Characteristics.
- Different modes of transportation: land way, waterway, airway. Merits and demerits of roadway and railway.
- General classification of roads.
- Selection and factors affecting road alignment.

Unit II: Geometric Design of Highway:

- Camber: Definition, purpose, types as per IRC - recommendations.
- Kerbs: Road margin, road formation, right of way.
- Design speed and various factors affecting design speed as per IRC - recommendations.
- Gradient: Definition, types as per IRC - Recommendations.
- Sight distance (SSD): Definition, types IRC - recommendations, simple numerical.
- Curves: Necessity, types: Horizontal, vertical curves.
- Extra widening of roads: numerical examples.
- Super elevation: Definition, formula for calculating minimum and maximum Super elevation and method of providing super-elevation.
- Standards cross-sections of national highway in embankment and cutting.

Unit III: Construction of Road Pavements:

- Types of road materials and their Tests: Test on aggregates - Flakiness and Elongation, Index tests, Angularity Number test, test on Bitumen-penetration, Ductility, Flash and Fire point test and Softening point test.
- Pavement: Definition, Types, Structural Components of pavement and their functions.
- Construction of WBM road. Merits and demerits of WBM & WMM road.
- Construction of Flexible pavement / Bituminous Road, Types of Bitumen and its properties, Emulsion, Cutback, Tar, Terms used in BR-prime coat, tack coat seal coat. Merits and Demerits of BR.
- Cement concrete road: methods of construction. Alternate and Continuous Bay Method. Construction joints, filler and sealers, merits and demerits of concrete road. Types of joints.

Unit IV: Basics of Railway Engineering:

- Classification of Indian Railways, zones of Indian Railways.
- Permanent way: Ideal requirement. Components, Railway Gauge. Types, factors affecting selection of a gauge.
- Rail, Rail Joints, requirements, types.
- Creep of rail: causes and prevention.
- Sleepers: functions and Requirement, types - concrete sleepers and their density.
- Ballast: function and types, suitability.
- Rail fixtures and fastenings: fish plate, spikes, bolts, keys, bearing plates, chairs-types of anchors.

Unit- V: Track geometrics, Construction and Maintenance

- Alignment: Factors governing rail alignment.
- Track Cross sections: Standard cross section of single and double line in cutting and embankment. Important terms-permanent land, formation width, side drains.
- Railway Track Geometrics: Gradient, curves, types and factors affecting grade compensation, super elevation, limits of super elevation cant deficiency, negative cant, coning of wheel, tilting of rail.
- Branching of tracks: points and crossings, turn out - types, components functions and inspection, track junctions crossover scissor cross over diamond crossing, track triangle
- Station: Purpose requirement of railway stations, important technical terms, types of railway stations, factors affecting site selections for railway stations.
- Station Yard: Classifications - Passenger, goods, locomotive and marshalling yards
- Track maintenance: Necessity classification, tools required for track maintenance with their functions, organisation of track maintenance, duties of permanent way inspector, gang mate and key man.

LIST OF EXPERIMENTS

1. Draw the sketches showing standard cross sections of expressways Freeways, NH/SH, MDR/ODR.
2. Flakiness and Elongation Index of aggregates.
3. Angularity number of aggregates.
4. Aggregate impact test.
5. Los Angeles Abrasion test.
6. Aggregate crushing test.
7. Softening point test of bitumen.
8. Penetration test of bitumen.
9. Flash and fire point of bitumen.
10. Ductility test of bitumen.
11. Visit the constructed road for visual inspection to identify the defects and suggest remedial measures.
12. Prepare the photographic report containing details for experiment No.11
13. Visit the hill road constructed site to understand its components
14. Prepare the photographic report containing details for experiment No.13
15. Visit the road of any one type (flexible or rigid) to know the drainage condition.
16. Prepare the photographic report suggesting the possible repairs and maintenance for experiment No.15.
17. Visit the railway track for visual inspection of fixtures, fasteners and yards.
18. Prepare the photographic report containing details for experiment No.17.

REFERENCES AND SUGGESTED READINGS

1. Kadiyali L. R., 'Transportation Engineering', Khanna Book Publishing Co., 2018.
2. Khanna S. K., Justo C. E. G., Veeraraghavan A., 'Highway Engineering', Nem Chand & Bros., Roorkee, 2014.
3. Arora N. L., 'Transportation Engineering', New India Pub., 1977.
4. Saxena S. C. and Arora S. P., 'A Textbook of Railway Engineering', Dhanpat Rai Publication.
5. Birdi, Ahuja, 'Road, Railways and Tunnel Engineering', Standard Book House, New Delhi.
6. Sharma S..K., 'Principles, Practice and Design of Highway Engineering', S. Chand Publishing, 2014.
7. Duggal Ajay K. and Puri V. P., 'Laboratory Manual in Highway Engineering', New Age International (P) Limited Publishers, New Delhi.
8. Subramanian K. P., 'Transportation Engineering', Scitech Publications, Chennai, 2015.

COURSE OUTCOMES

By the end of the course the students are expected to learn:

CO-1: To identify the types of roads as per IRC recommendations.

CO-2: To implement the geometrical design features of different highways.

CO-3: To perform different tests on road materials.

CO-4: To identify the components of railway tracks.

CO-5: To identify the defects in railway tracks.

Mapping of Course Outcomes with Programme Outcomes

Course Outcomes	Expected Mapping with Programme Outcomes (1- Weak Correlation; 2- Medium correlation; 3- Strong Correlation)						
	PO-1	**PO-2**	**PO-3**	**PO-4**	**PO-5**	**PO-6**	**PO-7**
CO-1	3	2	2	2	2	2	2
CO-2	3	3	3	3	1	3	3
CO-3	3	2	3	3	1	3	3
CO-4	3	2	2	3	2	2	2
CO-5	3	3	3	3	2	3	3

GUIDELINES FOR TEACHERS

To implement Outcome Based Education (OBE), knowledge level and skill set of the students should be enhanced. Teachers should take a major responsibility for the proper implementation of OBE. Some of the responsibilities (not limited to) for the teachers in OBE system may be as follows:

- Within reasonable constraint, they should manoeuvre time to the best advantage of all students.
- They should assess the students only upon certain defined criterion without considering any other potential ineligibility to discriminate them.
- They should try to grow the learning abilities of the students to a certain level before they leave the institute.
- They should try to ensure that all the students are equipped with the quality knowledge as well as competence after they finish their education.
- They should always encourage the students to develop their ultimate performance capabilities.
- They should facilitate and encourage group work and team work to consolidate newer approach.
- They should follow Blooms taxonomy in every part of the assessment.

Bloom's Taxonomy

Level	Teacher should Check	Student should be able to	Possible Mode of Assessment
Create	Students ability to create	Design or Create	Mini project
Evaluate	Students ability to justify	Argue or Defend	Assignment
Analyse	Students ability to distinguish	Differentiate or Distinguish	Project/Lab Methodology
Apply	Students ability to use information	Operate or Demonstrate	Technical Presentation/ Demonstration
Understand	Students ability to explain the ideas	Explain or Classify	Presentation/Seminar
Remember	Students ability to recall (or remember)	Define or Recall	Quiz

GUIDELINES FOR STUDENTS

Students should take equal responsibility for implementing the OBE. Some of the responsibilities (not limited to) for the students in OBE system are as follows:

- Students should be well aware of each UO before the start of a unit in each and every course.
- Students should be well aware of each CO before the start of the course.
- Students should be well aware of each PO before the start of the programme.
- Students should think critically and reasonably with proper reflection and action.
- Learning of the students should be connected and integrated with practical and real life consequences.
- Students should be well aware of their competency at every level of OBE.

ABBREVIATIONS AND SYMBOLS

List of Abbreviations

General Terms			
Abbreviation	**Full form**	**Abbreviation**	**Full form**
AADT	Annual Average Daily Traffic	IRB	Indian Railway Board
AEN	Assistant Engineers	IRC	Indian Roads Congress
AN	Angularity Number	IRI	International Roughness Index
ANC	Actual Nose Of Crossing	ISD	Intermediate Sight Distance
ATS	Actual Toe Of Switch	MC	Medium Curing Cutback Bitumen
BC	Bituminous Concrete	MDR	Major District Roads
BG	Broad Gauge	MG	Metre Gauge
BH	Bull Headed Rails	MoRT&H	Ministry Of Road Transport & Highways
BM	Bituminous Macadam	MSA	Million Standard Axles
CBE	Chief Bridge Engineer	NG	Narrow Gauge
CBR	California Bearing Ratio	NH	National Highways
CG	Centre of Gravity	NHAI	National Highways Authority Of India
CGE	Chief Engineer General	NHDP	National Highway Development Programme
CO	Course Outcome	NTPC	National Transport Policy Committee
CPDE	Chief Engineer Planning and Design	OBE	Outcome Based Education
CRRI	Central Road Research Institute	ODR	Other District Roads
CTE	Chief Track Engineer	OHE	Over Head Equipment
DBM	Dense Graded Bituminous Macadam	OSD	Overtaking Sight Distance
DEN	Divisional Engineer	PA	Passenger Address
DH	Dumb-Bell Or Double Headed Rails	PCU	Passenger Car Units
DSE	Divisional Superintending Engineers	PO	Program Outcome
EI	Elongation Index	PWI	Permanent Way Inspector
EIA	Environmental Impact Assessment	QR	Quick Response
FF	Flat Footed Rails	RC	Rapid Curing
FI	Flakiness Index	SC	Slow Curing

General Terms			
Abbreviation	**Full form**	**Abbreviation**	**Full form**
G	Gauge of track	SDBC	Semi Dense Bituminous Concrete
GDP	Gross Domestic Product	SEA	Switch Entry Angle
GMT	Gross Million Tonne per km per annum	SH	State Highways
HCV	Heavy Commercial Vehicle	Sr DEN	Senior Divisional Engineers
HRB	Highway Research Board	SSD	Stopping Sight Distance
HSD	Head light Sight Distance	TNC	Theoretical Nose Of Crossing
HV	Hourly Volume	UO	Unit Outcome
IR	Indian Railways		

LIST OF FIGURES

LIST OF TABLES

CONTENTS

UNIT 1
OVERVIEW OF HIGHWAY ENGINEERING

UNIT SPECIFICS

This unit covers the following aspects:

- Role of transportation in the development of a nation
- Different modes of transportation
- Merits and Demerits of roadway and railway
- Scope and importance of roads in India
- Characteristics of Road Transport
- Classification of roads
- Highway Alignment
- Factors controlling alignment of highways
- Selection of the best alignment of highways

A large number of multiple choice questions relevant to the topics covered in the unit as well as questions of short and long answer types, a list of references and suggested readings are given in the unit, so that one can go through them for practice. It is important to note that two dynamic QR codes are provided in different sections for more information on interesting topics which can be scanned for relevant supportive information. There is also a section called "KNOW MORE" that has been carefully designed so that the additional information provided in this part is useful to the users of the book. This section mainly contains some 'Activities' for the students to make them conversant with the topics he/she had studied, a timeline that begins with the development of the concerned topics up to the recent time, some interesting historical facts related with the contents of the unit.

RATIONALE

Road transport is one of the vital modes of transportation having desirable qualities like flexibility of travel, variety in usage of vehicles, and accessibility to remote areas. The road users are mainly concerned with smooth and comfortable riding quality, and high operating speed with safety in travel. The rapid growth in road traffic poses many challenging problems to the highway engineers in planning, design, construction and maintenance of the road infrastructure. Because of the consistent research and development activities going on worldwide in the field highway engineering, scientific and innovative solutions for many challenging issues are coming up. These include the use of better performing materials, improved structural design methods, advanced construction and maintenance practices, improved road safety/ traffic management measures, and so on.

UNIT OUTCOMES

After completing this unit, student will be able

U1-O1: To recognize the role of transportation system in the economic development of a nation.

U1-O2: To identify the relative merits and demerits of different modes of transport.

U1-O3: To identify the significance and characteristics of road transport in India.

U1-O4: To identify the type of road as per IRC recommendations

U1-O5: To select the best alignment of the proposed road from different alternatives.

Unit-1 Outcomes	**EXPECTED MAPPING WITH COURSE OUTCOMES** (1- Weak Correlation, 2-Medium Correlation, 3- Strong Correlation)				
	CO-1	CO-2	CO-3	CO-4	CO-5
U1-O1	3	1	-	1	-
U1-O2	3	2	-	-	-
U1-O3	3	2	-	1	-
U1-O4	3	3	-	-	-
U1-O5	2	2	1	-	-

1.1 ROLE OF TRANSPORTATION IN THE DEVELOPMENT OF A NATION

Transportation deals with the movement of men and/or goods from one place to another. The advancement in the transportation system is closely related with the development and well-being of a society. Transport has long been responsible for the development of civilization by meeting people's travel needs and goods transportation needs. The important roles played by any transportation system can be summarized as follows:

(i) **Economic Role**: Transportation system links places of production and consumption of goods and services at an economical cost. Increased productivity of agricultural and industrial products and their distribution through efficient transportation system can lower the cost of products. It also increases the employment opportunities.

(ii) **Social Role**: Transportation system facilitates social interaction, movement for education/ health/ recreation/ other social activities

(iii) **Spatial Development Role**: It facilitates area and infrastructure development for housing/ industrial/ educational and other activities.

(iv) **Cultural Role:** It enhances civilization, urbanization, education and enlightenment.

(v) **Political Role**: It promotes national integration, supports defence of the country, and helps to maintain law and order.

(vi) **Environmental Role**: Environmental role is generally a negative one. It leads to environmental pollution (air, water and noise pollution, vibrations), fuel consumption, lack of safety to life, increased consumption of land, etc.

(vii) **Others**: Transportation planning contributes to the aesthetics of the region. It also affects social life and pattern of a community. Planning and constructing new transport infrastructure requires relocation of residents.

1.2 DIFFERENT MODES OF TRANSPORTATION

The different modes of transportation can generally be classified as follows:

i. Land – Highways, railways, pipelines, conveyors, aerial ropeways

ii. Air – Airways

iii. Water – Waterways like river ways, canal ways, ocean ways

1.3 MERITS AND DEMERITS OF ROADWAYS AND RAILWAYS

1.3.1 Roadways

Merits

- Provides greater flexibility of travel
- Accommodates different classes of vehicles as well as pedestrians
- Provides door- to- door service for both passenger and freight movement
- Acts as feeder system for other modes of transport.

Demerits

- Consumes greater energy per passenger km and ton km than railways or waterways
- Rate of emissions of pollutants is higher than that of other modes of transport.
- Because of the flexibility of movement with a wide range of travel speeds along the same roadway, road transport is more prone to accidents compared to other modes. But, in other modes, even with various safety measures taken, major accidents do occur, which are more grievous.

1.3.2 Railways

Merits

- Since the resistance of steel wheels of railway wagons on railway track is much lower than the resistance of rubber tyres of vehicles on uneven road surface, the energy requirement for traction per unit weight of load is very less. Hence, bulk movement on long hauls through railways is more economical, compared to road transport.

- Railways can act as a high-speed public transportation system for suburban-to-urban travel and intra-urban travel.
- Lesser amount of emissions per unit weight of goods or passengers to be transported, if diesel locomotives being used, and negligible emissions in the case of electrified track.

Demerits

- To access intermediate parts and localities between stations, a feeder system is required.
- Less flexible as compared to roadways in terms of fixed time tables and routes
- Construction and maintenance cost is more than roadways.

Therefore, an integrated rail-cum-road network is essential for a developing country like India, to conserve energy and money.

1.4 SCOPE AND IMPORTANCE OF ROADS IN INDIA

For the integrated development of any country, a well-planned road network connecting all villages, district head quarters and commercial centres is very essential. Also, it is important to develop major highways and expressways connecting important urban, industrial and commercial centres for enhancing the mobility of travel. Thus, for a developing country like India, in order to meet the increasing travel demand, the road transportation system has to be upgraded in terms of quantity and quality, which in turn would result in increased employment potential as well as Gross Domestic Product (GDP).

In general, the roads in India perform the following functions to achieve the overall economic growth of the country through:

Rural connectivity – Since India is an agriculturally predominant country, connectivity to villages is essential for the economic and social uplift of the rural community, which can be accomplished only through a good system of road network.

Transportation in Hilly areas: A considerable portion of area covered in our country belongs to hilly or steep terrain, where the best feasible mode of transportation is roads for effective connectivity.

Strategic Importance: The defense of the country at borders depends greatly on road system available.

Freight and passenger traffic share: Short and medium distance passenger/freight traffic is taken care of by road network.

Forestry and Marine Products Trade: Trade and commerce related with forestry and marine products is facilitated through proper link roads penetrating the forests, and also along the coast line.

Tourism Development: Tourist centres can be well connected by proper road system.

Employment Potential: Employment opportunities can be will be enhanced with the development road sector.

Famine and flood relief: To relieve the hardships due to flood and famine, road system is highly beneficial.

Administrative convenience: For administrative convenience and maintenance of law and order, a good road system is essential.

1.5 CHARACTERISTICS OF ROAD TRANSPORT

As discussed in section 1.3.1, among all modes of transportation, road transport is the most accessible one for the movement of people or freight. Any class of vehicles, whether personal or public transport and also the pedestrians can make use of the road system. Also, the road network system could serve well the very remote villages or difficult terrains or even far-flung border areas located in high altitudes. Because of this flexibility, road transport gained maximum acceptability.

The characteristics of road transport can be briefly listed as below:

Advantages

i. Wide geographical coverage provided by Roads: Roads can be constructed to make a way into any interior places irrespective of terrain /topography conditions.

ii. Usage by wide variety of vehicles: Roads are used by different classes of vehicles like cars, buses, trucks, 3-wheelers, 2-wheelers, pedal cycles and animal drawn vehicles, and also the pedestrians.

iii. Low capital investment: Road transport infrastructure requires the lowest capital cost as well as maintenance cost, compared to other modes of transport. Even the best road is cheaper than a railway line.

iv. Quick and assured deliveries of articles are possible through road transport.

v. Road transport offers flexibility of service by any number of buses or trucks, flexibility in timings of travel, flexibility of routes of travel, and flexibility in the usage of personalized vehicles.

vi. Road transport offers door-to-door service from origin to destination, free from transshipments. For short hauls, road transport is the most economical one too.

vii. Road transport permits simpler packaging of goods.

viii. Road transport offers high employment opportunities.

Disadvantages

i. Road transport is more prone to accidents

ii. Road transport is one of the major sources of environmental pollution – in terms of noise, fumes, vibration, loss of aesthetics, ribbon development and clutter of advertisements along roadsides.

iii. Road transport leads to parking problems in urban areas.

iv. Road transport is not economical as that of railways for long hauls and high tonnage.

v. Road transport consumes more energy per passenger-kilometer and ton-kilometer than rail transport.

1.6 CLASSIFICATION OF ROADS

The different criteria adopted for classification of roads are listed below:

a) Seasonal condition in the usage of roads

b) Provision of surfacing on roads

c) Intensity of traffic volume

d) Load transported or tonnage

e) Location and function.

SCAN ME
for
Road Development Plans
in India

Of the above, the widely accepted criterion, and the one followed by the Ministry of Road Transport & Highways (MoRT&H) is 'location and function'. Thus, in the First Road Development Plan of India (Nagpur Plan 1943-'63), road classification was defined based on location and function, and it remained unchanged during the Second Plan (Bombay Plan 1961-'81). Later, the definition was modified in the Third Road Development Plan (Lucknow Plan 1981-2001).

Classification:

➢ Based on whether the roads can be used during different seasons of the year:

i. All-weather roads – negotiable during all seasons i.e. it remains functional irrespective of weather conditions

ii. Fair-weather roads – can be used during fair weather (dry season) only. Traffic on these roads may be disrupted during the monsoon season.

➢ Based on whether the paving (Surfacing) is provided or not:

i. Paved roads (Surfaced roads) – hard pavement (bituminous or concrete or paving block) surface is provided on the carriageway. They are also known as Metalled roads.

ii. Unpaved roads (Unsurfaced roads) – No hard surface provided (earth/gravel roads), also called Unmetalled roads.

➢ Based on traffic volume: Heavy/ Medium/Low Volume Roads

- Based on tonnage: Class I or II, or Class A, B.
- Based on **location and function**: (Generally used criterion)

As per Nagpur Road Plan (1st Road Development Plan 1943-'63)

i. National Highways (NH)
ii. State Highways (SH)
iii. Major District Roads (MDR)
iv. Other District Roads (ODR)
v. Village Roads (VR)

National Highways (NH) - are the main highways across the country connecting neighboring countries, major ports, state capitals, major industrial & tourist centers, including roads for strategic movements for the defence of India. The central government is responsible for the construction and maintenance of national highways. All NHs are serially numbered. For example, National Highway 1 connects Jammu & Kashmir with Ladakh.

State Highways (SH) – are the intrastate highway that connects the NHs of adjacent states, district headquarters, and major cities within the state, and serves as the primary thoroughfare for traffic to and from the major highways. Sharing the same design speed and geometric design specifications, NH and SH are designed to meet maximum mobility requirements rather than accessibility requirements. State governments are responsible for the construction and maintenance of SHs.

Major District Roads (MDR) – are the important roads within a district serving areas of production and markets, and connecting other major highways of the district. They are designed to meet almost equal levels of mobility and accessibility requirements. They have lower design speed and geometric design standards than NH/SH.

Other District Roads (ODR) – are the roads serving rural areas of production and providing access to market centres, railway stations, taluk/block development headquarters, etc. They act as a feeder system to MDRs, collecting traffic from village roads. They have lower design standards than MDRs.

Village Roads (VR) – are the roads connecting villages or groups of villages with each other to the nearest ODR. ODRs and VRs are designed to meet the maximum level of accessibility requirements, and have the same design standards. These are generally un-metalled roads.

Modified Classification System of Roads (As per Lucknow Plan- 3rd Road Development Plan, 1981-2001)

One of the outcomes of the 3rd 20-year Road Development Plan was the redefinition of road classification system. Based on location and function, the roads in India are generally classified into Non-urban roads (passing through non-urban area) and Urban roads (passing through urban area).

In order to provide higher degree of mobility of travel, "expressways", a superior class of divided highways with special design standards and full/partial control of access using grade separators at intersections, are also being constructed in the country. The expressways should permit only fast moving vehicles. India's first expressway was completed in 2002, connecting the two urban/industrial centres, Mumbai and Pune, having a length of 94.5 km. Thus, incorporating expressways too in the road network system, the Non-urban roads in our country are now classified into three systems for the purpose of transport planning, functional and location identification, assigning priorities and ear-marking administrative jurisdiction. They are:

i. **Primary system** – consists of Expressways and National Highways
ii. **Secondary system** – consists of State Highways and Major District Roads
iii. **Tertiary system** – consists of Other District Roads and Village Roads

Other District Roads and Village Roads together are renamed as "Rural Roads".

Classification of Urban Roads

The road system within an urban area is called "Urban Roads", which would be taken care of by the respective urban authorities. These roads are also classified as under:

i. Expressways
ii. Arterial Roads
iii. Sub-arterial Roads
iv. Collector Streets and
v. Local Streets

The function of expressways is the same whether they traverse through urban areas or non-urban areas.

The arterial roads have the highest mobility and the lowest accessibility, while the local streets offer the highest accessibility (door-to-door service). Collector streets have the function of collecting the traffic from local streets and feeding it to the arterials or sub-arterials. Local streets may be residential, commercial or industrial, depending on the predominant use of the adjacent land. Parking and pedestrian mobility are unrestricted on local streets. Urban road classification is illustrated in Fig. 1.1.

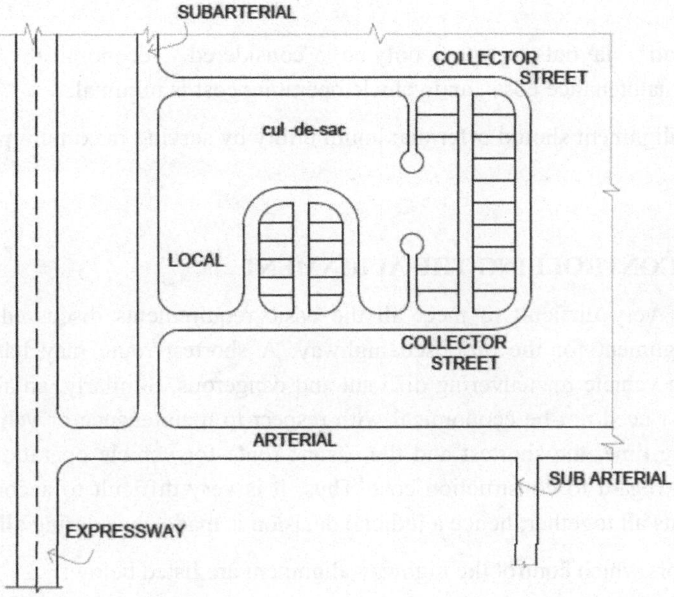

Fig 1.1 Classification of Urban Roads

1.7 HIGHWAY ALIGNMENT

The process of fixing/positioning the centre line of the proposed road on the ground is called the alignment. Alignment consists of horizontal and vertical alignments. Horizontal alignment includes the straight path, the deviations and horizontal curves, whereas, vertical alignment covers the changes in gradient, and vertical curves. Extra care should be given while aligning roads to reduce the construction / maintenance cost, vehicle operating cost and accident rate.

Hence, certain basic requirements are to be met for an ideal alignment between two stations, as listed below:

i. Shortness
ii. Easiness
iii. Safety and
iv. Economy.

Shortness: The shortest alignment between two stations is desirable as it reduces the expenses associated with construction, maintenance, and traffic operations. The straight path is the shortest one, though there may be other considerations making us to deviate from the straight path.

Easiness: The alignment should be such that it is easy to construct and maintain the road, and operate the traffic with ease gradients and curves.

Safety: The road's alignment needs to be safe for construction, maintenance, and traffic operation.

Economy: Road layouts can only be considered economical if the sum of capital costs, maintenance costs, and vehicle operating cost is minimal.

In addition, the alignment should offer maximum utility by serving maximum population and products.

1.8 FACTORS CONTROLLING THE ALIGNMENT

In practice, it is very difficult to meet all the basic requirements discussed above while selecting the alignment for the proposed highway. A shortest route may have very steep gradients making vehicle maneuvering difficult and dangerous. Similarly, an alignment with lowest initial cost need not be economical with respect to maintenance or vehicle operation cost. At the same time, the shortest and the easiest route for vehicle operation may not be economical with regard to construction cost. Thus, it is very difficult to accomplish all the basic requirements all together; hence a judicial decision is made considering all the factors.

The various factors which control the highway alignment are listed below:

- **i.** Obligatory or Control Points
- **ii.** Traffic factors
- **iii.** Geometric Design Elements
- **iv.** Economic Factors
- **v.** Other considerations

(i) *Obligatory or Control Points:* are points which govern/control the alignment of highways. They may be classified as :

a) Points through which the alignment should pass.

e.g. Mountain pass, bridge site, intermediate town

b) Points through which the alignment should not pass.

e.g. Religious places, marshy land, lakes, forests, parks, play grounds

a) *Points through which the alignment should pass*

The following options should be taken into account when a road alignment needs to traverse a hill, mountain, or high ridge: (a) cutting a tunnel across the hill; (b) going around the hill; or (c) deviating until a suitable hill pass is available. The decision between these options is influenced by a number of additional factors, including the terrain, site circumstances, and cost concerns. The straight path AB is diverted along a hill pass in Fig. 1.2(a), avoiding a deep cut or a tunnel.

While selecting a bridge site across a river, a number of factors are to be considered, viz. location where the river has straight and permanent path with less width, without a bend, pier and abutments can be properly founded and approach roads to the bridge are straight. Thus, mostly, the straight alignment across a river may have to be deviated to suit the bridge location, resulting in a longer path. See Fig. 1.2(b).

While aligning a road between two stations, in order to derive the maximum utility of the project, it may often be desirable to connect intermediate towns also. So the straight alignment AB may be shifted along ACB as shown in Fig. 1.2(c), in order to connect the intermediate station C. Station C can also be connected by a link road DC, so that the straight alignment AB is unchanged.

b) *Points through which the alignment should not pass*

There are control points through which the proposed straight (shortest) alignment should not pass and make it necessary to deviate from the shortest one. E.g. presence of religious places like temple, church, mosque, grave, tomb, location of reserve forest, parks, play ground, lakes, marshy land, etc. Acquisition of costly structures would result in increased budget for the project. So the shortest alignment has to be rerouted avoiding such critical places and going round the obstruction. See Fig. 1.2(d).

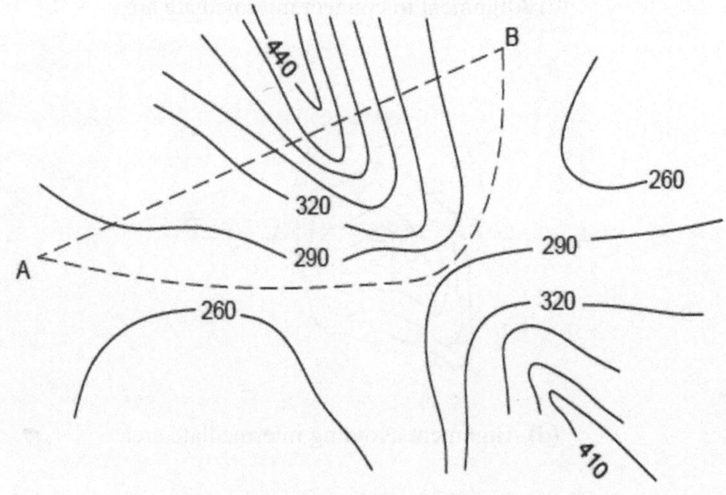

(a) Alignment along hill-side pass

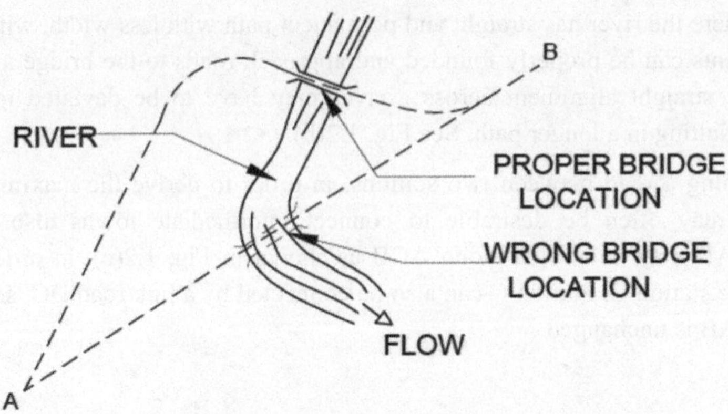

(b) Alignment to suite proper bridge location

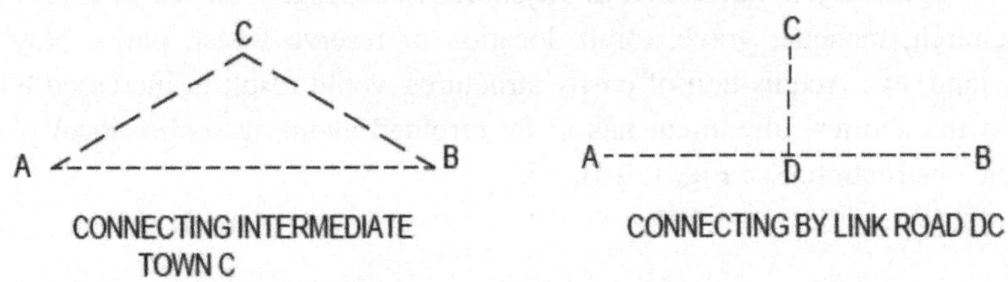

(c) Alignment to connect intermediate area

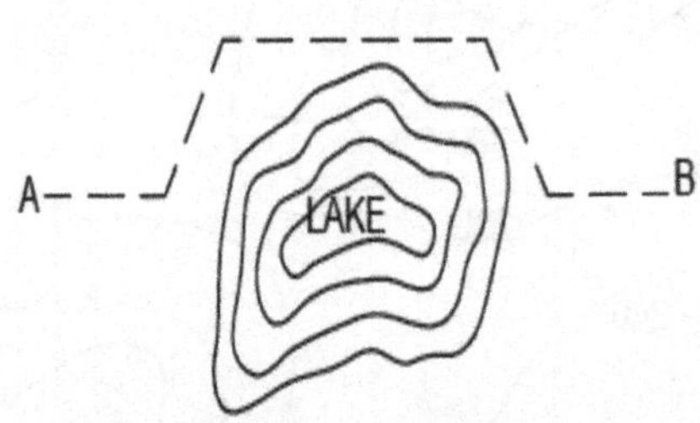

(d) Alignment avoiding intermediate area

Fig 1.2 Obligatory Points Controlling Alignment of Road

(ii) Traffic – The proposed alignment should match with the requirements of road traffic. Origin and Destination studies should be conducted in the area /region where an alignment is proposed and the 'desire lines' be drawn showing the desired trend of traffic flow. Fig. 1.3 explains the concept of desire lines. The band width of each line indicates the intensity of traffic potential to a scale, between origins and destinations. The new road to be aligned should keep in view the desire line pattern, anticipated traffic flow, classified traffic volume, their growth and future trends.

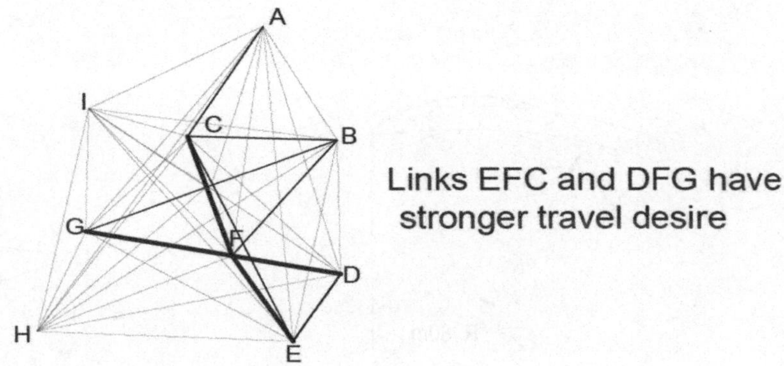

Fig 1.3 Concept of Desire Lines

(iii) *Geometric Design Elements* – The geometric design elements like gradient, radius of curve and sight distance would have a great influence in deciding the final alignment. It may be necessary to make changes in horizontal as well as vertical alignments of roads in order to conform to the standards specified by the Indian Roads Congress (IRC) for design speed, super elevation, skid resistance, sight distance requirements, radius of horizontal curves, length of transition curves and vertical curves, and gradient of roads. [These geometrical elements are explained in detail in Unit II].

SCAN ME for Indian Roads Congress (IRC)

IRC is the technical body constituted by the central government to provide standard specifications/guidelines for the planning, design, construction and maintenance of roads and bridges in the country, considering the safety and efficiency in traffic operation and management.

For e.g., as illustrated in Fig 1.4(a), the radius of the horizontal curve or sight distance may alter the alignment from a sharp curve to a wider one. Similarly, the design gradient may change the alignment from the straight path with steeper gradient to a longer path with ease gradient. See Fig. 1.4(b).

(iv) *Economic Factors*

The final alignment chosen based on the above factors should be economical or cost-effective. Highway economics include both highway costs and highway user benefits. In order to assess a certain alignment as economical, the benefits should exceed the costs. The highway costs consists of initial capital cost of construction and periodical maintenance, whereas the savings in vehicle operating cost and accident reduction are counted as user benefits. By considering the 'life cycle cost' of the project along with the annual benefits derived, the final selection of alignment from different alternative alignments may be done.

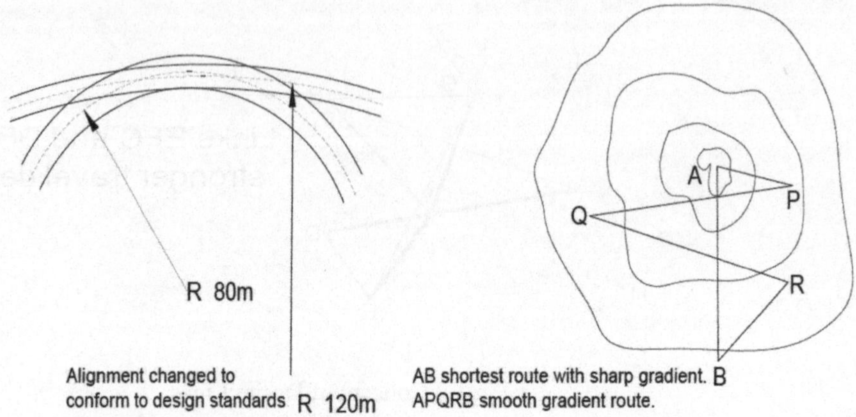

(a) Radius of Curvature / Sight Distance (b) Gradients

Fig 1.4 Impact of Geometric Design Elements on Alignment

(v) Other Considerations

Other factors which control the vertical /horizontal alignment of the road are:

- Drainage Considerations
- Hydrological factors
- Environmental considerations
- Social and Political considerations
- Monotony in driving

✓ The vertical alignment is often guided by drainage aspects including subsurface water level, seepage flow, high flood level, etc.

✓ Environmental Impact Assessment (EIA) is a mandatory requirement under Environmental Act 1986, for any project with investment more than Rs. 50 crores. The environmental impacts like pollution of air/water/noise/land, vibrations and visual intrusion are to be studied while fixing up the alignment.

✓ Social and economic dislocations warranting rehabilitation and resettlement of families should be lesser while selecting the alignment. Also, political interventions can change the alignment.

- ✓ In a flat terrain, it is always possible to have very long straight stretch of road without any horizontal curves, which would make drivers sleepy. Hence it is desirable to incorporate some slight bends deliberately after a few kilometers, so that the drivers shall be kept alert.

1.8.1 Special Considerations in the Alignment of Hill Roads

While aligning hill roads, special care should be taken in the following aspects:

(i) Stability of hill slopes during cutting and filling.

(ii) Drainage – align the road in such a manner that the number of cross drainage works is minimal.

(iii) Geometric design standards of hill roads should be ensured.

(iv) Ineffective rise and excessive fall should be kept minimal.

1.9 SELECTION OF THE BEST ALIGNMENT OF THE HIGHWAY

In order to select the best alignment from different alternatives, some engineering surveys are involved. These engineering surveys may be completed in the following four stages:

(i) Map Study – By studying the toposheets and remote sensing data products like aerial photos and satellite imageries, many possible/probable alignments could be arrived at.

(ii) Reconnaissance – With the help of simple or minor surveying instruments, all the above possible routes are studied on ground. The data collected from reconnaissance, may alter or change completely the proposed alignment. Thus, a few alternate alignments may be chosen for further investigation based on the data collected at site.

(iii) Preliminary Survey - In this stage, all the alternate alignments suggested from reconnaissance are subjected to detailed studies including drainage studies, soil survey, material survey, and traffic studies, with the help of more precise instruments, so that all options can be compared in terms of economic, social, engineering and environmental considerations. From the report of preliminary surveys, the best alignment is chosen, its grade lines are drawn and geometric elements designed at the office.

(iv) Final Location and Detailed Survey – The alignment selected after the preliminary survey is to be transferred to the ground by driving stakes at suitable intervals. Then detailed survey is carried out for the preparation of plans and construction details of the project.

UNIT SUMMARY

This unit gives an overview of highway engineering.

- Different roles played by transportation system in the development of a nation are:
    - Economic
    - Social
    - Spatial development
    - Cultural
    - Political

- Modes of Transportation:
    - Land – Highways, railways, pipelines, conveyors, aerial ropeways
    - Air – Airways
    - Water – Waterways like river ways, canal ways, ocean ways

- Relative Merits and Demerits of Roadways and Railways

Roadways	***Railways***
Higher flexibility of travel	Less flexibility
Accommodates all classes of vehicles and pedestrians	Only single type of vehicle
Provides door-to-door service	Not possible
Acts as feeder system for other modes	Not possible
Higher energy consumption	Less energy
Higher pollution level	Less pollution
Uneconomical bulk long hauls	Economical long hauls

- Important roles played by road transport in India are:
    - Rural connectivity
    - Transportation in hilly/difficult terrain
    - Trade and commerce
    - Strategic importance
    - Tourism development

- Employment generation
- Administrative convenience

➢ General Characteristics of Road Transport:

- Advantages:
    - Wide geographical coverage
    - Usage by different classes of vehicles
    - Low capital investment
    - Flexibility in service
    - High employment potential
- Disadvantages:
    - Lack of safety
    - Environmental issues
    - Parking problems
    - Uneconomical long hauls
    - Greater energy consumption

➢ General Classification of Roads by MoRT&H

✓ Based on Nagpur Plan:

- National Highways (NH)
- State Highways (SH)
- Major District Roads (MDR)
- Other District Roads (ODR)
- Village Roads (VR)

✓ Based on Lucknow Plan:

- Primary system –Expressways and National Highways
- Secondary system –State Highways and Major District Roads
- Tertiary system –Other District Roads and Village Roads

✓ Urban Roads Classification:

- Expressways
- Arterial Roads
- Sub-arterial Roads
- Collector Streets and

   - Local Streets

- Basic requirements of an ideal highway alignment:
   - Short
   - Easy
   - Safe and
   - Economical
- Factors controlling alignment
   - Obligatory points
   - Traffic
   - Geometric design
   - Economic
   - Other considerations – drainage, political intervention, monotony
- Engineering Surveys required for fixing final alignment:
   - Map Study
   - Reconnaissance
   - Preliminary survey
   - Final location survey

EXERCISES

Multiple Choice Questions

1.1 Which mode of transport is ideal for bulk and long haulage?

a) Highways b) Railways c) Airways d) Conveyor belts

1.2 Which mode of transport causes the least environmental issues?

a) Highways b) Railways c) Airways d) Waterways

1.3 Which mode of transport is ideal for door-to-door service?

a) Highways b) Railways c) Airways d) Waterways

1.4 Which mode of transport offers maximum flexibility of travel?

a) Highways b) Railways c) Airways d) Waterways

1.5 Which mode of transport does not require a feeder system for getting access?

a) Highways b) Railways c) Airways d) Waterways

1.6 Classification of roads as per Nagpur Plan is

a) NH, SH, MDR, ODR, VR b) All-weather & Fair-weather Roads

c) Primary, Secondary & Tertiary System d) Paved & Unpaved Roads

1.7 The criterion adopted for classification of roads in Nagpur Plan is

a) Surface condition b) Intensity of traffic volume

c) Tonnage d) Location and function

1.8 Classification of roads into three systems viz. Primary, Secondary and Tertiary systems is the outcome of which Road Development Plan?

a) First b) Second c) Third d) Fourth

1.9 Roads connecting district headquarters of a state would come in the category of

a) NH b) SH c) MDR d) ODR

1.10 Secondary system of roads comprises of

a) Expressways & NH b) NH & SH c) SH & MDR d) MDR & ODR

1.11 Which type of the following roads has maximum level of mobility?

a) NH b) Arterials c) Sub Arterials d) Expressways

1.12 Which type of the following roads has almost 50:50 level of mobility: accessibility?

a) Expressways b) Arterials c) Sub Arterials d) Collector streets

1.13 If you have to choose between an alignment of highway through cutting/ embankment/ pavement at ground level itself/ tunnel, the best choice is

a) Road nearer to ground level b) Embankment c) Cutting d) Tunnel

1.14 While aligning a road bridge across a river, the site conditions to be considered favourably are

a) Location where the river has straight, permanent path with least width

b) Where pier and abutments can be properly founded

c) Approach roads are straight

d) All the above

1.15 In the alignment of hill roads, the important factor to be considered is

a) Stability of slopes

b) Drainage

c) Geometric standards of hill roads

d) All the above

1.16 The stage of engineering survey in which the selection of final alignment is made

a) Map Study

b) Reconnaissance

c) Preliminary survey

d) Detailed Survey

Answers to Multiple Choice Questions

1.1 (b), 1.2 (d), 1.3 (a), 1.4 (a), 1.5 (a), 1.6 (a), 1.7 (d), 1.8 (c), 1.9 (b), 1.10 (c), 1.11(d), 1.12 (c), 1.13 (b), 1.14 (d), 1.15 (d), 1.16 (c).

Short and Long Questions

Category I

1.1 Discuss the role of transportation in the development of a nation.

1.2 What are the economic roles played by a transportation system in our society?

1.3 Explain the importance of roads in a developing country like India.

1.4 Enumerate the characteristics of road transportation.

1.5 What are the different modes of transportation and their specific functions?

1.6 Discuss the relative merits and demerits of roadways and railways.

1.7 Explain the role of transportation in rural development of India.

1.8 What are the various methods of classifying roads? Explain the classification based on location and function as suggested in Nagpur Plan.

1.9 Explain briefly the modified classification system for roads in India as per Lucknow Road Plan.

1.10 What are the various requirements of an ideal highway alignment? Explain briefly.

Category II

1.1 Compare the classification of roads suggested by Nagpur Plan and Lucknow Plan.

1.2 Explain with sketches the various factors controlling the alignment of a road.

1.3 What are obligatory points in highway alignment? Explain their significance with necessary sketches.

1.4 What are the precautions to be taken in hill road alignment?

1.5 Briefly explain the importance of different stages of engineering surveys in highway alignment.

KNOW MORE

Activity:

1.1 Collect the history of the oldest road as well as the bridge constructed in your locality. The data may include the year of construction, connecting places, length of the road, type of the bridge, etc.

1.2 List out the National Highways and the State Highways passing through your locality. Check whether they are intersecting each other, or interlinked by any District Road.

1.3 Indicate any three live examples of obligatory points which changed the alignment of any road constructed in your place.

1.4 Identify the longest bridge in your locality. Check whether that bridge location was an obligatory point during the alignment of the respective highway, with the help of maps available.

Time lines:

1928 : Jayakar Committee Report

1929: Central Road fund

1934: Indian Roads Congress (IRC)

1939: Motor Vehicles' Act

1943: First Road Development Plan (Nagpur plan) 1943 - 1963

1950: Central Road Research Institute (CRRI)

1956: National Highways Act

1960: Border Roads Organisation (BRO)

1961: Second Road Development Plan (Bombay plan) 1961 -1981

1973: Highway Research Board (HRB)

1978: National Transport Policy Committee (NTPC)

1981: Third Road Development Plan (Lucknow plan) 1981 - 2001

1995: National Highways Authority of India (NHAI)

1999: National Highway Development Programme (NHDP)

2001: Fourth Road Development Plan (Vision- 2021) 2001- 2021

2005: Rural Road Development Plan (Vision-2025) 2005 – 2025

Interesting Facts:

India's First Highway - the Grand Trunk Road – the Road Connecting Four Nations

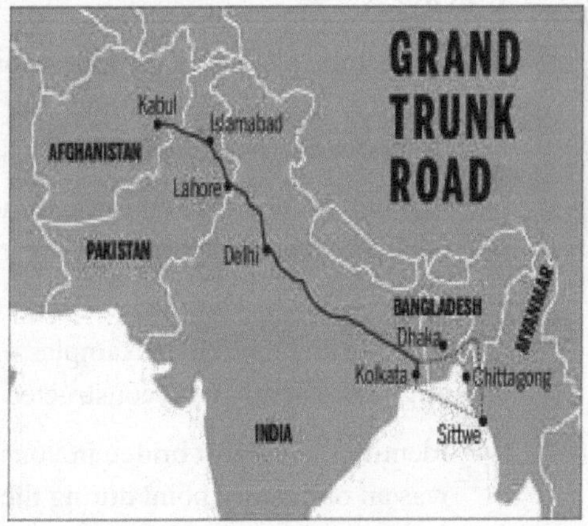

In the 16th century, Sher Shah Suri, the emperor of Northern India, built a major road named, **"Sadak-e-Azam"**, later renamed as **"the Grand Trunk Road"**, covering a distance of over 2,500 kilometers. It starts from Chittagong in **Bangladesh**, and then through **India**, it enters Lahore in **Pakistan**, then through Khyber-pass it enters **Afghanistan** and continues through Jalalabad and ends at Kabul. Within India, the major portion of the road: the stretch between Howrah to Kanpur is National Highway-2 and Kanpur to Delhi, is National Highway-91, and between Delhi and Wagah, the border with Pakistan, is National Highway-1.

Rudyard Kipling called it 'a river of life', but for the modern driver it's a nightmare.

How America became rich?

"American roads are not good because America is rich, but America is rich because American roads are good, *"US President John F Kennedy once said famously.*

The transportation system through different modes allowed Americans to take advantage of the continent's vast territory and natural resources, and to build an industrial economy on a national scale, in the 19th century itself.

History of Development of Road Construction

a) Roman Roads (312 B.C.)

Very deep construction, built straight, without cross slope. Drainage was not considered.

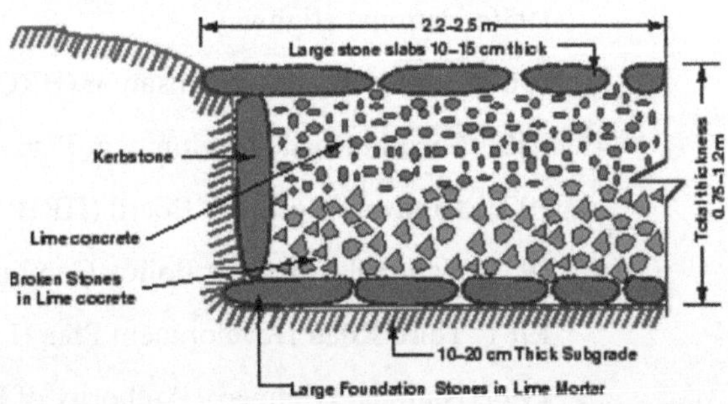

b) French Roads (1764 A.D.)

Large foundation stones varying in size to give a straight cross slope of 1 in 45 for drainage purpose.

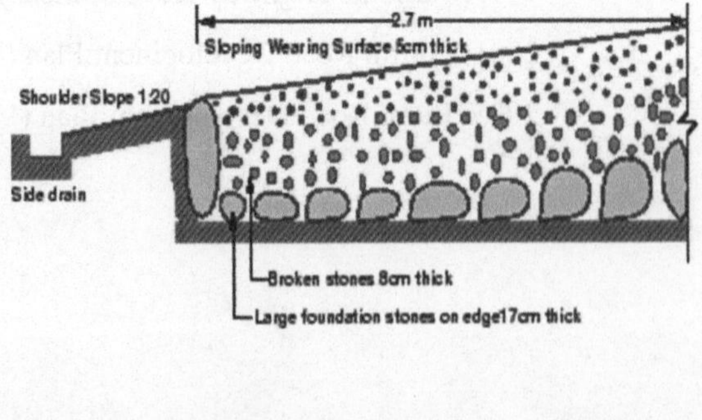

c) British Roads (1815 A.D.)

Layered construction using different grades of materials, with a parabolic cross slope of 1 in 36 in all layers, from sub grade to top, providing broken stones as foundation, instead of heavy boulders. Present day construction is the modified version of this concept.

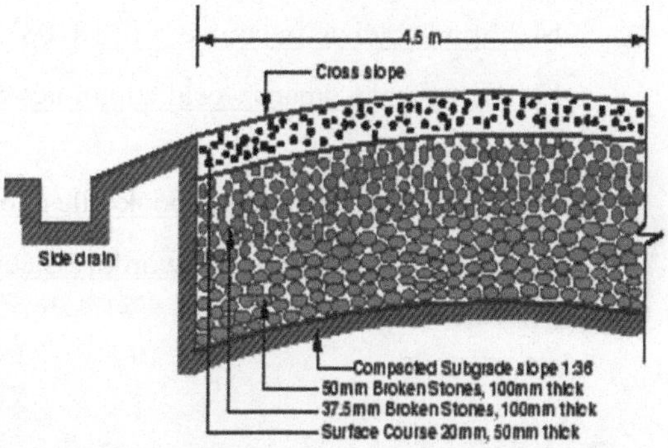

REFERENCES AND SUGGESTED READINGS

1. William W. Hay, 'An Introduction to Transportation Engineering", Wiley, New York, 1977.
2. Morlok Edward K., 'Introduction to TransportationEngineering and Planning', McGraw-Hill Book Company, New York, 1978.
3. Kadiyali L. R., 'Transportation Engineering', Khanna Book Publishing Co., 2018.
4. Khanna S. K., Justo C. E. G., Veeraraghavan A., 'Highway Engineering', Nem Chand & Bros., Roorkee, 2014.
5. Arora N. L., 'Transportation Engineering', New India Pub., 1977.
6. Subramanian K. P., 'Transportation Engineering', Scitech Publications, Chennai, 2015.
7. Sharma S.K., 'Principles, Practice and Design of Highway Engineering', S. Chand Publishing, 2014.
8. Ministry of Transport and Communication, 'Road Development Plan for India, 1961-1981', Department of Transport, Government of India.
9. Ministry of Shipping and Transport, Roads Wing, 'Road Development Plan for India, 1981-2001', Indian Roads Congress, 1984.
10. 'Report of the National Transport Policy Committee', Planning Commission, Government of India, 1980.
11. Ministry of Road Transport and Highways, (Government of India), 'Road Development Plan Vision: 2021, Indian Roads Congress, 2001.
12. Ministry of Rural Development, (Government of India), 'Rural Road Development Plan: Vision 2025', National Rural Roads Development Agency, New Delhi, 2007.
13. Ministry of Road Transport and Highways, (Government of India), 'Pocket Book for Highway Engineers', Indian Roads Congress, 2002.

14. https://nptel.ac.in/courses/105101087

15. https://www.smartzworld.com/notes/transportation-engineering-pdf-notes-te-pdf-notes/

16. https://jntukucen.ac.in/ebook_files/166.pdf

17. https://knowledge4civil.wordpress.com/2016/12/12/highway-alignment-and-survey/

UNIT 2
GEOMETRIC DESIGN OF HIGHWAYS

UNIT SPECIFICS

This unit discusses the following aspects:

- Geometric design - definition and significance
- Geometric elements to be designed
- Factors controlling Geometric design
- Highway cross sectional elements
- Design of sight distance
- Design of horizontal alignment
- Design of vertical alignment

Multiple-choice questions along with answers, short and long answer type questions including numerical problems and a practical work, relevant to the topics covered in the unit, are added. A list of references and suggested readings are also given. It should be noted that dynamic QR codes are provided for additional reading in different sections, which can be scanned for relevant supportive information. A "KNOW MORE" section is also given at the end, which has been carefully designed so that additional information relevant to this unit is provided for the users of the book. This section mainly contains some 'Activities' for the students to make them conversant with the topics he/she had studied, and some interesting facts related with the contents of the unit.

RATIONALE

For a highway engineer, the most important phase in a highway project is its geometric design. The geometrics should be designed carefully to render maximum efficiency and safety in traffic operations on that highway. Though it is possible to design and construct the pavement of a highway in stages, it is very difficult and expensive to modify its geometric elements in stages at future date. Hence, utmost care should be taken in the design of each geometric element of a highway taking into consideration the future trend of traffic potential.

Additionally, it should be noted that highway geometrics are greatly influenced by the topography or terrain through which the highway is aligned, the locality, the traffic characteristics and the requirements of design speed.

UNIT OUTCOMES

After completing this unit, student will be able

U2-O1: To identify the cross sectional details and other geometric elements of a highway.

U2-O2: To understand the importance of design speed in geometric design of highways.

U2-O3: To identify the significance and design features of sight distances required under different conditions.

U2-O4: To design the horizontal alignment features of road as per IRC recommendations

U2-O5: To design the vertical alignment features of road as per IRC recommendations.

Unit-2 Outcomes	EXPECTED MAPPING WITH COURSE OUTCOMES (1- Weak Correlation, 2-Medium Correlation, 3- Strong Correlation)				
	CO-1	CO-2	CO-3	CO-4	CO-5
U2-O1	3	3	-	-	-
U2-O2	3	2	-	-	-
U2-O3	3	3	-	-	-
U2-O4	3	3	-	-	-
U2-O5	3	3	-	-	-

2.1 GEOMETRIC DESIGN - DEFINITION AND SIGNIFICANCE

Geometric design of any structure means the fixing up of it size and shape. Thus, for a highway, its cross section, horizontal and vertical alignments, sight distances and intersections are to be designed. The design should aim at maximum efficiency in traffic operation with maximum safety at reasonable cost. During the planning and design process of a highway, the existing and the anticipated traffic, as well as the possibility of upgradation, if any, should be considered, as it is very expensive and difficult to change the features at a later date. The road user, that is, whoever uses the road – driver /motorist /cyclist /passenger /pedestrian - is concerned with three aspects, viz: speed, safety and comfort of travel. So the objective of the highway engineer is to plan and design the highway structure in such a manner that the above requirements are met simultaneously. Therefore, utmost care has to be taken in the design of geometrics of the highway.

2.2 GEOMETRIC ELEMENTS TO BE DESIGNED

The various geometric elements to be designed for a highway are listed below:

i. Cross sectional elements

ii. Sight distance requirements

iii. Horizontal alignment features

iv. Vertical alignment features and

v. Intersectional elements.

The design of intersection elements does not come under the scope of this text book.

2.3 FACTORS CONTROLLING GEOMETRIC DESIGN OF HIGHWAYS

The Geometric design of highways depends on several factors as listed below:

a) Design speed of the highway

b) Topography or Terrain condition

c) Traffic factors

d) Environmental and other factors

2.3.1 Design speed

Putting in simple terms, the speed adopted for the geometric design of a highway is called 'design speed', and it is also the most important factor controlling the geometric design. The design speed is considered as the maximum safe speed that can be maintained for a vehicle over a road stretch, given the geometric and traffic operating conditions are favourable. The design speed varies with the class of the road, like Expressways/National Highway/State Highway/Major District Road/Other District Road/Village Road and also with the terrain conditions, like plain or mountainous, etc., through which the road passes. Similarly, urban roads have a different set of design speeds.

The design of each geometric element discussed in the section 2.2 is dependent primarily on design speed.

2.3.2 Topography (Terrain conditions)

The topographical conditions greatly influence the design speed of the vehicle and in turn the design of geometric elements. Since speed of a vehicle is dependent on the slope of the road on which it is moving, the design speed adopted for a highway should also be suiting to the terrain conditions. Thus, the speed adopted for a plain terrain will not be possible for a steep terrain. Hence, considering the general cross slope of the country, IRC has classified the terrains into four categories viz. plain, rolling mountainous and steep. Design speeds are specified for each of these terrain conditions and for each class of the road. The terrain classification suggested as per IRC standards is given in Table 2.1 and the design speeds specified for different classes of roads and with respect to terrain classification is given in Table 2.2.

Table 2.1 Terrain Classification by the IRC

Terrain Classification	General cross slope of the country, %
Plain	0-10
Rolling	10-25
Mountainous	25-60
Steep	>60

Table 2.2 Design Speeds for different classes of roads (IRC)

Road Classification	Design speed in kmph							
	Plain		Rolling		Mountainous		Steep	
	Ruling	Minimum	Ruling	Minimum	Ruling	Minimum	Ruling	Minimum
Expressways	120	100	100	80	80	60	80	60
NH & SH	100	80	80	65	50	40	40	30
MDR	80	65	65	50	40	30	30	20
ODR	65	50	50	40	30	25	25	20
VR	50	40	40	35	25	20	25	20

There are two values of designs speeds specified in the Table 2.2 viz. ruling design speed and minimum design speed. E.g. The ruling design speed for a national highway or state highway on plain terrain is 100 km per hour whereas its minimum design speed is 80 km per hour. This implies that wherever possible, the geometric design of the highway should be done based on 'ruling design speed', but 'minimum design speed' can be adopted, if there are any site/economic constraints. The design speeds suggested for urban roads are given in Table 2.3.

Table 2.3 Suggested design speeds for urban roads in India (IRC)

Road Class	Design Speed, kmph
Expressways	120
Arterials	80
Sub arterials	60
Collector streets	50
Local streets	30

2.3.3 Traffic Factors

Since the roads are for operating the traffic, obviously, the characteristics of traffic will affect the design of road infrastructure. The traffic characteristics include vehicular characteristics and road user characteristics.

The traffic factors influencing the geometric design of highways are:

i. Characteristics of the components of the traffic (vehicle and road user)

ii. Design Traffic Volume

iii. Directional distribution of traffic

iv. Traffic composition

v. Future traffic demand

Vehicular Characteristics: Since in mixed traffic condition, as prevalent in our country, different classes of motorised vehicles like cars, buses, trucks, two/three-wheelers and non-motorised vehicles like bicycles, animal carts, etc. having different speed/acceleration characteristics, as well as physical dimensions, are being operated on our roads. Hence, it is very difficult to select a 'design vehicle' and a 'standard traffic lane'. For geometric design of highways, a design vehicle is considered.

The characteristics of the vehicle can be classified as *static* and *dynamic*. The *static* characteristics include: length, width, height and weight of the vehicle. The length of the vehicle affects design of road geometrics like radius of curve, sight distance, minimum turning radius, safe overtaking sight distance; the width of the vehicle affects lane width, shoulders and parking geometries; and the height of the vehicle affects clearances (such as clearance heights for over-bridges, under- bridges, electric and other service lines). On the other hand, weight of vehicle affects the structural design of pavements and structures.

The *dynamic* characteristics like speed and acceleration rates affect the design of horizontal curves, transition curves, vertical curves and sight distance.

Road user characteristics: include the physical, mental and psychological characteristics of driver and pedestrians which would affect the traffic behaviour, and sight distance requirements.

Design traffic volume: is the number of vehicles passing a section of road per unit interval of time, say, an hour, expressed as vehicles/hour. The traffic volume varies with respect to hour/day/week/month/season. If we take hourly volume, there will be peak hours and off-peak hours. To design a road on the basis of peak hour traffic may not be economical. So a reasonable value of traffic volume, a little less than the highest volume, is taken for design purpose. Thus, in general, the 30th highest hourly volume (30 HV) is adopted for geometric design, on the assumption that there are only 29 times the traffic volume will exceed that value during a year, which can be ignored. All other traffic volumes will be less than this value. IRC suggests that 10% of annual average daily traffic (AADT) may be assumed as the 30th highest hourly volume under Indian conditions.

Directional distribution of traffic: For two-lane highways, the total traffic in both directions is taken for calculating the design hourly volume, whereas, for roads with more than two lanes, 67% of total traffic travelling in one direction is considered for design.

Traffic composition: Since the traffic in our country is of heterogeneous in character consisting of both fast-moving and slow-moving vehicles using the same lane of the road, it is customary to express the traffic volume in terms of a standard vehicle, say, passenger car. Thus, all types of vehicles in our country or converted in terms of Passenger Car Units (PCU), using equivalency factors, as suggested by the IRC. For example, while a car is given an equivalency factor of 1.0, bus and truck are given 3.0, two-wheelers 0.5 and bullock cart 8.0. For urban conditions, there are slight changes in the above values. Particularly in the design of intersection elements, the traffic volume has to be taken in terms of PCUs.

Future traffic demand: Obviously the geometrics of any highway are to be designed to meet the future travel demand requirements. Generally, the design period adopted is 20 years. So the existing traffic volume data has to be projected for the design year assessing the prevailing growth rate of vehicle population. Annual growth rate of the traffic varies from 7.5% to 8%.

Environmental and other factors: It includes aesthetics, landscaping, pollution levels, etc. These factors are very significant in the case of design of intersections.

2.4 CROSS SECTIONAL ELEMENTS OF THE HIGHWAY

These include:

i. Typical cross-section of a highway
ii. Pavement surface characteristics
   - Friction (skid resistance) – lateral and longitudinal
   - Unevenness of the pavement
iii. Camber (cross-slope)
iv. Carriageway width
v. Median (Traffic Separator)
vi. Kerb
vii. Road margins
viii. Roadway width
ix. Right-of-way

2.4.1 Typical Cross Section of Highway

Fig 2.1 shows the typical cross section of a highway in embankment as well as in cutting.

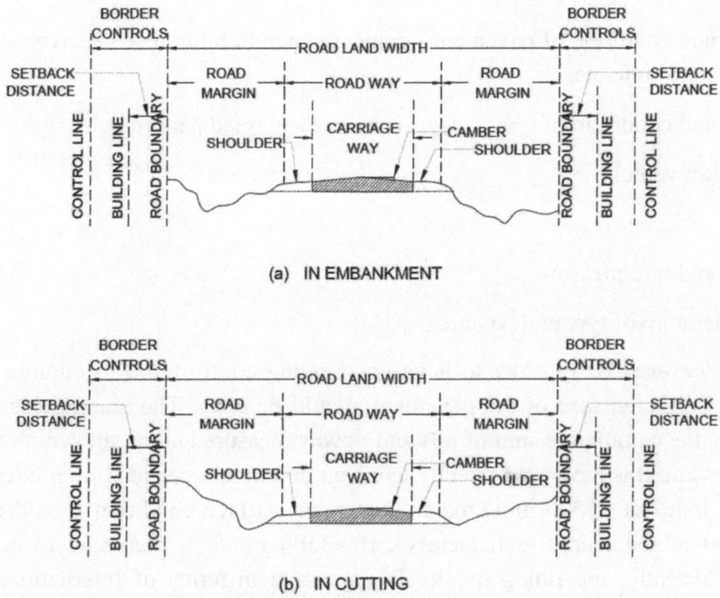

Fig 2.1 Cross section details of highway in embankment and cutting

2.4.2 Pavement surface characteristics

Friction (skid resistance): It is the resistance between the tyres of vehicles and the surface of road. It is an important factor which influences the design of horizontal alignment and sight distance requirements. Two types of skid resistances are considered in design. (i) Lateral skid resistance – used in the design of horizontal curves and superelevation and (ii) longitudinal skid resistance - used in the design of stopping sight distance. Sight distance is explained in sect. 2.5.

When a vehicle negotiates in a horizontal curve, centrifugal force would be induced on the vehicle resulting in lateral skidding of the vehicle. The design of the curve is done in such a manner that this centrifugal force is counteracted by the friction between tyre and pavement in the lateral direction, along with the component of the weight of the vehicle due to the super elevation provided at curves. Super elevation is raising of outer edge of the horizontal circular curve than its inner edge. Refer sect. 2.6.1.

Similarly, for the safe and efficient operation of a vehicle on road, a visible distance free from any obstruction should be made available, so that on emergencies the driver should be able to stop the vehicle without hitting the obstruction. This visible distance which is called 'stopping sight distance' which is a function of frictional resistance offered between tyre and road surface in the longitudinal direction, but opposite to the movement of the vehicle, along with many other factors. The numerical values of lateral skid resistance and longitudinal resistance taken for design are quite different. The former is 0.1 to 0.15, whereas the latter is 0.35 to 0.4, as suggested by the IRC.

The skid resistance depends on the following factors:

- Type and condition of pavement - cement concrete/bituminous /gravel roads; wet/dry; smooth/rough, etc.
- Type and condition of tyres - new/worn-out and tread pattern
- Speed of vehicle
- Brake efficiency
- Load and tyre pressure
- Temperature of tyre and pavement.

Pavement Unevenness: In order to have good riding comfort and to minimise the vehicle operating cost, the surface of the pavement should be even. The unevenness index can be expressed as the cumulative sum of ups and downs measured along the length of the road in terms of mm/km. It is measured directly using an instrument called 'Bump integrator'. If the unevenness index is <1500 mm/km, the pavement surface condition is said to be 'good', 1500 - 2500 is considered 'satisfactory', if >3500 mm/km, then said to be 'repairs are required'. Currently, the riding quality is expressed in terms of International Roughness Index (IRI) in terms of 'metre per kilometre' which can be measured directly by another new instrument called Roughometer. IRI is correlated with bump integrator values (BI) as given by equation 2.1:

$$BI = 630(IRI)^{1.12} \qquad \text{Eq. 2.1}$$

2.4.3 Camber or Cross slope

It is the slope provided to the road surface in the transverse direction for drainage purpose. Usually, a raised camber is provided to the pavement surface to serve two functions: (i) to drain off the rainwater falling on the surface easily and (ii) to prevent the entry of water from the sides or shoulders to the pavement layers. The degree of camber is expressed as 1 in N or x per cent and it depends on two factors: (i) type of pavement surface and (ii) rainfall intensity. IRC has recommended the following ranges of degree of camber with respect to pavement type and rainfall intensity (Table 2.4).

Table 2.4 Recommendations of camber for different pavement types

Sl. No.	Pavement Type	Range of Camber
1	Cement concrete and high type Bituminous pavements	1.7 to 2.0% or 1 in 60 to 1 in 50
2	Thin Bituminous pavements	2.0 to 2.5% or 1 in 50 to 1 in 40
3	Water Bound Macadam/ Gravel roads	2.5 to 3.0% or 1 in 40 to 1 in 33
4	Earth road	3.0 to 4.0% or 1 in 33 to 1 in 25

Here, the lower values shown in the ranges are to be adopted for low rainfall areas (if annual rainfall less than 1000 mm) and higher values for heavy rainfall areas (if annual rainfall is greater than 1000 mm). However, excessive camber i.e., > 4.0%, even in the case of earth roads, is not desirable because of many reasons like: it would result in tilting of highly laden commercial vehicles, discomfort in riding, unequal wear of tyres and pavement, early rutting failure of pavements, etc.

Types of Camber: Different shapes of camber are adopted in the field as shown in Fig 2.2. They are parabolic, straight, and combination of straight and parabolic shapes.

In order to provide the camber required, camber boards are prepared with the desired shape and degree of camber. Using these boards, the final transverse profile of the pavement will be checked and corrected, if necessary. If parabolic camber is used, the equation of parabola $y = x^2 /a$ may be used. Thus, for a pavement of width 'w' and cross slope 1 in N,

$$a = N.\frac{w}{2}$$

and hence,

$$y = 2x^2 /(N.w) \qquad \text{Eq. 2.2}$$

2.4.4 Carriageway width

Carriageway is the central portion of the road which carries the load. The area designated for the movement of one row of vehicle is known as a traffic lane. The number of lanes and lane width are used to determine the width of the carriageway. The lane width is decided by considering the lateral placement of a heavy commercial vehicle (HCV) on roads, allowing sufficient lateral clearance on either side of a moving vehicle. Number of lanes required will depend on the design traffic volume. Fig 2.3 illustrates the lateral placement of vehicle(s) on a pavement leaving the clearances.

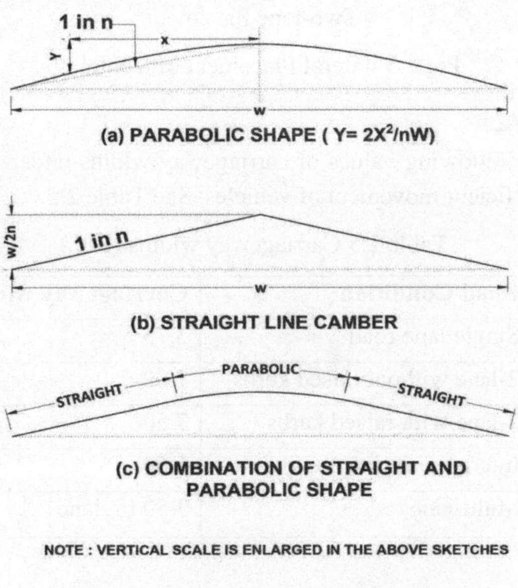

Fig 2.2 Different shapes of camber

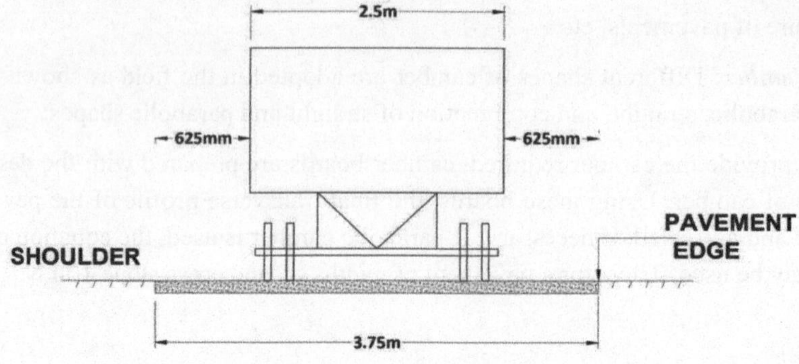

a) Single lane Pavement

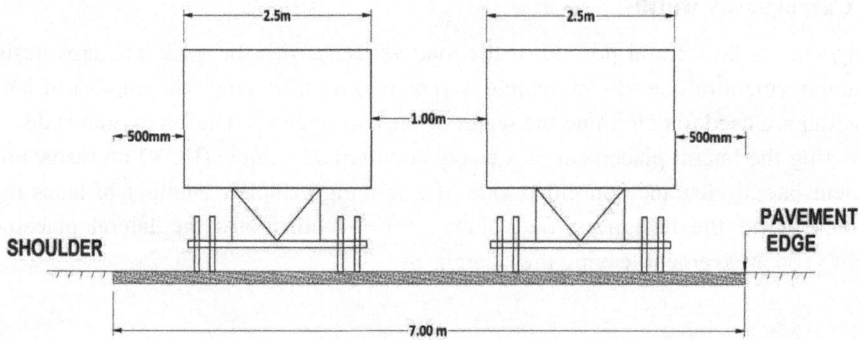

Two-lane Pavement

Fig 2.3 Lateral Placement of Vehicles

IRC has suggested the following values of carriageway widths under different conditions of the road for safe and efficient movement of vehicles. See Table 2.5.

Table 2.5 Carriageway widths (IRC)

Sl. No.	Road Condition	Carriageway width in m
1	Single lane road	3.75
2	2-lane without raised kerbs*	7.00
3	2-lane with raised kerbs	7.50
4	Intermediate lane	5.50
5	Multi-lane	3.50 m /lane

*See section 2.4.6

Notes:

- For expressways, lane width adopted is 3.75 m/per lane in plain and rolling terrains and 3.5 m in mountainous terrain.
- For urban roads without raised kerbs, lane width is 3.5 m/ lane
- Minimum width for kerbed urban road is 5.5 m to accommodate a parked vehicle.
- For local streets in residential areas, lane width may be 3m only.

2.4.5 Median or Traffic Separators

A traffic separator or a median is provided to separate the traffic in order to prevent head-on collisions between vehicles driving in opposing directions on adjacent lanes. Generally, the desirable width of median is 5m and minimum is 1.2m. The width is decided based on the availability of land. Wider medians will avoid glare due to opposite vehicles during night driving, whereas, in narrower medians, glare may be reduced by planting shrubs on the median. See Fig 2.4.

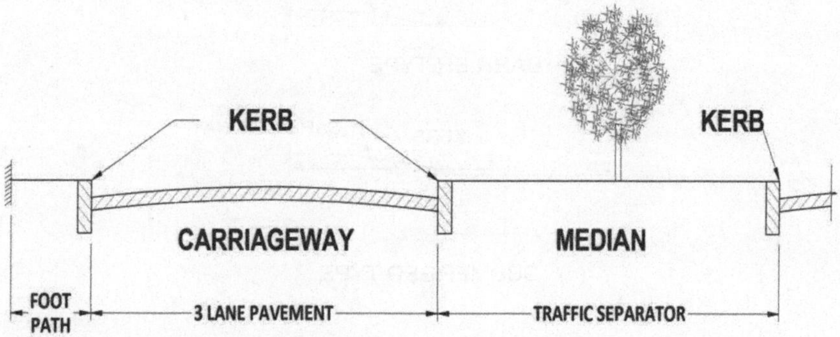

Fig 2.4 Kerb and Median

2.4.6 Kerbs

Kerb is the boundary stone provided between the carriageway and the footpath/median. Its primary function is to prevent or arrest the movement of vehicles from the carriageway to the footpath. Also, it prevents the flow of materials from the carriageway to its sides while doing the surfacing work of pavement.

Different types of kerbs generally used are given below: (See Fig 2.5)

i. **Low/Mountable type**: It allows the vehicle to mount over the kerb on eventualities.

ii. **Semi-barrier type**: Provided where pedestrian traffic is considerable. On very emergency condition vehicle can drive over the kerb.

iii. **Barrier type**: Provided at places of high pedestrian traffic; not possible to mount over

iv. **Submerged type**: Provided in rural areas where pavement and shoulders are to flush each other; at the same time act as a supportive structure for pavement layers.

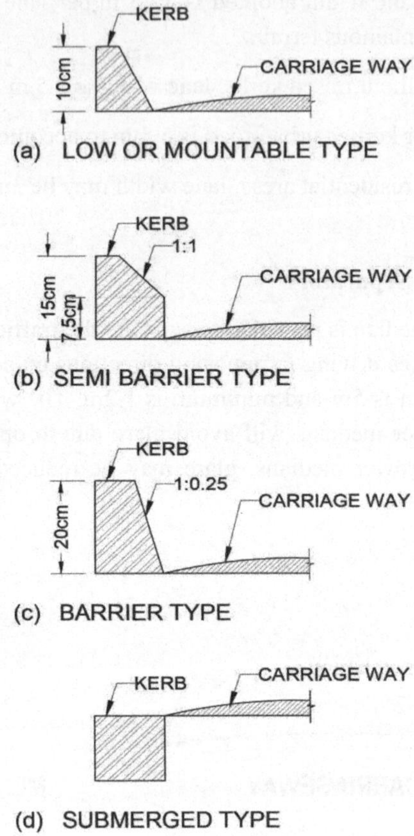

Fig 2.5 Different types of Kerbs

2.4.7 Road margins

These include various structures; viz. Shoulders, Footpath, Drive way, Cycle track, Parking lane, Bus bay, Lay bye, and Frontage road.

Shoulders: are provided on the both sides of the carriageway to provide structural stability and support to the edges of the pavement (See Fig 2.1). Shoulders can be paved or unpaved depending on the intensity of traffic flow, so that on emergencies, vehicles can make use of it. IRC recommends a minimum width of 2.5 m for shoulders to accommodate brake-down vehicles on it and for emergency parking. The surface of shoulder shall be rough and distinct in colour with respect to the carriageway, in order to discourage drivers from using it as carriageway.

Guard rails or Guard stones: are provided to safeguard vehicles from running out of the embankment particularly when embankment height exceeds 3 m.

Footpath: is provided for the safe movement of pedestrians along the road way, if both the pedestrian traffic and vehicular traffic are high. IRC suggests an absolute minimum width of 1.5 m and a desirable minimum with of 2.0 m, with a cross slope of 2.5 to 3%. It should be well-maintained too to encourage the pedestrian for using it.

Drive ways: are used to give access to fuel station or service station, etc. from the highway. They should be located away from junctions, provided with easy curves at entry and exit.

Cycle tracks: are provided where cycle traffic is high. Minimum width is 2 m, increased at the rate of 1 m for every additional lane.

Parking lanes: are provided to facilitate on-street parking. Minimum width suggested is 3 m for parallel parking.

Bus bays: are provided to stop the buses safely at specified locations without interfering with other traffic. They are constructed by recessing the kerb sufficiently for accommodating the buses; located at least 75 m away from junction.

Lay byes: where vehicles can stop without interrupting other traffic; minimum length required is 30m, 3m wide with the tapered ends.

Frontage roads or Service roads: are provided running parallel to parallel to the highway, giving access to other properties and with controlled access to highway facility.

2.4.8 Roadway

Carriageway together with the shoulders and separators (median), if any, is called road way. (See Fig 2.1). In embankment, the top width is considered for roadway, whereas in cutting, the bottom width is taken. Roadway widths suggested by the IRC for different classes of roads with respect to the road category and the nature of terrain conditions are given in Table 2.6.

Table 2.6 Roadway widths for different classes of roads (IRC)

Sl. No.	**Road Class**	**Roadway width, m in**	
		Plain & Rolling terrain	**Mountainous & Steep terrain**
1	NH & SH		
	(a) Single lane	12.00	6.25
	(b) 2-lane	12.00	8.80
2	MDR		
	(a) Single lane	9.00	4.75
	(b) 2-lane	9.00	-
3	ODR		
	(a) Single lane	7.50	4.75
	(b) 2-lane	9.00	-
4	VR		
	Single lane	7.50	4.00

2.4.9 Right of way

It is the area acquired by the authorities for the construction of the highway. The transverse distance between the two road boundaries is the width of the right of way and is known as 'right of way width' or 'land width'. Its length will be the length of the highway. (See Fig 2.1) The land widths recommended by the IRC for different classes of roads under different terrain conditions are given in Table 2.7. Also, note that the land widths recommended for Urban roads are given Table 2.8.

Table 2.7 Land widths (m) for different classes of roads (IRC)

Sl. No.	Road Class	Plain & Rolling terrain		Mountainous & Steep terrain	
		Open Area	**Built up Area**	**Open Area**	**Built up Area**
1	Expressways	90	-	60/30	-
2	NH & SH	45	30	24	20
3	MDR	25	20	18	15
4	ODR	15	15	15	12
5	VR	12	10	9	9

Table 2.8 Land widths (m) for Urban roads (IRC)

Road Class	Land width, m
Arterials	50-60
Sub arterials	30-40
Collector streets	20-30
Local streets	10-20

2.5 SIGHT DISTANCE

Sight Distance: Definition, Significance and Types

For a safe driving, the visibility available for a driver is very important. The term "sight distance" refers to the length of the road where a driver with an eye level at certain height above the pavement can see things that are a certain height above the pavement while they are driving. It is measured along the road surface from the driver to the object concerned.

One of the important criteria considered in the design of vertical curves, design of set-back distance at horizontal curves and at intersections is sight distance. Sight distance is essential at different instances like, (i) for stopping a vehicle moving at a design speed suddenly (ii) for overtaking another slow moving vehicle ahead by a vehicle running with the design speed (iii) for avoiding collision between vehicles entering an intersection area (iv) for safe driving during night on a deep valley curve, etc. Some of the instances showing the importance of sight distance and how it is measured in the field are illustrated in Fig 2.6.

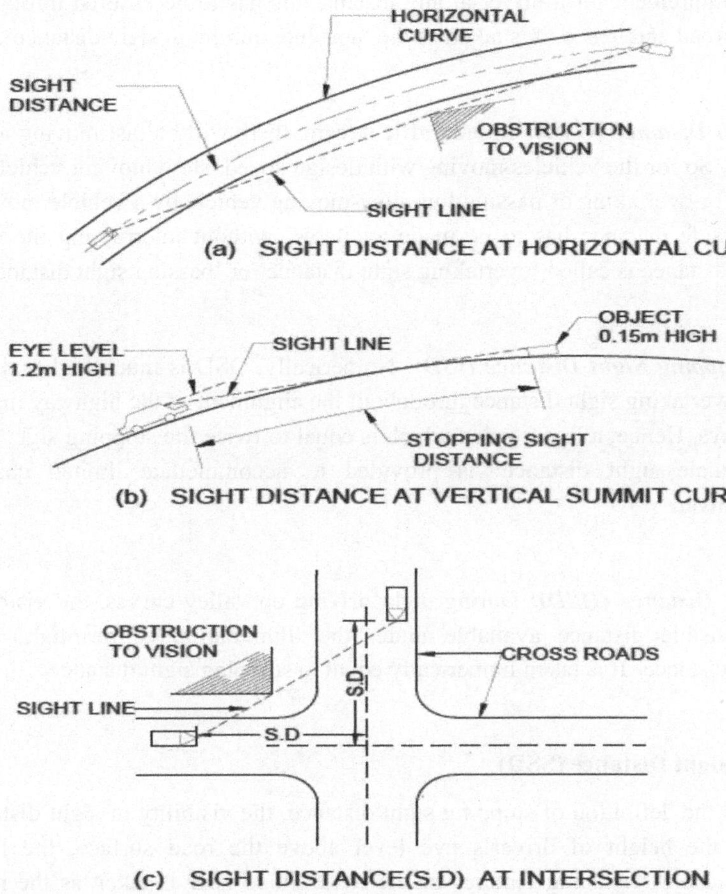

Fig 2.6 Significance of sight distance and its measurement in the field

Depending on the purpose for which the sight distance is designed, sight distances are classified as under:

a) Stopping sight distance (absolute minimum sight distance)

b) Overtaking sight distance or passing sight distance

c) Intermediate sight distance and

d) Headlight sight distance.

SCAN ME
for
Sight Distances

Stopping Sight Distance (SSD): is the safe minimum distance required for a driver travelling at design speed, whose eye level is at a specified height of 1.2 m to stop the vehicle when he sees an object having a minimum height of 0.15 m, without hitting that obstruction. Since this is an essential requirement for a driver at any instant, this has to be ensured throughout the alignment of the road and hence, it is taken as the 'absolute minimum sight distance'.

Overtaking Sight Distance (OSD): In the traffic stream, there will be fast-moving and slow-moving vehicles. So for the vehicles moving with design speed, slow moving vehicle will be an obstruction. For overtaking or passing this slow-moving vehicle by a vehicle moving with design speed, a safe distance has to be made available, without interrupting the opposing traffic.This safe distance is called 'overtaking sight distance' or 'passing sight distance'.

Intermediate Stopping Sight Distance (ISD): Numerically, OSD is much higher than SSD. To provide the overtaking sight distance throughout the alignment of the highway may not be economical always. Hence, a lesser value which is equal to twice the stopping sight distance, called 'Intermediate sight distance' is provided to accommodate limited chances of overtaking maneuver.

Headlight Sight Distance (HSD): During night driving on valley curves, the visibility is a problem. The visible distance available under the illumination of headlight is called 'headlight sight distance'.It is taken numerically equal to stopping sight distance.

2.5.1 Stopping Sight Distance (SSD)

As mentioned in the definition of stopping sight distance, the visibility or sight distance will be affected by the height of driver's eye level above the road surface, the height of obstruction and also the existing features of the road. Since SSD is taken as the minimum distance required for a driver of a vehicle travelling at design speed to stop safely the vehicle at any moment when he sees an obstruction on the road, without hitting the obstruction. Hence, obviously, considering this process, the SSD will depend upon the following factors:

- Speed of the vehicle
- Reaction time of the driver (time taken by the driver to react to that new situation). That is, time when the driver sees the object to the instant he starts application of brakes, or, it is the sum of perception time and brake-reaction time, which is considered as the 'total reaction time'"t" of the driver.Generally, it is taken us 2.5 seconds for design purpose.
- Skid resistance (longitudinal) between the tyre and the road surface
- Brake efficiency
- Gradient or slope of the road, if any.

Essentially, SSD comprises of two components:

i. Distance travelled by the vehicle moving at design speed,v, during the reaction time of the driver, t, which is called 'lag distance', and

ii. Distance travelled by the vehicle during the application of brakes till it comes to stop (braking distance).

Lag Distance: If v is the design speed of the highway at which the vehicle is assumed to travel in m/s; t, is the reaction time of the driver in seconds; then distance travelled by the vehicle during the reaction time,

i.e. lag distance, $d_1 = v \times t$ m.

If v is in kilometre per hour and t in seconds then $d1 = \frac{v \times t \times 1000}{60 \times 60} = 0.278 v.t$ m.

Braking distance: It is obtained by equating the work done by the vehicle during the application of brakes and the kinetic energy of the vehicle travelling at design speed. If W is the weight of the vehicle, v speed in m/s, then,

kinetic energy $= \frac{Wv^2}{2g}$

If f is the skid resistance (longitudinal) between the tyre and road surface and braking distance is 'l',

Work done by the vehicle $= f \times W \times l$

Now equating work done to Kinetic Energy,

$$f \times W \times l = \frac{Wv^2}{2g}$$

Or, $l = \frac{v^2}{2gf} = \frac{v^2}{254 f}$ {putting v in kmph and g as 9.81 m/s^2}

Thus, SSD = Lag distance + Braking distance

i.e. SSD= $v.t + \frac{v^2}{2gf}$ {putting v in m/s, t in s, and g in m/s^2} Eq. 2.3a

Or, SSD= $0.278 V.t + \frac{V^2}{254 f}$ {putting v in kmph, t in s, and g as 9.81 m/s^2} Eq.2.3b

(f ranges from 0.4 at 20 kmph to 0.35 at 100 kmph).

SSD at Slopes:

If there is an ascending gradient of n per cent, then component of weight of vehicle adds to frictional force. Since α, the angle of slope of the road is very small,

Wsinα = Wtanα = W.n/100 [n% is the slope of road]

Equating kinetic energy and work done,

$$(f.W + \frac{W.n}{100})l = \frac{Wv^2}{2g}$$

Or $$l = \frac{v^2}{2g[f + \frac{n}{100}]}$$

If it is a descending gradient, braking distance l becomes $\frac{v^2}{2g[f - \frac{n}{100}]}$

Thus, $$SSD = v.t + \frac{v^2}{2g(f \pm \frac{n}{100})}$$ Eq. 2.4a

Or, $$SSD = 0.278V.t + \frac{V^2}{254(f \pm 0.01n)}$$ Eq. 2.4b

This is for a single lane road with traffic in one direction only. If two-way movement is allowed on a single lane road, then SSD is twice that given by Eq. 2.4.

Example 2.1:

Design the safe SSD on a national highway passing through rolling terrain (design speed 80kmph) (i) at a level stretch (ii) at an ascending gradient of 2%. Take skid resistance as 0.35, reaction time as 2.5s.

Solution:

Given: V= 80 kmph= (80 x 1000)/(60 x 60) = 22.2 m/s

t = 2.5 s, f = 0.35

On the level stretch:

n =0

$$SSD = v.t + \frac{v^2}{2g(f \pm \frac{n}{100})}$$

= 22.2 x 2.5 + 22.22 / (2 x 9.81 x 0.35)

= 55.5 + 71.77 = 127.27 m say 128 m

On the ascending gradient of 2%

n= 0.02

SSD = 22.2 x 2.5 + 22.22 / [(2 x 9.81 x (0.35+0.02)]

= 55.5 + 67.95 = 123.45m say 124m

Example 2.2:

Design the SSD for single lane level highway having a design speed of 50kmph, and a skid resistance of 0.36, if (i) only one-way traffic is permitted (ii) if 2-way traffic permitted and (iii) one-way traffic with f = 0.65 and brake efficiency = 60%.

Solution:

Given: V = 50kmph; v= 50/3.6 = 13.9 m/s

Assume t = 2.5s, f= .36; n=0

$$SSD = v.t + \frac{v^2}{2g(f \pm \frac{n}{100})}$$

If one-way traffic permitted:

SSD = 13.9 x2.5 +13.92 /(2 x 9.81 x 0.36) = 34.75+27.35

=62.1m say 63m

If two-way traffic permitted:

SSD = 2 x SSD for one-way = 2 x 62.1 =124.2m say 125m

One-way traffic with f = 0.65, brake efficiency X = 60%.

Effective f = f x X = 0.65 x 60/100 = 0.39

SSD = 13.9 x2.5 +13.92 /(2 x 9.81 x 0.39) = 34.75+25.25

=60.0m

Example 2.3:

Design the headlight sight distance and intermediate sight distance for a two-lane highway with two-way traffic permitted, having a design speed of 65kmph and f = 0.35.

Solution:

Given: V= 65 kmph; v = 18m/s

t = 2.5s, f = 0.35; n=0

Headlight Sight Distance, HSD = SSD

$$SSD = v.t + \frac{v^2}{2g(f \pm \frac{n}{100})}$$

HSD = 18 x2.5 +182 /(2 x 9.81 x 0.35) = 45+47.18

=92.18m say 93m

Intermediate sight distance , ISD = 2 x SSD

= 2 x 92.18

= 184.36m say 185m

2.5.2 Overtaking Sight Distance (OSD)

On our roads, all the vehicles are not moving at uniform speed or design speed, some will be following lower speeds than the design speed. For vehicles moving with design speed, slow-moving vehicle ahead is an obstruction. If fast-moving vehicles have to overtake the slow ones, sufficient sight distance should be made available to them for the safe operation. Thus, overtaking sight distance is defined as the visible distance measured along the road surface for a driver moving with design speed to overtake another slow-moving vehicle ahead, without interrupting the opposing traffic.

The overtaking process is illustrated in the following Fig 2.7, which would help in the analysis of OSD.

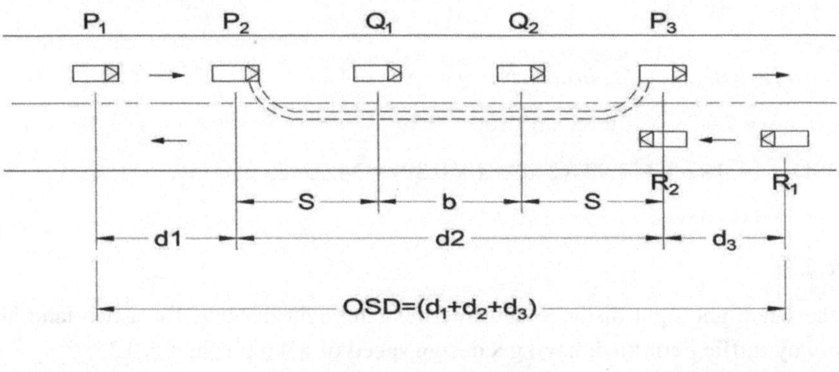

Fig 2.7 Overtaking process

Analysis of OSD

Assume, P and R are vehicles moving with design speed, v m/s (or V kmph)

R - vehicle moving with slow speed, v_b m/s (or V_b kmph)

V_b = (V - 16) kmph   (as per IRC)

t = reaction time of overtaking driver = 2s (as per IRC)

T = acceleration time of vehicle, P in s

b = distance travelled by slow vehicle, Q during the acceleration time T in m a = acceleration rate of the vehicle, P in m/s^2 (Generally assumed as 1m/s^2)

s = safe gap between successive vehicles in m

Now, assume the vehicle, P has been running at design speed 'v' up to the point P_1, and when he sees the slow-moving vehicle Q ahead, he naturally reduces his speed at least equal to that of Q i.e. v_b and it travels a distance $P_1$to P_2 = d_1 in time, t (his reaction time), leaving a safe gap 's' behind Q.

So, $d_1 = v_b \times t$ -------- (a)

Then, vehicle P accelerates from P_2, enters the other lane, passes the vehicle, Q and comes back to the original lane at P_3, leaving again a safe gap 's' ahead of Q. The distance travelled is

$d_2 = s + b + s = b + 2s$ ------- (b)

During the acceleration time 'T' of vehicle P, the opposing vehicle, R has moved fromR_1 to R_2 at design speed v. So,

$d_3 = v \times T$ ---------(c)

Now, 'b' is the distance travelled by the slow vehicle Q fromQ_1 to Q_2 during 'T' at speed v_b.

i.e., $b = v_b \times T$ ------- (d)

Also, $d_2 = b + 2s$

Using the equation of motion, $S = ut + \frac{1}{2}at^2$, distance travelled, $d_2 = v_b T + \frac{1}{2}aT^2$

Therefore, $$b + 2s = v_b T + \frac{1}{2}aT^2$$

But, $b = v_b.T$, So, $$2s = \frac{1}{2}aT^2$$

Or, $$T = \sqrt{\frac{4s}{a}}$$

Where, safe gap $s = (0.7v_b + 6)$ m (v_b in m/s) [As per IRC]

Hence, OSD = $(d_1 + d_2 + d_3) = (v_b.t + v_b.T + 2s + v.T)$ m Eq. 2.5a

Or, OSD = $(0.28V_b.t + 0.28V_b.T + 2s + 0.28V.T)$ m Eq. 2.5b

Note: If the road is one-way, there will not be opposing traffic, hence $d_3 = 0$.

So, OSD = $(d_1 + d_2)$ only.

Overtaking Zones: These are the designated areas where overtaking of vehicles can be allowed. It should be noted that such areas should be properly indicated in the field by installing sign posts meant for that purpose. Fig 2.8 illustrates such an area. According to IRC, the minimum length of overtaking zone = 3 x OSD, while desirable length is 5 x OSD.

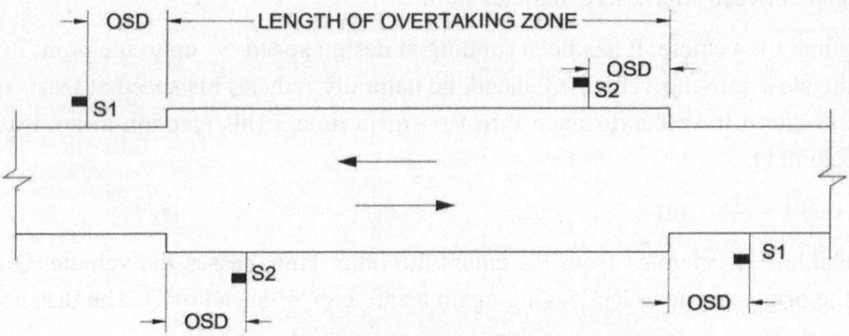

S1 - Sign indicating "overtaking zone ahead"

S2 - Sign indicating "overtaking zone ends"

Fig 2.8 Features of Overtaking zone

Example 2.4:

Design the overtaking sight distance required for a State Highway (two-lane, two-way) passing through rolling terrain. What is the length of the overtaking zone? Assume all data as per IRC specifications.

What will be the OSD if the stretch is one-way?

Solution:

Assumptions: Design speed V = 80 kmph (SH, Rolling terrain)

$$v = 80/3.6 = 22.2 \text{ m/s}$$

$V_b = V - 16 = 80 - 16 = 64$ kmph

$v_b = 64/3.6 = 17.8$ m/s

$t = 2$ s; $a = 1 \text{m/s}^2$;

$s = (0.7v_b + 6)$ m $= (0.7 \times 17.8) + 6 = 18.46$ m

$$T = \sqrt{\frac{4s}{a}}$$

$$= \sqrt{\frac{4 \times 18.46}{1.0}} = 8.59 \text{ s}$$

$\text{OSD} = (d_1 + d_2 + d_3) = [v_b.t + (v_b.T + 2s) + v.T]$ m

$= 17.8 \times 2 + 17.8 \times 8.59 + 2 \times 18.46 + 22.2 \times 8.59$

$= 416.12$m say 417m

Minimum Length of Overtaking zone = 3 x OSD = 3 x 417 = 1251m

Desirable Length of Overtaking zone = 5 x OSD = 5 x 417 = 2085 m

If only one-way permitted, OSD = $d_1 + d_2$ = (17.8 x 2 + 17.8 x 8.59 + 2 x 18.46) = 225.42 m

2.6 DESIGN OF HORIZONTAL ALIGNMENT

The alignment of the highway with respect to horizontal plane is called 'horizontal alignment'. As discussed in section 1.8 of Unit 1, many a times we have to change the alignment from a straight path, resulting in curves or bends. Such deviations should be carefully designed in such a manner that safe and efficient travel is ensured for the road users. The design of horizontal alignment comprises of a number of geometric elements as listed below:

i. Design speed
ii. Super elevation
iii. Radius of circular curve
iv. Extra widening at curves
v. Length of transition curve
vi. Set-back distance at curves

2.6.1 Design Speed

It is the main factor on which the design of all geometric elements depends. It is already detailed in section 2.3. The design speed varies with respect to the class of the road and type of terrain through which the road passes. Two values of design speeds - ruling designs speed and the minimum design speed are suggested by the IRC. Always, the design of all geometrics are to be done using the ruling design speed but, if there is any constraint due to land or others, then only we would change the design as per minimum design speed specified by the IRC.

2.6.2 Super elevation

Whenever there is a change in alignment in the horizontal plane, it has to be accomplished through a smooth circular curve. But, when the vehicle traverses this circular curve, centrifugal force acts radially outward through the centre of gravity of the vehicle, tending the vehicle to either overturn or skid laterally outward. So, for the stability of the vehicle on this curve, super elevation (banking of the outer edge with respect to inner edge) is provided. Thus, the centrifugal force will be counteracted by the horizontal component of the weight of the vehicle along with the frictional resistance offered by the tyre and road surface (lateral skid resistance). So, in order to maintain the design speed on the horizontal curve, super elevation and radius of the curve are to be designed accordingly.

Further, if there is a change in alignment for the straight stretch which is done through a circular curve, the straight end shall not be directly connected to the circular curve, because it will affect the stability as well as riding comfort of vehicles. Hence, it is always safe to connect straight road with the circular curve through a transition curve only, whose radius decreases gradually from infinity at the tangent point to the radius of the circular curve at its start. Also, transition curve helps in introducing the super elevation and extra widening at horizontal circular curves.

Super elevation is the raising of outer edge of the highway with respect to inner edge of a horizontal circular curve, to counteract the centrifugal force acting on the vehicle moving on it, so that the vehicle is protected from over turning or lateral skidding.

Rate of super elevation is defined as the ratio of difference in height between inner and outer edges of the curve to the width of the road.

Analysis of super elevation: If a vehicle traverses a circular curve provided with super elevation having a radius R at a speed v m/s, the different forces acting on the vehicle are illustrated in the Fig 2.9.

i. Weight of the vehicle 'W' acting vertically downward through its centre of gravity

ii. The centrifugal force 'P' acting outward through the centre of gravity of the vehicle

iii. Frictional forces 'F_A' and 'F_B' between tyres and pavement acting along the pavement against P

iv. Reactions 'R_A' and R_B' on Tyres A and B against W.

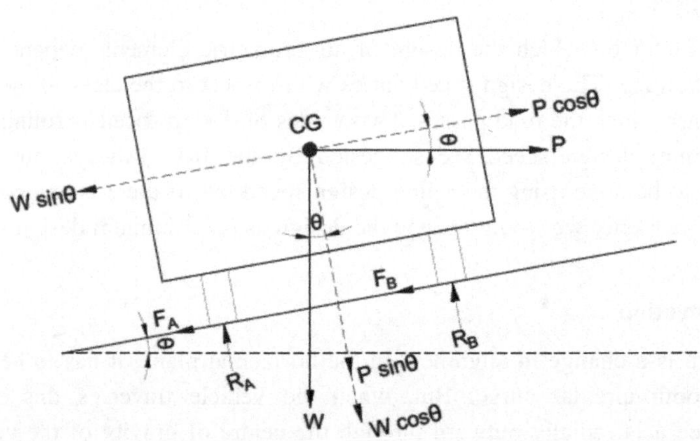

Fig 2.9 Analysis of Superelevation

For equilibrium, resolving for horizontally,

$P \cos \theta = W \sin \theta + F_A + F_B$ (a)

Resolving vertically,

$P \sin \theta + W \cos \theta = R_A + R_B$ (b)

Eq (a) becomes,

$P \cos\theta = W \sin\theta + f(R_A + R_B)$

$= W \sin\theta + f(P \sin\theta + W \cos\theta)$

ie., $P(\cos\theta - f\sin\theta) = W(\sin\theta + f\cos\theta)$

Or, $\frac{P}{W} = \frac{\sin\theta + f\cos\theta}{\cos\theta - f\sin\theta}$

Dividing by $\cos\theta$, $\frac{P}{W} = \frac{\tan\theta + f}{1 - f\tan\theta}$; where $\tan\theta = e$, the rate of super elevation and

P/W is centrifugal ratio $= v^2/gR$

So, $$\frac{v^2}{gR} = \frac{e+f}{1-f.e}$$

Since f and e are very small (0.15 and 0.07 respectively), their product will be still smaller, hence negligible.

Therefore, $$e + f = \frac{v^2}{gR} \qquad \text{Eq. 2.6a}$$

Putting V in kmph, R in m and $g = 9.81$ m/s^2,

$$e + f = \frac{V^2}{127R} \qquad \text{Eq. 2.6b}$$

Notes:

i. In general, IRC suggests that the maximum value of 'e' is limited to 0.07 or 7%, whereas in hill roads not bound by snow it is 10%. On urban roads with frequent intersections, maximum super elevation may be limited to 4%.

ii. If the calculated value of 'e' as per equation 2.6 comes to less than the camber of the road, then the super elevation to be provided in the field is camber itself, to meet drainage requirements also.

Design of super elevation: IRC suggests certain steps for designing super elevation in the field, as mixed traffic condition is prevalent in our country. The steps are described below:

Step (i) Calculate the super elevation for 75% of design speed, and neglecting friction using Eq. 2.6.

i.e., $$e = \frac{(0.75v)^2}{gR} \qquad \text{[v in m/s, R in m]} \qquad \text{Eq. 2.7a}$$

OR,
$$e = \frac{(0.75V)^2}{127R}$$

i.e.,
$$e = \frac{V^2}{225R}$$
[V in kmph, R in m] Eq. 2.7b

Step (ii) If the calculated value of e < 0.07, provide the calculated value as the design value of 'e'. Else, provide e as 0.07 and proceed with steps (iii) or (iv).

Step (iii) Check the value of skid resistance 'f' for the maximum value of e = 0.07 at full design speed v.

i.e., $$f = (\frac{v^2}{gR} - 0.07)$$ Eq. 2.8a

Or, $$f = (\frac{V^2}{127R} - 0.07)$$ Eq. 2.8b

If f is ≤ 0.15, the e provided as 0.07 is safe. Else, we have to increase the radius or restrict the speed for e=0.07 and f=0.15 using the equation 2.6 as given in step (iv).

Step (iv) The restricted speed or allowable speed 'v_a' can be calculated as

$$e + f = 0.07 + 0.15 = \frac{v_a^2}{gR}$$

$$v_a = \sqrt{0.22gR} = \sqrt{2.156R} \text{ m/s}$$ Eq. 2.9a

$$Va = \sqrt{27.94R} \text{ kmph}$$ Eq.2.9b

Put a 'speed limit sign board' indicating the v_a in kilometre per hour, well in advance of the curve. Or, for the specified design speed, calculate the revised radius as

$0.07 + 0.15 = v^2/(gR) = 0.22$

Or, $R = v^2/(0.22g) = 0.464v^2$ m Eq.2.10a

$R = 0.358V^2$ m Eq.2.10b

Note: If e is the rate of super elevation, B the width of the road in metres, then the total amount of super elevation to be provided in the field in metres will be

E = e x B m Eq.2.11

This 'vertical raise' E which is to be provided against calculated/specified superelevation 'e' across the width and is maintained throughout the circular curve length.

Example 2.5:

Design the super elevation required for a two-lane SH passing through rolling terrain at a horizontal curve radius 400 m. Calculate the amount of super elevation also. Assume data suitably.

Solution:

Design speed, V = 80 kmph [SH, rolling terrain]

= 80/3.6 = 22.2 m/s

R = 420 m

For 75% v, and neglecting friction,

$$e = \frac{(0.75v)^2}{gR} = \frac{(0.75 \times 22.2)^2}{9.81 \times 420} = 0.067 \subset 0.07$$

So, design e = 0.067

B = 7.00 m (2-lane)

Therefore, amount of super elevation, E = e x B = 0.067 x 7.0 = 0.47 m

Example 2.6:

Design the super elevation for a national highway passing through plain Terrain at a horizontal curve of radius 550 m. Assume data suitably.

Solution:

V = 100 kmph [NH, plain terrain]

=100/3.6 =27.8 m/s

Step (i)

For 75% v, and f =0,

$$e = \frac{(0.75 \times 27.8)^2}{9.81 \times 550} = 0.081 > 0.07$$

So, provide a limiting value of e as 0 07, and check for f with full design speed.

i.e.,

$$f = \frac{v^2}{gR} - e = \frac{27.8^2}{981 \times 550} - 0.07 = 0.073 \subset 0.15$$

Hence safe.

Example 2.7:

Design the super elevation for MDR passing through rolling terrain (designs speed 65 km per hour) at a horizontal curve of radius 150 m.

V = 65 kmph, R = 150 m, f = 0.15

Step 1 For 75% V, and f=0,

$e = V^2 / 225\ R = 65^2 / (225 \times 120) = 0.156 > 0.07.$

Maximum e is limited to 0.07.

Step 2

So, provide e = 0.07, and check for f for full V.

i.e., $$f = \frac{V^2}{127R} - 0.07$$

$$f = \frac{V^2}{127R} - 0.07 = \frac{65^2}{127 \times 120} - 0.07 = 0.21 > 0.15$$

Since, f >0.15, the speed has to be restricted or increase the radius of the curve.

Step 3

Allowable Speed, $V_a = \sqrt{(27.94R)}$ kmph

$= \sqrt{(27.94 \times 120)} = 57.9$ kmph say 55 kmph.

OR, Revised $R = 0.0358\ V^2 = 0.0358 \times 65^2 = 151.26$ m say 152 m.

Example 2.8:

Design the super elevation required for a state highway with high type bituminous pavement passing through rolling terrain in heavy rainfall area having a horizontal curve of radius 1500 m.

Solution:

Design speed, V = 80 kmph (SH, rolling terrain)

R = 1500m

$e = V^2 / 225R = 80^2 / (225 \times 1500) = 0.0189 < 0.07$ [OK]

But, e obtained (0.0189) is less than the camber required for that highway too. The camber suggested for high type bituminous pavement in heavy rainfall area is 2%. Here, the obtained value is 1.89%. So provide a super elevation of 2% on that curve.

Method of provision of super elevation in the field: As discussed earlier, the design super elevation has to be provided invariably throughout the entire length of the circular curve. Also, it is not possible to connect the straight stretch with the circular curve, as the cross sectional shapes of straight and circular curve are different. The straight portion has a cambered section with crown at centre whereas, for circular curve, the peak point is at outer edge. See Fig 2.10. This transformation of shapes is facilitated through the provision of a transition curve between straight and circular curve. Thus, the super elevation 'E' is attained gradually along the length of transition curve through two stages:

(a) Eliminating the crown of the cambered section of the straight stretch by either rotating outer edge with respect to crown [Fig 2.11(a)] or shifting the crown slightly outward [Fig 2.11(b)].

(b) Rotating the pavement with respect to centre line or inner edge [Fig 2.12].

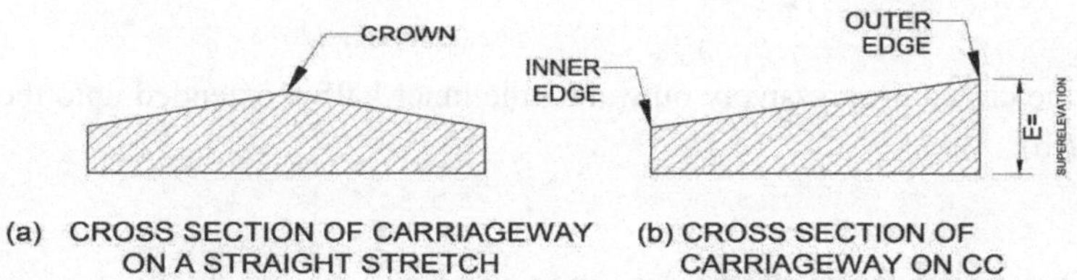

Fig 2.10 Shapes of carriageway cross sections at straight stretch and circular curve

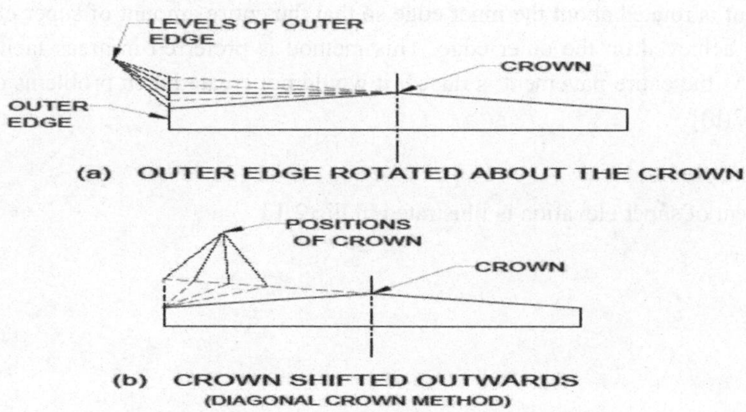

Fig 2.11 Elimination of crown of cambered section

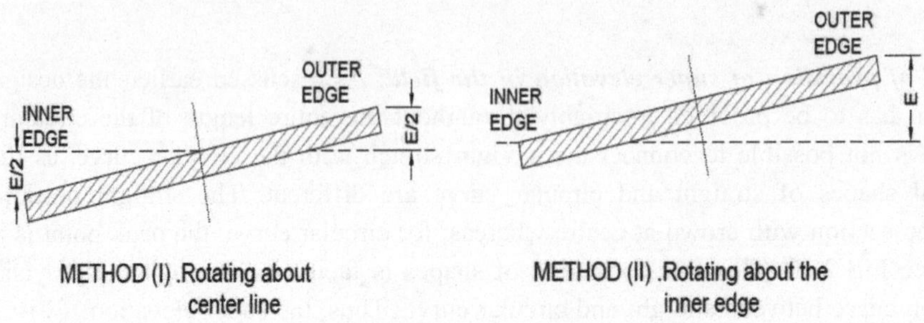

Fig 2.12 Rotation of pavement section to attain full superelevation

Elimination of crown: As shown in Fig 2.11(a), the outer half of the pavement is rotated with respect to the crown at desired rate such that this portion falls on the same plane as the inner portion.

By shifting the crown progressively outwards, the inner half is extended upto the outer edge. See Fig 2.11(b).

Rotation of pavement: It can also be done in two ways:

i. Pavement is rotated in such a manner that the inner edge is depressed and outer edge is raised, resulting in an advantage of balancing the earth work. But it may lead to drainage problem, if sufficient care is not taken. [Fig 2.12(a)]

ii. Pavement is rotated about the inner edge so that the entire amount of super elevation 'E' shall be achieved on the outer edge. This method is preferred in areas facing drainage issues. As the entire pavement is raised, it would not create much problems of drainage. [Fig 2.12(b)]

The attainment of super elevation is illustrated in Fig 2.13.

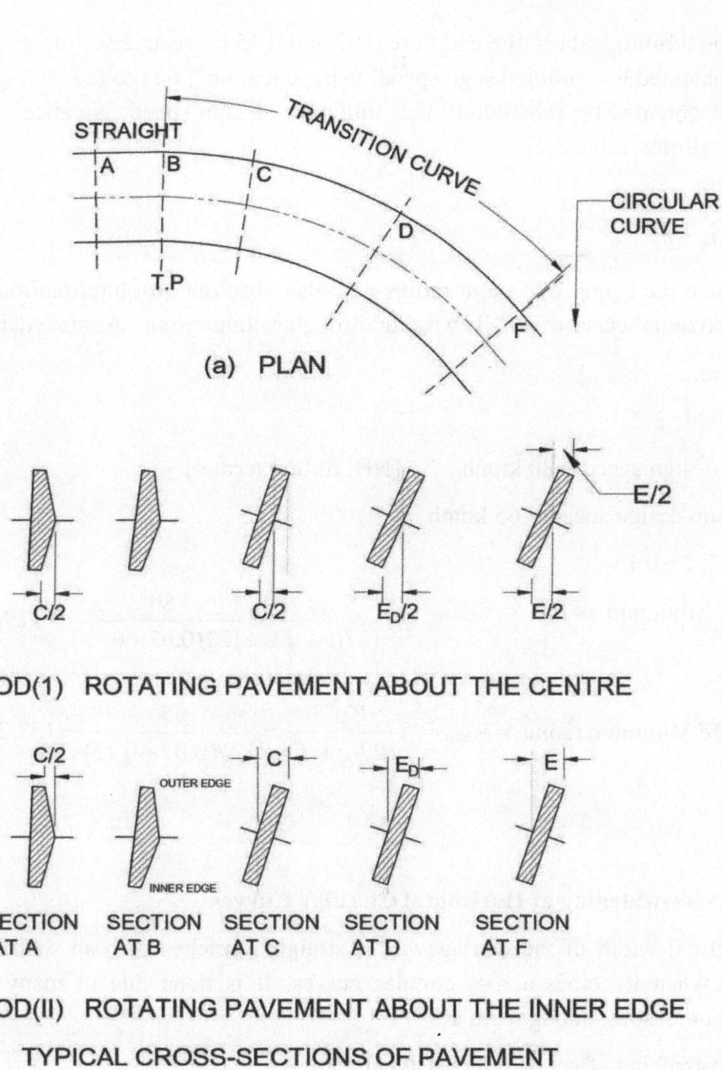

Fig 2.13 Attainment of Super elevation

2.6.3 Radius of horizontal circular curve

Generally, horizontal curves are designed to satisfy the 'ruling design speed' of the highway. But, sometimes it may not be possible to design for ruling design speed, because of certain site constraints; hence, they may be designed for "minimum design speed". As already discussed, if a vehicle negotiates a horizontal curve, centrifugal force would act on the vehicle tending it to skid laterally or to overturn. These effects are avoided by designing the curve in such a manner that this centrifugal force is counteracted by super elevation and lateral skid resistance. The relation connecting these variables is given in Eq. 2.6.

$$e + f = \frac{v^2}{gR} = \frac{V^2}{127R}$$

Here, the limiting values of e and f are 0.07 and 0.15 respectively. Adopting these values, the radius obtained for 'ruling design speed' using equation 2.6 is called '*ruling minimum radius*' and that obtained by substituting the 'minimum design speed' is called '*absolute minimum radius*'. [Refer Table 2.2]

Example 2.9:

Determine the ruling minimum radius and also absolute absolute minimum radius required for a horizontal curve of an NH passing through rolling terrain. Assume data suitably.

Solution:

From Table 2.2

Ruling design speed = 80 kmph [NH, rolling terrain]

Minimum design speed = 65 kmph

e = 0.07; f = 0.15

Ruling Minimum radius = $R_{ruling} = \dfrac{V_{ruling}^2}{127(e+f)} = \dfrac{80^2}{127(0.07+0.15)} = 229m$ say 230m

Absolute Minimum radius = $R_{min} = \dfrac{V_{min}^2}{127(e+f)} = \dfrac{65^2}{127(0.07+0.15)} = 151.2m$ say 152m

2.6.4 Extra-widening at Horizontal Circular Curves

The normal width of the carriageway at straight stretches of road will be widened a little further when it comes across circular curves. It is done due to many reasons. The two important reasons among them are :

i. Off-tracking effect of vehicles at curves.

ii. Psychological reasons for the driver.

Off-tracking of vehicles (Mechanical widening)

Automobiles have rigid wheel bases, and only their front wheel can be turned.When the vehicle negotiates a circular curve, the rear wheels will not follow the exact path of the front wheels.There will be a shift for the inner rear wheel path towards inner side of the curve. See Fig 2.14.

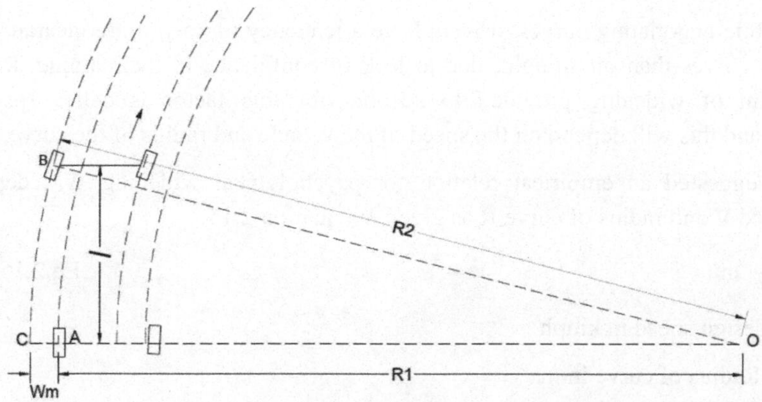

Fig 2.14 Off-tracking and mechanical widening on horizontal curve

However, if the inner front wheel takes a path on the inner edge of the pavement, the inner rear wheel will be off the pavement. This phenomenon is called 'off-tracking of the vehicle'. The amount off-tracking depends on length of wheel base of the vehicle and turning angle or radius of the horizontal curve traversed.The widening of carriageway provided to account for off-tracking of vehicles is generally called 'Mechanical Widening', 'W_m'. It is calculated as explained below: (Refer Fig 2.14)

Let, R_1 = Radius of outer rear wheel path in metre.

R_2 = Radius of outer front wheel path in metre.

$R_2 - R_1 = W_m =$ Mechanical Widening.

l = Length of wheelbase of vehicle in metre.

For the right triangle, OAB,

$OB^2 = OA^2 + AB^2$

$R_2^2 = R_1^2 + l^2$

$R_2^2 - R_1^2 = l^2$

$(R_2+R_1)(R_2-R_1) = l^2$

$2R \times W_m = l^2$ since $R_1 \approx R_2 = R$

or $W_m = \frac{l^2}{2R}$ This is for single lane.

If n lanes are there, vehicle in each lane requires this W_m.

So, total $W_m = \frac{nl^2}{2R}$ Eq.2.14

Psychological Widening

Further, while negotiating curves, drivers have a tendency to keep more clearances between vehicles at curves than on straight, due to lack of confidence in maintaining design speed. The amount of widening provided to account for this factor is called 'psychological widening' and this will depend on the speed of the vehicle and radius of the curve.

IRC has suggested an empirical relation for psychological widening W_{PS} depending on design speed V and radius of curve R as given in equation 2.15.

$$W_{PS} = \frac{V}{9.5\sqrt{R}} \text{ m} \qquad \text{Eq.2.15}$$

where V- design speed in kmph

R- Radius of curve in m

Hence, the total extra width W_e required for the highway at curve

= Mechanical Widening + Psychological Widening

$= W_m + W_{PS}$

$$W_e = \frac{nl^2}{2R} + \frac{V}{9.5\sqrt{R}} \qquad \text{Eq. 2.16}$$

Where, n = radius of curve

V = design speed in kmph

l = wheel base of vehicle in m (taken as 6 m, generally)

The extra widths recommended by the IRC for single and two-lane pavements are given in Table 2.9.

Table 2.9 Extra width of pavement on horizontal curves (IRC)

Radius of curve (m)	**Extra width (m)**	
	Single-lane	**Two-lane**
Upto 20	0.9	1.5
21-40	0.6	1.5
41-60	0.6	1.2
61-100	Nil	0.9
101-300	Nil	0.6
Above 300	Nil	Nil

Normally, extra width is provided equally on each side of the curve ($W_e/2$). But, on sharp curves, the entire W_e may be provided on the inner side of the curve. Also, this W_e or $W_e/2$

shall be attained gradually along the length of the transition curve, so that at the start of the circular curve, the required W_e is attained and maintained throughout.

Example 2.10

Calculate the extra width required for a two-lane MDR with design speed 65 kmph at a horizontal curve of radius 240 m.

Solution:

V = 65 kmph, R = 240 m, n = 2, l = 6.0 m (assumed)

Extra width,

$$W_e = \frac{nl^2}{2R} + \frac{V}{9.5\sqrt{R}}$$

$$= \frac{2\times 6^2}{2\times 240} + \frac{65}{9.5\sqrt{240}} = 0.15 + 0.44$$

$$= 0.59 \text{ m}$$

Example 2.11

There is a horizontal curve of radius equal to ruling minimum radius on an NH passing through plain terrain. Calculate the total width of the pavement on that curve.

Solution:

V = 100 kmph (NH plain terrain), n = 2, l = 6.0 m (assumed), W = 7.0 m

$$R = \frac{V^2}{127(e+f)} = \frac{100^2}{127(0.07+0.15)} = 357.9m \cong 360m$$

Extra width,

$$W_e = \frac{nl^2}{2R} + \frac{V}{9.5\sqrt{R}}$$

$$\frac{2\times 6^2}{2\times 360} + \frac{100}{9.5\sqrt{360}} = 0.1 + 0.56 = 0.66m$$

So total width, B = (W+W_e) = 7.0 + 0.66 = 7.66 m

2.6.5 Transition curves

If a circular curve is connected abruptly to a straight stretch, it causes a sudden jerk or discomfort to travelers when they enter the circular curve from straight stretch because of the sudden application of centrifugal force on the vehicle. So transition curves are provided to connect straight stretches of road with circular curve by which smooth introduction of centrifugal force as well as super elevation is made possible. The radius of transition curve changes from point to point, ranging from infinity at the start of the transition curve (or end of straight) to a minimum value equal to radius of the circular curve. See Fig 2.15.

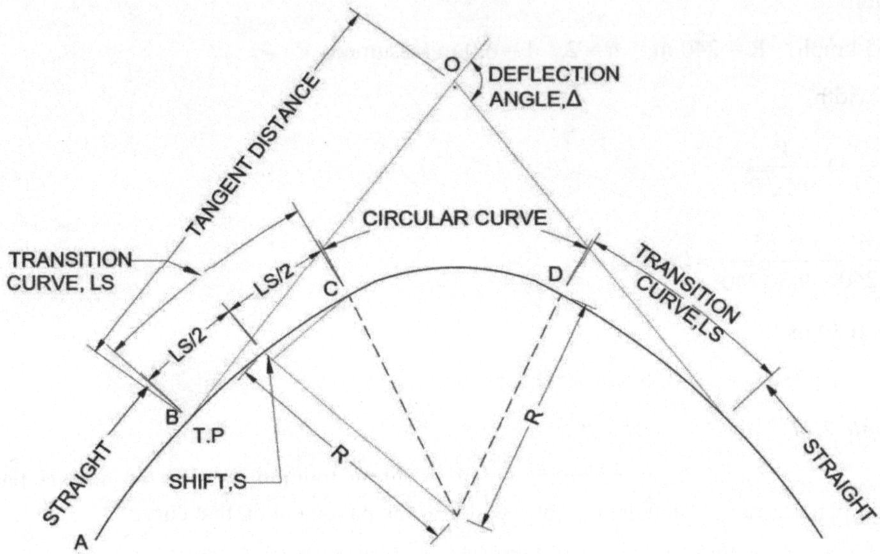

Fig 2.15 Transition Curve in Horizontal Alignment

Functions of Transition Curves in Highways

- To introduce the centrifugal force gradually on the vehicle.
- To provide riding and steering comfort to the vehicle.
- To introduce the superelevation and extra widening gradually along the length of transition curve.
- To provide an aesthetic appearance of the road.

Though there are different types of transition curves like spiral, lemniscate and cubic parabola in use, spiral type is said to be the most ideal one for highway transition curves.

Design of transition curve

The design of transition curve means we have to find the 'length' and 'shift' of the curve. The length is decided on the basis of three criteria, which are to be satisfied simultaneously. These criteria are listed below:

i. Gradual introduction of rate of change of centrifugal acceleration.

ii. Gradual introduction of rate of change of superelevation.

iii. Minimum length by empirical formula, suggested by the IRC.

In order to fulfill all the above three criteria, the highest of the three values is taken as the final length of transition curve.

i. Length of transition curve based on rate of change of centrifugal acceleration

Let 'L_s' the length of transition curve in metre,

'R' the radius of circular curve in metre,

't' time taken in seconds by the vehicle to travel 'L_s' at design speed v m/s, $t = L_s/v$

'α' the maximum centrifugal acceleration attained at the end of transition (start of circular curve) $= \frac{v^2}{R}$ m/s^2,

Rate of change of centrifugal acceleration, 'C' $= \frac{\alpha}{t} = \frac{v^2}{Rt} = \frac{v^2 \times v}{R \times Ls} = \frac{v^3}{Ls \times R}$ m/s^3

or $L_s = \frac{v^3}{CR}$ [v in m/s, R in m] Eq. 2.17a

$L_s = \frac{0.0215\, V^3}{CR}$ [V in kmph, R in m] Eq. 2.17b

where, $C = \frac{80}{75+V}$ [C in m/s^3, V in kmph] Eq. 2.18

The minimum and maximum values of C are 0.5 and 0.8 respectively.

ii. Length of transition curve based on rate of introduction of super elevation

IRC has suggested the rate ofintroduction of superelevation depending on the terrain conditions as:

In open country	- 1 in 150
In built-up areas	- 1 in 100
In hill roads	- 1 in 60

If e is the rate of superelevation, B total width of pavement including extra width, the amount of superelevation 'E' to be achieved at the start of the circular curve through the length of transition curve is E = B×e.

If the pavement it is rotated with respect to inner edge, the length of transition curve will be,

L_s = E×N = B×e×N Eq. 2.19a

If the pavement is rotated with respect to center line only, E/2 need be achieved through L_s. Hence L_s will also become EN/2 = eNB/2 Eq. 2.19b

iii. Empirical relation suggested by the IRC

IRC has suggested the following empirical relations for finding 'L_s' with respect to terrain conditions as

a) for plain and rolling, $L_s = 2.7V^2/R$ Eq. 2.20a

b) For mountainous and steep, $L_s = V^2/R$ Eq. 2.20b

[V in kmph, R in m]

Adopt the highest value of L_s from equations 2.17, 2.19 and 2.20 given above as the design length of transition curve. These transition curves are provided between the tangent points of the straight stretches and the ends of the circular curve on both sides as shown in Fig 2.15.

If the length of transition curve is L_s and the radius of the circular curve is R, the shift 'S' of the transition curve is given by the Eq. 2.21.

$$S = \frac{L_s^2}{24R} \qquad \text{Eq. 2.21}$$

Example 2.12

Design the length and shift of the transition curve required for a circular curve of radius 240m in a MDR passing through plain terrain (V=65 kmph). Assume the pavement is rotated with respect to centre line for the introduction of superelevation.

Solution :

Given : V = 65 kmph, R= 240 m, N = 150 (rate of change of e)

Pavement rotated with respect to centre line.

Total width of pavement,B= W + W_e

$$W_e = \frac{nl^2}{2R} + \frac{V}{9.5\sqrt{R}} = \frac{2\times6^2}{2\times240} + \frac{65}{9.5\sqrt{240}}$$

$$= 0.15 + 0.44 = 0.59 \text{ m}$$

Total width, B = 7.00+ 0.59 = 7.59 m

Length of transition curve based centrifugal acceleration:

$$L_s = \frac{0.0215V^3}{CR}$$

$$C = \frac{80}{75+V} = \frac{80}{75+65} = 0.57m/s^3 = 0.57m/s^3 \quad [0.5 < C < 0.8] \qquad \text{(OK)}$$

$$L_s = \frac{0.0215\times65^3}{0.57\times240} = 43.2m \text{ -------} \qquad \text{(a)}$$

Design of e

for 0.75 V and f = 0

$$e = \frac{V^2}{225R} = \frac{65^2}{225 \times 240} = 0.078 > 0.07$$

So provide e= 0.07 and check for 'f' with full 'V'

$$f = \frac{V^2}{127R} - e = \frac{65^2}{127 \times 240} - 0.07 = 0.06 < 0.15$$

(OK)

Hence design e = 0.07

Length of transition curve for e

Since pavement is rotated with respect to centre line,

$$L_s = \frac{EN}{2} = \frac{e(W + W_e)N}{2} = \frac{0.07 \times 7.59 \times 150}{2} = 39.84m$$ ------- (b)

Length as per empirical formula by IRC (plain terrain)

$$L_s = \frac{2.7V^2}{R} = \frac{2.7 \times 65^2}{240} = 47.53m$$ ------(c)

Adopt the highest of (a), (b), (c) as 47.53m say 48m as the design length of transition curve.

$$Shift = S = \frac{L_s^{\,2}}{24R} = \frac{48^2}{24 \times 240} = 0.40m$$

Example 2.13

Design the transition curve required for an NH passing through plain terrain in heavy rainfall area at a horizontal curve of radius equal to ruling minimum radius. Assume data suitably.

Solution

V = 100 kmph (NH plain terrain)

Rate of change of e, N = 150

Normal width of carriageway = 7.0 m

Heavy rainfall area implies that the pavement has to be rotated with respect to inner edge for the introduction of e.

For centrifugal acceleration

$$R = \frac{V^2}{g(e+f)} = \frac{V^2}{127(e+f)} = \frac{100^2}{127 \times 0.22} = 358m$$ say 360m

$$L_s = \frac{0.0215V^3}{CR}$$

$$C = \frac{80}{75+V} = \frac{80}{75+100} = 0.457 < 0.5$$

take C = 0.5

$$L_s = \frac{0.0215 \times 100^3}{0.5 \times 360} = 119.4m$$

For super elevation

$$W_e = \frac{nl^2}{2R} + \frac{V}{9.5\sqrt{R}} = \frac{2 \times 6^2}{2 \times 360} + \frac{100}{9.5\sqrt{360}} = 0.1 + 0.55 = 0.65m$$

Total width B = (W + W_e) = 7.0 + 0.65 = 7.65m

L_s = N × e × B = 150 × 0.70 × 7.65 = 80.3m

Empirical formula

$$L_s = \frac{2.7V^2}{R} = \frac{2.7 \times 100^2}{360} = 75m$$

Adopting the highest of three values L_s = 119.4m say 120m

$$Shift = \frac{L_s^{\,2}}{24R} = \frac{120^2}{24 \times 360} = 1.67m$$

2.6.6 Set-back Distance on horizontal curves

It is important to ensure sight distance along the inner side of the curve while laying out horizontal curves for highway alignment. No obstruction should enter the sight line along the curve in order to assure sight distance (SSD, ISD, or OSD), leaving enough space between the obstruction and the road's centre line. See Fig 2.16.

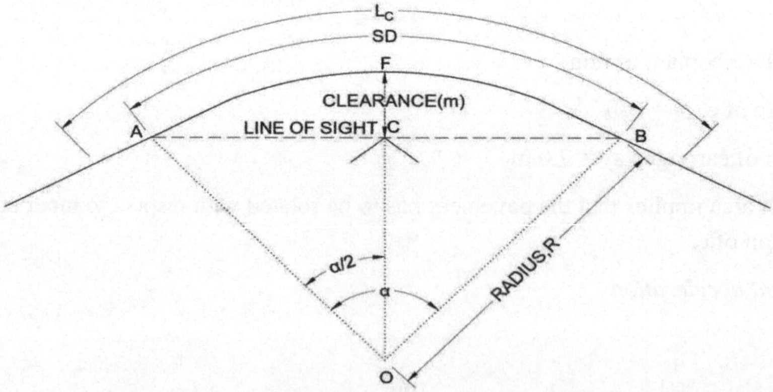

Fig 2.16 Set-back distance when length of curve > sight distance

The distance to any obstruction inside a curve from the centre line of the carriageway providing sufficient sight distance is called 'setback distance'. It will depend upon the following factors:

a) Required sight distance 'S' (SSD or ISD or OSD

b) Radius of horizontal circular curve (R)

c) Length of horizontal circular curve (L_c), which may be less than or greater than S.

Refer Fig 2.16.

Two cases are considered: if length of curve (L_c) greater than sight distance (S) or less than sight distance.

Case (i): $L_c > S$

from the geometry of Fig 2.14,

Setback distance m = OF - OC = R - Rcos α/2

i.e., $m = R(1 - \cos \alpha/2)$ Eq.2.22a

where, α= S/R radians = $\frac{180}{\pi} \times \frac{S}{R} \deg rees$

OR $\frac{\alpha}{2} = \frac{180}{2\pi} \times \frac{S}{R} \deg rees$ Eq. 2.22b

If there are two or more lanes, set-back distance has to be ensured with respect to the visibility of the innermost lane. Thus, if 'd' is the distance between the centre line of the road and the center line of the innermost lane in m, sight distance is measured along the center line of the innermost lane, and the set-back distance 'm' is given by:

$$m' = R - (R-d)\cos\frac{\alpha'}{2}$$

Eq.2.23

$$\frac{\alpha}{2} = \frac{180}{2\pi} \frac{S}{(R-d)} \deg rees$$

Case (ii) : $L_c < S$ (Refer Fig 2.17)

As shown in Fig 2.17, α is measured with respect to length of curve L_c only, not sight distance.

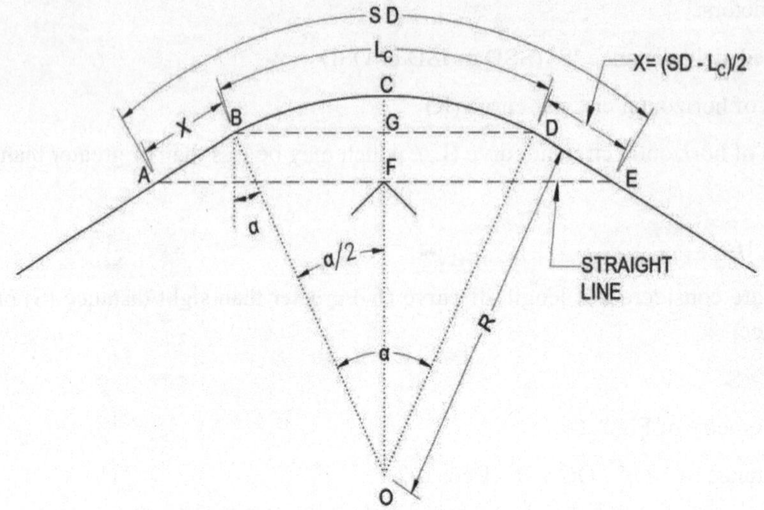

Fig 2.17 Set-back distance when length of curve < sight distance

Total Set-back Distance = FC = FG + GC

$= R\ (R\text{-}d)\ \cos\alpha/2 + (S\text{-}\ L_c)/2x\ \ \sin\alpha/2$ Eq. 2.24

where, $\alpha/2 = (180\ x\ L_c)/\ ((2\pi(R\text{-}d))$ degrees.

Example 2.14

A 2-lane state highway has a horizontal curve of radius=280m, length = 320m, total width of pavement = 7.6m. Design the set-back distance in order to facilitate a sight distance of 250m.

Solution:

Given $R = 280m$, $L_c = 320m$, $B = 7.6m$, $S = 250m$, $d= 7.6/4 = 1.9m$

$\alpha/2 = (180\ x\ S)/\ ((2\pi(R\text{-}d))$ degrees = $(180\ x\ 250)\ /\ ((2\pi(280\text{-}1.9)$

= 25.8 degrees

Since, $L_c > S$, Set-back distance, $m = R\ (R\text{-}d)\ \cos\alpha/2 = 280\ (280\text{-}1.9)\ \cos 25.8$

= 29.62m say 30m

Example 2.15

A national highway with 4 lanes has a horizontal curve of radius = 320m, length = 340m, sight distance = 400m, width of pavement including extra width = 14.8m. Design the set - back distance required for this curve.

Solution:

Given $R = 320m$, $L_c = 340m$, $B = 14.8m$, $S = 400m$, $d = 14.8/2 - 3.7/2 = 5.55m$

$\alpha/2 = (180 \times L_c)/((2\pi(R-d))$degrees $= (180 \times 340) / ((2\pi(320-5.55)$

$= 30.98$ degrees

Since, $L_c<S$, Set-back distance, $m = R (R-d) \cos \alpha/2 + (S- L_c)/2 \times \sin \alpha/2$

$= 320 (320-5.55) \cos 30.98 + (400- 340) /2 \times \sin 30.98$

$= 65.85m$ say 66m.

2.7 DESIGN OF VERTICAL ALIGNMENT

Vertical alignment of a highway deals with the alignment with respect to vertical plane. It includes the design of gradient and vertical curves. Vertical alignment influences mainly speed and acceleration of vehicles, sight distance, riding comfort, and vehicle operating cost.

Gradient: If the rate of rise or fall along the length of the road with respect to horizontal plane. It is expressed as a ratio of 1 in x or n% or y degrees.

Types of gradients: Depending on the site conditions and the requirements of the highway, different types of gradient are employed:

i. Ruling gradient
ii. Limiting gradient
iii. Exceptional gradient
iv. Minimum gradient
v. Compensated gradient

SCAN ME
for
Vertical alignment
(Module-3, Lecture-17)

Ruling gradient: It is the maximum gradient which can be adopted for a highway such that there will not be extra consumption of fuel or energy or tractive power for the vehicle and extra fatigue for animals in the case of animal-drawn vehicles.

Limiting gradient: It is the gradient steeper than the ruling gradient, provided at places where it compels to do so because of increased cost of construction. But they are allowed for limited distances only and shall be separated by flatter gradient.

Exceptional gradient they are still steeper than limiting one, provided in extraordinary situations for short stretches only. IRC recommends the maximum value of ruling, limiting and exceptional gradient with respect to different terrain conditions which are given in Table 2.10.

Table 2.10 Gradients recommended by IRC

Terrain	**Gradient**		
	Ruling	**Limiting**	**Exceptional**
Plain/Rolling	3.3% (1 in 30)	5.0% (1 in 20)	6.7% (1 in 15)
Mountainous & Steep, with elevation > 3000m above mean sea level	5.0% (1 in 20)	6.0% (1 in 16.7)	7.0% (1 in 14.3)
Steep terrain upto 3000m elevation	6.0% (1 in 16.7)	7.0% (1 in 14.3)	80% (1 in 12.5)

Minimum gradient it may be possible to construct a road with even zero gradient; but it will cause drainage problem. Though the water falling on the pavement can be drained off to the sides by providing proper camber or cross-slope to the pavement as well as shoulders, deep cutting will be required for the side drain to maintain the longitudinal slope for the drainage of water collected there. Hence, it is desirable to have a 'minimum gradient' on roads matching with the bed slope of the side drains. The minimum gradient depends on factors like amount of rainfall and run-off, type of soil, topography and other site conditions. IRC suggests a minimum gradient of 1 in 500, if concrete drains are provided, and 1 in 200 to 1 in 100, if soil drains are provided.

Compensated gradient: If an ascending gradient equal to ruling gradient or maximum permissible gradient is coming along with a horizontal circular curve at the same chainage of a highway, then for a vehicle negotiating such a gradient, there will be a reduction in the tractive effort available for the vehicle to climb that gradient. It is called 'curve resistance' which has developed due to the horizontal curve. That is, when a vehicle negotiates a curve, due to the turning angle α of the horizontal curve, the tractive effort P on the vehicle if it were on a straight stretch, will be reduced to $P\cos\alpha$, resulting in decrease in speed. Hence, to overcome this curve resistance and grade resistance, two options are available either increase the radius of the curve for which extra land acquisition is required, or decrease the gradient of the road at that section for which only extra earthwork is involved. Generally, the latter option is desirable as it is economical and also it will not affect the surrounding land. Thus, this reduced gradient adopted on that horizontal curve to accommodate the curve resistance is called 'compensated gradient' and the amount of reduction in gradient is called 'grade compensation'. IRC has suggested an empirical relation for calculating grade compensation depending on radius of the circular curve as follows:

Grade compensation, % = (30+R)/R %, Eq. 2.25

subject to a maximum value of 75/R %.

where R is the radius of circular curve in m.

i.e., Compensated gradient = Ruling gradient - Grade compensation

Example 2.16

In the alignment of a MDR on a hilly terrain, a horizontal curve of radius 90m has come simultaneously at a stretch with a ruling gradient of 5%. Determine the actual gradient to be provided at the curve.

Solution:

Given: R = 90 m, Ruling gradient = 5%

Grade compensation, % = (30+R)/R % = (30+90)/90 %

= 120/90 = 1.33%

Maximum limit of Grade compensation, % = 75/R % = 75/90 = 0.83 %

So, Grade compensation to be adopted = 0.83%

$\therefore$ Compensated gradient (actual gradient to be provided) =5.0 - 0.83 = 4.17%.

Vertical curves

Whenever there is a change in gradient in the vertical alignment of a highway, it has to be connected by a smooth vertical curve, providing adequate sight distance and riding comfort

There are two types of vertical curves:

(i) Summit curves (Vertical curve with convexity upwards)

(ii) Valley curves (Vertical curves with convexity downwards)

Summit curves: As shown in Fig 2.18, there are different instances at which summit curves are to be designed. If two gradients $n_1$and $n_2$are meeting at a point, the deviation angle, Nis computed as the algebraic difference between them, as shown in the Fig 2.18.

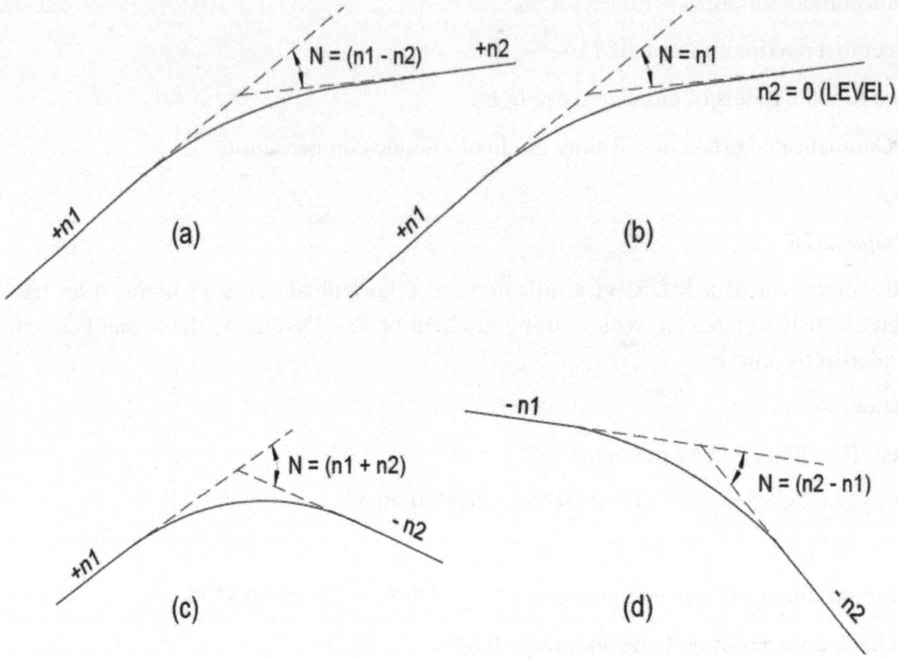

Fig 2.18 Types of Summit Curves

The length of summit curve is designed on the basis of SSD or ISD / OSD.Since the height of objects concerned in the SSD and OSD are different, separate equations are suggested for the computation of length of summit curve.

Also, two cases of length of curve in relation to sight distance i.e., L>S and L<S, are suggested by the IRC as follows:

(a) For Stopping Sight Distance (SSD)

$$L = \frac{NS^2}{4.4} \; for L > S \qquad \text{Eq.2.26}$$

$$L = 2S - \frac{4.4}{N} \; for L < S \qquad \text{Eq.2.27}$$

(b) For Overtaking Sight Distance (OSD) and Intermediate Sight Distance (ISD):

$$L = \frac{NS^2}{9.6} \; for L > S$$

Eq.2.28

$$L = 2S - \frac{9.6}{N} \, for L < S \qquad \text{Eq.2.29}$$

where, L= length of summit curve, S = Sight distance (SSD or ISD/OSD) and N = deviation angle.

Notes:

(i) During the design of vertical curves, we may first assume one condition say L>S and calculate the value of L, and if the assumed condition is satisfied, then the length obtained can be taken as the design length of the curve. Otherwise, proceed with the second condition L<S, by which the result will be obtained.

(ii) Generally for submit curves, OSD is the criterion for design. If that is not feasible, ISD has to be considered then only; then only the SSD need be considered, which will give the absolute minimum length for the curve.

IRC has recommended the minimum length of vertical curves for different speeds and for maximum grade change (%) which do not require vertical curve. These are given in Table 2.11.

Table 2.11 Minimum length of vertical curves (IRC)

Design speed, kmph	**Max. grade change (%) not requiring vertical curve**	**Min. length of vertical curves (m) (for higher grade change values)**
35	1.5	15
40	1.2	20
50	1.0	30
65	0.8	40
80	0.6	50
100	0.5	60

Valley curves: Valley curves are sag curves with convexity downwards as shown in Fig 2.19. Deviation angle N is the algebraic difference between the successive gradients.

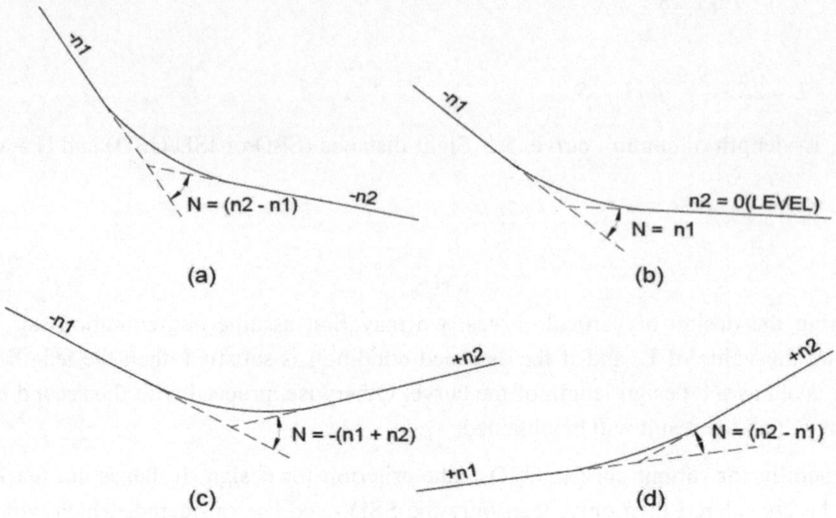

Fig 2.19 Types of Valley Curves

While driving during day time on valley curves, visibility or sight distance is not a problem. But during night, the sight distance available will be restricted with respect to the gradients of the valley curve. Hence, headlight sight distance has to be taken into account. Further, unlike the case of summit curves, here, there is a possibility of sudden jerk to the passengers in the vehicle, while negotiating deep valley curves at high speeds. It is because, when a vehicle travels along a valley curve, the centrifugal force as well as weight of the vehicle act in the same direction, that is downward, causing an impact to the vehicle, resulting in discomfort to passengers.Whereas, in the case of summit curve, when the self weight of vehicle act downward, centrifugal force will be upward, resulting in a balanced condition of forces; hence no discomfort to passengers sitting in the vehicle.

Thus, two criteria are to be considered in the design of valley curve: (a) headlight sight distance and (b) riding comfort. Adopt the highest of the two values as the design length of the curve as both criteria are to be met.

Length for HSD: Two cases are considered, viz: L>S and L<S where, L is the length of valley curve and S is the headlight sight distance.

$$L = \frac{NS^2}{1.5 + 0.035S} \; for L > S \quad \text{Eq. 2.30}$$

$$L = 2S - \frac{1.5 + 0.035S}{N} \; for L < S \quad \text{Eq. 2.31}$$

Length for riding comfort:

$$L = 2\left[\frac{NV^3}{C}\right]^{1/2} \qquad \{V \text{ in m/s, } C = 0.6 m/s^3\} \qquad \text{Eq. 2.32a}$$

Or, $$L = 0.38(NV^3)^{1/2} \qquad \text{Eq. 2.32b}$$

Deepest point on the valley curve: The deepest or lowest point on a valley curve is significant with respect to drainage considerations, which indicate the position of cross drainage work or culvert. If the two grade n_1 and n_2 are equal, then the lowest point will be at the centre of the length of the curve. If the curve is asymmetrical the lowest point lies on the side of flatter grade and its distance from the tangent point of grade n_1 is given by the equation:

$$X_o = L.\sqrt{\frac{n_1}{2N}} \qquad \text{Eq.2.33}$$

from the side of n_1.

Example 2.17

Design the summit curve required to provide SSD when two gradients + 3.0 and -5.0 per cent are meeting at a point in a MDR passing through rolling terrain. Assume data suitably.

Solution:

Given: Design speed, V = 65kmph (MDR, rolling terrain)

n_1= +3.0%, n_2= -5.0%, f=0.35, t=2.5s

$$SSD = 0.278V.t + \frac{V^2}{254(f \pm 0.01n)}$$

Neglecting the slope in SSD calculation,

$$SSD = 0.278 \times 65 \times 2.5 + \frac{65^2}{254(0.35 \pm 0)} \qquad = 92.7m \text{ say } 93m$$

Deviation angle, N =+0.03-(-0.05) = 0.08

Assuming L>SSD, L= NS^2 / 4.4 = (0.08 93^2) / 4.4

=157.25m > 93m × OK

Hence, length of summit curve = 158m

From Table 2.11,

Minimum length suggested for 65kmph by IRC = 40m (satisfied)

Example 2.18

Two grades +1/100 and -1/120 are meeting at a point to form a summit curve on an NH passing through rolling terrain. Design the summit curve to satisfy the requirements of a) SSD of 190 m b) OSD of 600 m. Due to site constraints length of vertical curve is restricted to a maximum of 500 m. So if OSD cannot be fulfilled, check the design for ISD instead.

Solution:

$$N = \frac{1}{100} - \left(-\frac{1}{120}\right) = \frac{1}{100} + \frac{1}{120} = \frac{11}{600}$$

V = 80 kmph (NH, rolling terrain)

SSD = 190 m, OSD = 600m

a) For SSD: Assume L>S

$$L = \frac{NS^2}{4.4} = \frac{11 \times 190^2}{600 \times 4.4} = 150.4m < 190m$$

As L<S, assumption is not correct

Assuming L<S, $L = 2S - \frac{4.4}{N} = 2 \times 190 - \frac{4.4 \times 600}{11} = 140m < 190m$ (OK)

b) For OSD Assume L>S

$$L = \frac{NS^2}{9.6} = \frac{11 \times 600^2}{600 \times 9.6} = 687.5m > 600m$$ (OK)

But it is suggested that due to site constraints, length should not be greater than500m.

So check for ISD.

ISD = 2 × SSD = 2 × 190 = 380m

Assume L>S

$$L = \frac{NS^2}{9.6} = \frac{11 \times 380^2}{600 \times 9.6} = 275.8m < 380m$$ (not OK)

Hence assume L<S

$L = 2S - \frac{9.6}{N} = 2 \times 380 - \frac{9.6}{11} \times 600 = 236.4m < 380m$ (OK)

So L = 237m and also less than 500m.

Hence provide a length of 237m to fulfill ISD, instead of OSD.

Example 2.19

Two grades -1/25 and +1/30 are meeting at a point in a highway with design speed 100kmph. Design the valley curve required in order to meet the requirements of a headlight sight distance and comfort condition. Take C = 0.6 m/s³.Also find the lowest point to locate cross drainage work.

Solution:

V = 100kmph = 27.8 m/s, $N = \frac{-1}{25} - \frac{1}{30} = \frac{-11}{150}$

a) for headlight sight distance (HSD)

$$HSD = SSD = v.t + \frac{v^2}{2gf} = 27.8 \times 2.5 + \frac{27.8^2}{2 \times 9.81 \times 0.35} = 182.16 \cong 183m$$

Assuming L>S,

$$L = \frac{NS^2}{1.5 + 0.035 \times S} = \frac{11 \times 183^2}{150(1.5 + 0.035 \times 183)} = 310.67m > 183m \quad \text{(OK)}$$

Comfort condition:

$$L = 2(\frac{Nv^3}{C})^{1/2} = 2[\frac{11}{150} \times \frac{27.8^3}{0.6}]^{0.5} = 102.5m$$

Therefore, highest of the two, L = 310.67, say 311m.

Lowest point

$$X_0 = L\sqrt{\frac{n_1}{2N}} = 311 \times \sqrt{\frac{1/12}{2 \times (11/150)}} = 234.4m$$

$$X_o = L\sqrt{\frac{n_1}{2N}} = 311 \times \sqrt{\frac{1/25}{2 \times (11/150)}} = 162.41m$$

i.e. At 162.41m from the side of -1/25 grade is the location of CDW.

UNIT SUMMARY

Geometric elements of the highway

i. Cross sectional elements

ii. Sight distance

iii. Horizontal alignment

iv. Vertical alignment

v. Intersectional elements.

Factors Controlling Geometric Design

i. Design speed

ii. Topography

iii. Traffic

iv. Environmental and other factors

Terrain classification by the IRC

Plain	0-10%
Rolling	10-25%
Mountainous	25-60%
Steep	>60%

Design Speeds for different classes of roads (IRC)

Road Classification	Design speed in kmph							
	Plain		Rolling		Mountainous		Steep	
	Ruling	Minimum	Ruling	Minimum	Ruling	Minimum	Ruling	Minimum
Expressways	120	100	100	80	80	60	80	60
NH & SH	100	80	80	65	50	40	40	30
MDR	80	65	65	50	40	30	30	20
ODR	65	50	50	40	30	25	25	20
VR	50	40	40	35	25	20	25	20

Cross Sectional Elements

i. Typical cross-section of a highway

ii. Pavement surface characteristics

iii. Friction (skid resistance) – lateral and longitudinal

iv. Unevenness of the pavement

v. Camber (cross-slope)

vi. Carriageway width

vii. Median (Traffic Separator)

viii. Kerb

ix. Road margins

x. Roadway width

xi. Right-of-way

Friction (skid resistance):2 types

i. Lateral skid resistance–to design horizontal curves&super elevation, f=0.10-0.15

ii. Longitudinal skid resistance - to design stopping sight distance.f= 0.35-0.40

Pavement Unevenness- cumulative sum of ups and downs measured along the length of the road (mm/km). Measured using 'Bump integrator'.

$BI = 630(IRI)^{1.12}$

Camber or Cross slope

Depends on type of pavement surface and rainfall intensity

Types of Camber: parabolic, straight, and combination of straight & parabolic shapes

Carriageway widths (IRC)

Single lane road	3.75m
2-lane without raised kerbs	7.00m
2-lane with raised kerbs	7.50m
Intermediate lane	5.50m
Multi-lane	3.50m /lane

Median or Traffic Separators desirable width is 5.0 m and minimum is 1.2 m

Kerbs: Types - Low/Mountable, Semi-barrier, Barrier, Submerged.

Road margins: Shoulders, Footpath, Drive way, Cycle track, Parking lane, Bus bay, Lay bye, and Frontage road.

Roadway: Carriageway plus shoulders and separators (median).

Right of way: area acquired for the construction of the highway.

Sight Distances:

i. Stopping sight distance(SSD) = absolute minimum sight distance
ii. Overtaking sight distance(OSD)
iii. Intermediate sight distance = 2×SSD
iv. Headlight sight distance = SSD

$SSD = v.t + \frac{v^2}{2gf}$ {putting v in m/s, t in s, and g in m/s²}

$$0.278V.t + \frac{V^2}{254f}$$

SSD={putting V in kmph, t in s, and g as 9.81 m/s²}

$OSD = (d_1 + d_2 + d_3) = (v_b.t + v_b.T + 2s + v.T)$ m {putting v in m/s, t & T in s}

$OSD = (0.28V_b.t + 0.28V_b.T + 2s + 0.28V.T)$ m {putting V in kmph, t in s}

Minimum length of overtaking zone = 3 x OSD, desirable length = 5 x OSD

Elements of Horizontal Alignment

i. Design speed

ii. Super elevation

iii. Radius of circular curve

iv. Extra widening at curves

v. Length of transition curve

vi. Set-back distance at curves

Super elevation

$$e+f=\frac{v^2}{gR}$$ v in m/s, R in m and g in m/s²

$$e+f=\frac{V^2}{127R}$$ V in kmph, R in m and g= 9.81 m/s²

Attainment of super elevation in the field

- Elimination of crown
- Rotation of pavement

Radius of horizontal circular curve

$$R_{ruling}=\frac{V_{ruling}^2}{127(e+f)}$$

$$R_{min}=\frac{V_{min}^2}{127(e+f)}$$

Extra-widening

i. Off-tracking effect of vehicles

ii. Psychological reasons for driver.

$$W_e=\frac{nl^2}{2R}+\frac{V}{9.5\sqrt{R}}$$

where, n = number of lanes

R = radius of curve

V = design speed in kmph

l = Wheel base of vehicle in m (taken as 6 m, generally)

Transition curves

i. *For rate of change of centrifugal acceleration*

$L_s = \frac{v^3}{CR}$ [v in m/s, R in m]

$L_s = \frac{0.0215\,V^3}{CR}$ [V in kmph, R in m]

where, $C = \frac{80}{75+V}$ [C in m/s³, V in kmph]

ii. *For rate of change of superelevation.*

$L_s = E \times N = B \times e \times N$ (pavement rotated with respect to inner edge)

$L_s = E \times N/2 = B \times e \times N/2$ (pavement rotated with respect to center line)

iii. *By empirical formula (IRC)*

for plain and rolling, $L_s = 2.7V^2/R$

For mountainous and steep, $L_s = V^2/R$

[V in kmph, R in m]

Adopt the highest value as L_s; Shift, $S = \frac{L_s^2}{24R}$

Set-back Distance

$$m' = R - (R-d)\cos\frac{\alpha'}{2}$$

$$\frac{\alpha}{2} = \frac{180}{2\pi}\frac{S}{(R-d)}\deg rees$$

m = R (R-d) Cosα/2 + (S- L_c)/2x sin α/2

where, α/2 = (180 xL_c)/ ((2π(R-d))degrees.

Vertical Alignment: Gradient and Vertical curves

Types of gradients

i. Ruling gradient
ii. Limiting gradient
iii. Exceptional gradient
iv. Minimum gradient
v. Compensated gradient

Gradients Recommended by IRC

Terrain	Gradient		
	Ruling	**Limiting**	**Exceptional**
Plain/Rolling	3.3% (1 in 30)	5.0% (1 in 20)	6.7% (1 in 15)
Mountainous & Steep , with elevation > 3000m above mean sea level	5.0% (1 in 20)	6.0% (1in 6.7)	7.0%(1in14.3)
Steep terrain upto 3000m elevation	6.0%(1in 6.7)	7.0% (1in 4.3)	80%(1in 12.5)

Minimum gradient 1 in 500 (concrete drains)

1 in 200 to 1 in 100 (soil drains)

Grade compensation, % = (30+R)/R %, subject to a maximum value of 75/R % .

where R is the radius of circular curve in m.

i.e., Compensated gradient = Ruling gradient - Grade compensation

Vertical curves:

(iii) *Summit curves (convexity upwards)*

(c) *For Stopping Sight Distance (SSD)*

$$L = \frac{NS^2}{4.4} \, for L > S$$

$$L = 2S - \frac{4.4}{N} \, for L < S$$

(d) *For OSD and ISD:*

$$L = \frac{NS^2}{9.6} \, for L > S$$

$$L = 2S - \frac{9.6}{N} \, for L < S$$

(iv) Valley curves (convexity downwards)

Length for HSD:

$$L = \frac{NS^2}{1.5 + 0.035S} \, for L > S$$

$$L = 2S - \frac{1.5 + 0.035S}{N} \quad for L < S$$

Length for riding comfort:

$$L = 2\left[\frac{NV^3}{C}\right]^{1/2} \qquad \{V \text{ in m/s}, C = 0.6 m/s^3\}$$

Deepest point on the valley curve:

$$X_o = L.\sqrt{\frac{n_1}{2N}}$$

EXERCISES

Multiple Choice Questions

2.1 The portion of a road surface, which is meant for vehicular traffic is known as

a) carriageway b) shoulder c) expressway d) all of the above

2.2 Carriageway is protected by ______ wide shoulders.

a) 0.5 to 1.25m b) 1.25 to 2m c) 2 to 4m d) 4 to 6m

2.3 For thin bituminous macadam roads, the recommended camber is

a) 1.7 to 2.0% b) 2 to 2.5% c) 2.5 to 3.0% d) 3 to 4%

2.4 The highest point on the road surface is called

a) camber b) crown c) gradient d) berm

2.5 The slope of the line joining crown and edge of the road surface is known as

a) cross-fell b) cross-slope c) camber d) any of the above

2.6 A camber of 2% means that for a 7m wide pavement, the cross will be _____ cm above the edge of the road.

a) 14cm b) 7cm c) 3.5cm d) 1.4cm

2.7 The primary object of providing camber is

a) easy drainage b) improved appearance c) easy separation of up and down traffic d) easy overtaking

2.8 The maximum value of coefficient of lateral friction is

a) 1.0 b) 0.5 c) 0.4 d) 0.15

2.9 The maximum value of coefficient of longitudinal friction is

a) 1.0 b) 0.5 c) 0.4 d) 0.15

2.10 Minimum superelevation on a curve is

a) 0% b) 7% c) camber d) gradient

2.11 Super elevation is

a) directly proportional to speed ofvehicle

b) inversely proportional to speed of vehicle

c) directly proportional to radius of the curve

d) inversely proportional to the width of pavement

2.12 Maximum super elevation in general cases is

a) 10% b) 3% c) 5% d) 7%

2.13 Maximum super elevation in hill roads is

a) 5% b) 7% c) 10% d) 12%

2.14 The maximum rate of super elevation (neglecting friction) is given by

a) e = $\frac{V^2}{127R}$ b) e = $\frac{V^2}{225R}$ c) e = $\frac{V^2}{540R}$ d) e = $\frac{V^2}{1.27R}$

2.15 Superelevation + lateral friction should not be greater than

a) $\frac{V^2}{127R}$ b) $\frac{V^2}{225R}$ c) $\frac{V^2}{7.4R}$ d) $\frac{V^2}{27R}$

2.16 If the radius of curve is R, and wheel base of physical is 'l', then mechanical widening is

a) $\frac{l^2}{R}$ b) $\frac{l^2}{2R}$ c) $\frac{2l^2}{R}$ d) $\frac{l^2}{2R^2}$

2.17 Psychological widening required for a curve of radius at a speed of V kmph is

a) $\frac{V^2}{9.5R}$ b) $\frac{V^2}{9.5\sqrt{R}}$ c) $\frac{9.5\sqrt{R}}{V}$ d) $\frac{9.5\sqrt{R}}{V^2}$

2.18 On sharp curves, widening of the carriageway is done by providing extra width

a) fully on inner side of the curve.

b) fully on outer side of the curve.

c)half each on inner and outer sides of the curve.

d)3/4thon the outer side and 1/4thon the inner side.

2.19 In Plains the minimum length of transition curve is

a) $\frac{V^2}{R}$ b) $\frac{2.7V^2}{R}$ c) $\frac{V^2}{1.5R}$ d) $\frac{V^2}{24R}$

2.20 Reaction time of driver taken for SSD calculation is ____ seconds.

a) 1.5 b) 2.5 c) 3.0 d) 2.0

2.21 Reaction time taken for OSD calculation is ____ seconds.

a) 1.5 b) 2.0 c) 3.0 d) 2.5

2.22 Height of driver's eye level is assumed as _____ for sight distance calculation

a) 1.0m b) 1.2m c) 0.15m d) 1.5m

2.23 For stopping sight distance, height of object is considered as

a) 10cm b) 15cm c) 50cm d) 25cm

2.24 SSD is given by

$a) v.t + \dfrac{v^2}{2g(f \pm n/100)}$ $b) v.t^2 + \dfrac{v}{2gfn/100}$ $c) (v.t + \dfrac{v^2}{2g}) f$ $d) v.t + \dfrac{v^2 f}{2gn}$

2.25 Length of vehicle controls the design of

a) SSD b) super elevation c) extra widening d) gradient

2.26 Weight of vehicle controls the design of

a) thickness of pavement b) camber c) extra widening d) transition curve

2.27 Minimum gradient required for concrete drains is

a) 1 in 500 b) 1 in 100 c) 1 in 200 d) 1 in 1000

2.28 Ruling gradient in Plains is

a) 1 in 20 b) 1 in 30 c) 1 in 40 d) 1 in 50

2.29 Limiting gradient in Plains is

a) 1 in 15 b) 1 in 20 c) 1 in 30 d) 1 in 40

2.30 Exceptional gradient in Plains is

a) 1 in 15 b) 1 in 20 c) 1 in 30 d) 1 in 40

2.31 Maximum value of grade compensation is

a) 175/R b) 75/R c) R/75 d) $75/R^2$

2.32 The type of transition curve ideally suited for horizontal alignment of highways is

a) cubic parabola b) spiral c) lemniscate d) none of the above

2.33 The expression for length of transition curve in metre is

a) $L=\dfrac{V^3}{CR}$ b) $L=\dfrac{V^2}{CR}$ c) $L=\dfrac{V^3}{CR^2}$ d) $L=\dfrac{CV^3}{R}$

where, C is the rate of change of centrifugal acceleration in m/s^3, R is the radius of curve in m, V is the design speed in m/s.

2.34 Rate of change of centrifugal acceleration C used in the design of transition curve in m/s³ is

a) $\frac{80}{75+V}$ b) $\frac{75}{80+V}$ c) $\frac{80}{75+V^2}$ d) $\frac{75+V}{80}$

2.35 Shift of a transition curve is given by

a) $\frac{L^2}{12R}$ b) $\frac{L^2}{48R}$ c) $\frac{L^2}{24R}$ d) $\frac{L^2}{24R^2}$

2.36 If S is the SSD and N the deviation angle, then the length of Summit curve, if S>L is given by

a) $\frac{NS^2}{4.4}$ b) $\frac{NS^2}{9.6}$ c) $2S - \frac{9.6}{N}$ d) $2S - \frac{4.4}{N}$

2.37 If S is the OSD and N the deviation angle, then the length of Summit curve, if S<L is given by

a) $\frac{NS^2}{4.4}$ b) $\frac{NS^2}{9.6}$ c) $2S - \frac{9.6}{N}$ d) $2S - \frac{4.4}{N}$

2.38 According to IRC, the length of Valley curve when L>S is given by

a) $\frac{NS^2}{1.5+0.035S}$ b) $\frac{1.5+0.035S}{NS^2}$ c) $2S - \frac{1.5+0.035S}{N}$ d) $2S - \frac{N}{1.5+0.035S}$

2.39 If N is the deviation angle, V- design speed in m/s, C- rate of change of centrifugal acceleration in m/s³, then length of Valley curve to fulfill comfort condition is

a) $2(\frac{Nv^3}{C})^{1/2}$ b) $2(\frac{Nv^3}{C})^2$ c) $\frac{Nv^3}{C}$ d) $2(\frac{C}{Nv^3})^{1/2}$

2.40 The lowest point in a valley curve is located at a distance X_o = _______ from the end of grade n_1.

a) $L\sqrt{\frac{2N}{n_1}}$ b) $\sqrt{\frac{L.n_1}{2N}}$ c) $\sqrt{\frac{2N}{L.n_1}}$ d) $L\sqrt{\frac{n_1}{2N}}$

Answers of Multiple Choice Questions

2.1 (a), 2.2 (b), 2.3 (b), 2.4 (b), 2.5 (d), 2.6 (b), 2.7 (a), 2.8 (d), 2.9 (c), 2.10 (c), 2.11(a), 2.12 (d), 2.13 (c), 2.14 (b), 2.15 (a), 2.16 (b), 2.17 (b), 2.18 (a), 2.19 (b), 2.20 (b), 2.21 (b), 2.22 (b), 2.23 (b), 2.24 (a), 2.25 (c), 2.26 (a), 2.27 (a), 2.28 (b), 2.29 (b), 2.30 (a), 2.31 (b), 2.32 (b), 2.33 (a), 2.34 (a), 2.35 (c), 2.36 (d), 2.37 (b), 2.38 (a), 2.39 (a), 2.40 (a).

Short and Long Answer Type Questions

2.1 Explain the significance of Geometric design of highways.

2.2 List the various geometric elements to be designed while constructing a new highway.

2.3 How frictional resistance affects Geometric design of highways?

2.4 Sketch the cross section of a highway on embankment and its details.

2.5 What is camber? What is its significance in highway Geometric design?

2.6 Explain different types of camber. How is it introduced in the field?

2.7 What are the reasons for avoiding excessive camber in the field?

2.8 What are the functions and features of Shoulders?

2.9 Differentiate: carriageway, Roadway, right-of-way.

2.10 Define sight distance.What are the factors on which sight distance depends?

2.11 Calculate the SSD for an NH passing through a plain terrain at a descending gradient of 1.5 %. Assume data suitably.

2.12 Enumerate the factors on which OSD depends.

2.13 What are overtaking zones? How are they designated?

2.14 Find the overtaking sight distance for an NH passing through plain terrain. Assume data suitably.

2.15 Enumerate the design elements to be considered in horizontal alignment of highways.

2.16 Explain the significance of design speed in geometric design of highways.

2.17 Define superelevation. What are the factors on which design of superelevation depends?

2.18 What are the IRC standards for minimum and maximum super elevation?

2.19 Design the super elevation required for a state highway passing through rolling terrain (V= 65 km per hour) at a horizontal curve of radius equal to 320 m. Assume suitable data.

2.20 Differentiate ruling minimum radius and absolute minimum radius of a highway curve.

2.21 Calculate the absolute minimum and the ruling minimum radii required for a national highway passing through plain terrain.

2.22 Enumerate the functions of a transition curves in highways.

2.23 What are the objects of widening of carriageway at horizontal curves in highways?

2.24 Explain the factors on which the extra-width required at horizontal curve depends.

2.25 How extra widening is introduced in the field?

2.26 Design the extra-width required for a national highway passing through plain terrain at a horizontal curve of radius equal to ruling minimum radius.

2.27 What are the factors on which transition curve length depends?

2.28 Derive an expression for finding the length of transition curve on highways.

2.29 What is meant by grade compensation? How is it calculated?

2.30 Find the compensated gradient required for a road stretch with a horizontal curve of radius 80m, if its ruling gradient is 4%.

2.31 What are the factors controlling vertical alignment of highways?

2.32 Differentiate ruling, limiting, and exceptional gradient. Give IRC specifications for plain terrain.

2.33 Sketch different instances at which summit and valley curves are needed. What are the deviation angles in each case?

2.34 What are the design criteria for vertical curves?

2.35 Given the deviation angle = 0.05, OSD = 400m, determine the length of summit curve required.

Category II

2.1 Differentiate lateral and longitudinal skid resistances used in the design of highways.What are their limiting values for design?

2.2 Discuss the factors which control the degree of camber to be provided in the field. Specify the IRC standards followed.

2.3 Explain briefly the various factors on which geometric design of highways depends.

2.4 Explain briefly the important pavement characteristics affecting geometric design of highways.

2.5 What are the factors on which the width of the carriageway depends? Give the IRC specification for carriageway widths for different classes of roads.

2.6 Explain the role of skid resistance in Geometric design of highways.

2.7 Derive the expression for finding stopping sight distance at level road and at a gradient.

2.8 The speeds of overtaking and overtaken vehicles 80 and 60 km per hour respectively.If the acceleration of the overtaking vehicle is 2.5 kmph per second, calculate the the safe overtaking sight distance for the following conditions:(a) one-way traffic (b) two-way traffic.Also, sketch the overtaking zoneshowing all its details.

2.9 Derive an expression for finding super elevation.

2.10 Enumerate the steps for design of super elevation in the field.

2.11 Design the super elevation required for a national highway passing through plain terrain at a horizontal curve of radius 400 m. Assume suitable data.

2.12 Design the super elevation required for a state highway passing through plain terrain at a horizontal curve of radius 260 m. Should there be restriction in speed? If speed is not restricted, what should be the revised radius of the curve?

2.13 Explain with sketches how super elevation is introduced in the field.

2.14 Derive an expression for finding extra width of pavements at horizontal curve.

2.15 Explain the phenomenon of off-tracking of vehicles. How is it accounted in geometric design of highways.

2.16 Given Radius of curve = 360 m, total width of pavement = 7.7m, super elevation = 0.07, V = 100 kmph. Assuming pavement rotated with respect to centre line, design the length and shift of the transition curve required.

2.17 Design the transition curve for a state highway passing through rolling terrain at a horizontal curve of radius equal to ruling minimum radius. Assume data suitably.

2.18 Calculate the set-back distance required for a two-lane highway having a sight distance of 120m at a horizontal curve of radius 320m, assuming length of curve greater than sight distance.

2.19 Design the set-back distance required for a horizontal curve of radius 350 m and length 190m on a 2-lane NH with OSD 400m.

2.20 Explain why riding comfort is not a considered in the design of summit curve.

2.21 Given two ascending grades 1/25 and 1/125 are meeting at a point in a highway with a design speed of 80 km per hour. Design the length of vertical curve required in order to fulfill stopping sight distance.

2.22 Two gradients + 1/50 and -1/75 are meeting at a point in a highway. Design the length of summit curve to provide a) ISD of 180 m b) OSD of 320m.

2.23 Design a valley curve for a national highway passing through rolling terrain when two grades -1/40 + 1/30 are meeting at a point. Also, locate the position for constructing the culvert.

PRACTICAL

Experiment on Design of Geometrics of highway

Draw the sketches showing standard cross sections of

a) Expressway
b) National Highway
c) State Highway
d) Major District Road
e) Rural Road

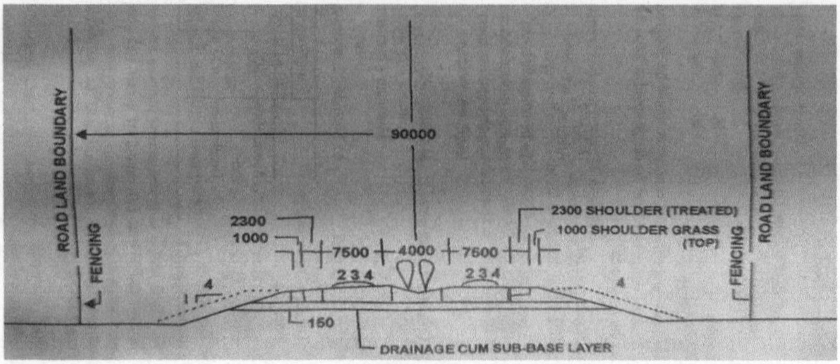

Fig 2.P(a) Typical Cross section of an expressway

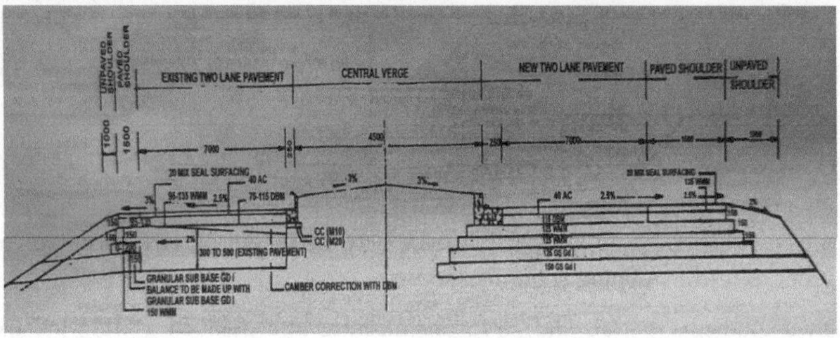

Fig 2.P(b) Typical Cross section of a 4-lane National Highway

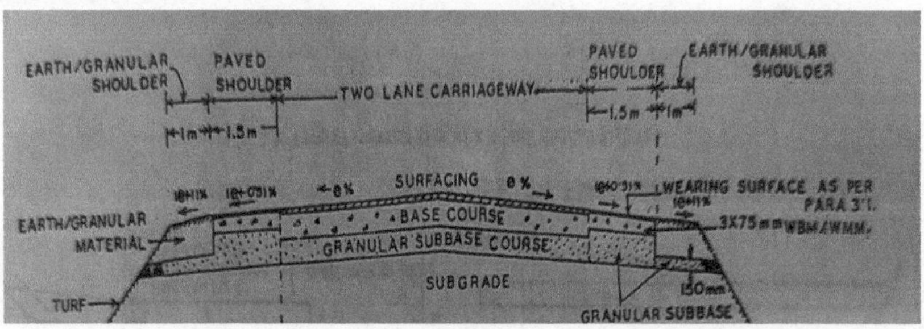

Fig 2.P(c) Typical Cross section of a 2-lane State Highway

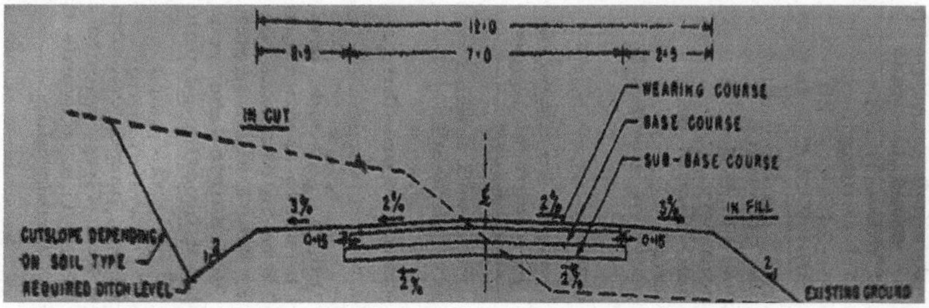

Fig 2.P(d) Typical Cross section of a 2-lane Major District Road

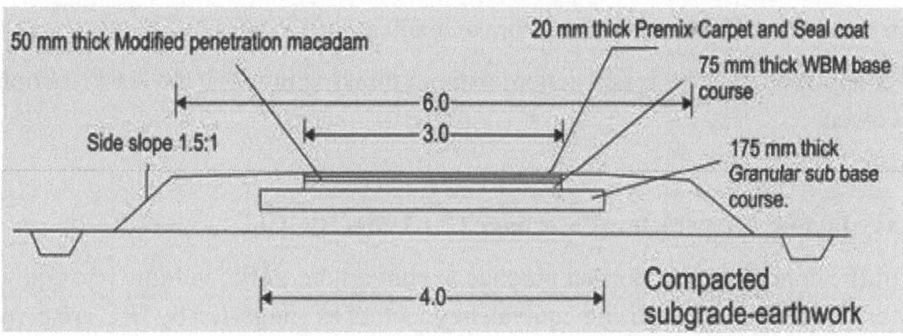

Fig 2.P(e) Typical Cross section of a Rural Road

KNOW MORE

Activity:

2.1 Identify three road stretches belonging to three different classes of road category, whose geometrics are properly designed, constructed and well-maintained. Take photographs of these stretches and prepare a report on it.

2.2 Identify a horizontal curve in a nearby state highway and check whether the set-back distance available satisfies the stopping sight distance requirements.

2.3 Collect the road accident data during the last three years in your locality and identify the reasons for the same. If any of them is due to improper geometric design, suggest remedial measures for the same.

2.4 Identify the pavements failed in any of roads in your locality due to lack of camber or drainage.

Interesting Facts:

PIEV Theory of Reaction Time of Driver:

This theory supports the amount of reaction time of drivers to be taken for the design of sight distances. PIEV stands for Perception, Intellection, Emotion, and Volition.

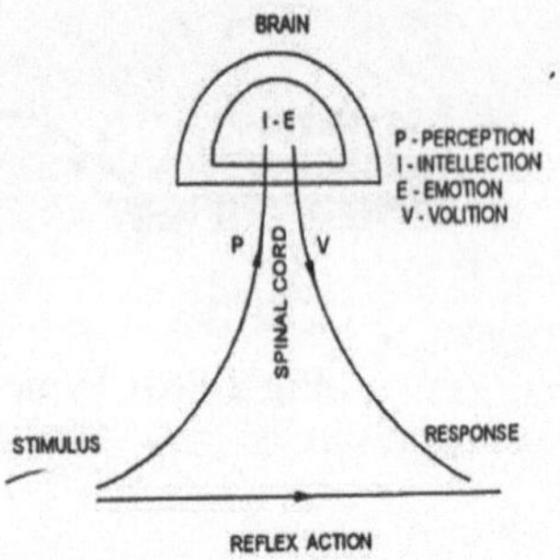

a) Perception time: Time required to perceive an object or situation

b) Intellection time: Time to rearrange different thoughts and to understand the situation by brain.

c) Emotion time: Time elapsed in emotional sensation.

d) Volition time: Time for final action or brake application.

If the driver applies brakes by reflex action, without thinking process, the least reaction time will be involved.

Equivalency factors for vehicles (Passenger Car Units -PCU)

In mixed traffic condition, it is normal practice to convert the traffic volume into equivalent passenger car units (PCUs), by using equivalency factors as suggested by IRC are given in Table 2.12.

Table 2.12 Equivalency factors for vehicles (PCUs) on rural roads

Sl. No.	Vehicle Type	Equivalency factor
1	Motor cycle/scooter	0.50
2	Passenger car, auto-rickshaw	1.00
3	Agricultural tractor, LCV	1.50
4	Truck / Bus	3.00
5	Truck-trailer, agricultural tractor-trailer	4.50
6	Cycle	0.50
7	Cycle-rickshaw	2.00
8	Hand cart	3.00
9	Horse-drawn vehicle	4.00
10	Bullock cart	8.00

About National Highways:

- The Indian road network is the second largest road network in the world after the United States. The total length of roads in India was around 6.4million kilometers as on December 2021. Of which, national highways is only around 2%, but they carry 40% of road traffic in the country!

- Since 2010, NHs directed from north to south are numbered in *even* digits and from east to west in *odd* digits. Also, NHs numbered in three digits are branches to a main highway and are numbered such that its main and branch can be identified. Eg: NH 144 is a branch of NH44. They are further broken into sub-divisions such as 144A, 244A, etc.

Mega highway projects in India:

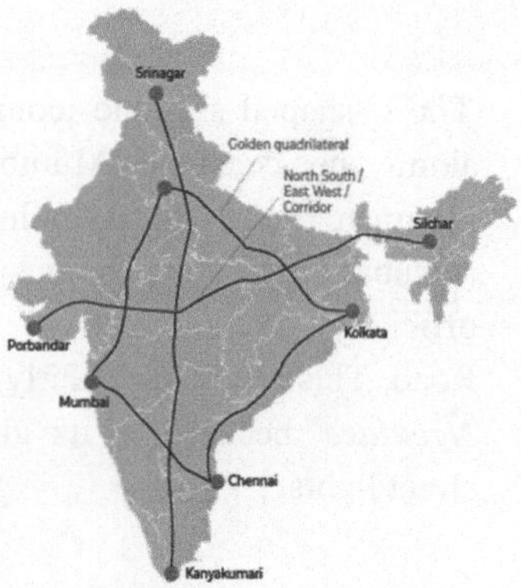

- **Golden Quadrilateral (GQ)** and **North-South-East-West corridor (NS-EW)** launched in 2001 as part of National Highways Development Project (NHDP) consist of four/six-lane highways.GQ stretch connects the four metro cities of India (Delhi, Mumbai, Kolkata and Chennai)- 5,846km. NS corridor stretches from Srinagar in J&K to Kanyakumari, the southern most tip of India, while the EW corridor connects Porbandar in Gujarat with Silchar in Assam.- 7300 km. NS and EW Super Highways meet at Jhansi in Madhya Pradesh.

- First 4-lane Expressway in India is Ahmedabad - Vadodara

- First 6-lane expressway in India is Mumbai - Pune Expressway

- World's Tallest highway (as on 2022)- **Manali-Leh** (Himachal Pradesh- Kashmir) with an average height of 4270 m.

- India's **Umling La Pass**, located in eastern Ladakh at an altitude of 19,300 feet above sea level, is the world's highest motorable road.

- The C-shaped six lane iconic concrete road along the coast of Mumbai which links Nariman point to Babulnath Road and Malabar Hills is the famous 'Marine Drive', officially, Netaji Subash Chandra Bose Road. This road is popularly called ***'Queen's Necklace'*** because of its glowing string of street lights.

- Delhi-Gurgaon Expressway Toll Plaza is India's largest or perhaps Asia's largest toll plaza with a total of 32 toll lanes and 4 reversible toll lanes.

- Portions of NHs will be converted as air strips to facilitate landing of aircrafts. The Indian Air Force (IAF) has identified 28 Emergency Landing Facilities (ELF) in the country. NH-925 is India's first ELF.

Other Important Road Development Schemes:

- ***Pradhan Mantri Gram Sadak Yojana (PMGSY)*** -Fully centrally sponsored rural development scheme to connect all habitation with 500^+ population by roads, launched in December 2000.
- ***Pradhan Mantri Bharat Jodo Pariyojana (PMBJP)*** will cover the entire nation, particularly state capitals and trading centres, with 4-lane highways, launched in January 14, 2004.
- ***Bharatmala Pariyojana*** envisages development of about 26,000km length of Economic Corridors, which along with GQ and NS-EW corridors are expected to carry majority of the freight traffic on roads.
- ***Green Highways*** (Plantation, Transplantation, Beautification & Maintenance) Policy launched in 2015 to promote greening of highway corridors with participation of the community, farmers, private sector, NGOs, and government institutions.

Mile stones are painted in different colours for different types of roads, like

- NH: Yellow and White
- SH: Green and White
- City Roads: Black and White
- Rural Roads: Orange and White

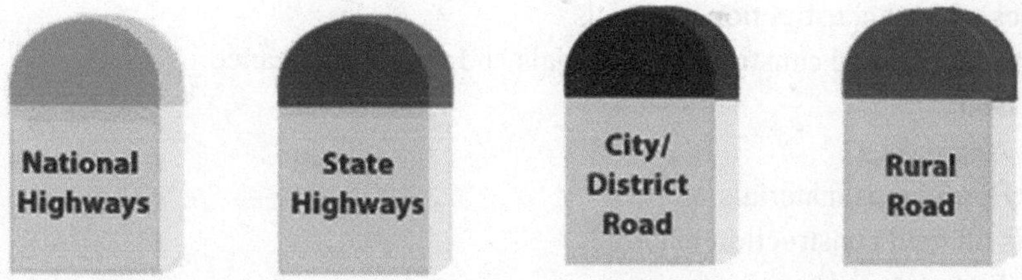

REFERENCES AND SUGGESTED READINGS

1. *Kadiyali L.* R., 'Transportation Engineering', Khanna Book Publishing Co., 2018.
2. *Khanna S.* K., Justo C. E. G., Veeraraghavan A., 'Highway Engineering', Nem Chand & Bros., Roorkee, 2014.
3. *Arora N.* L., 'Transportation Engineering', New India Pub., 1977.
4. *Subramanian K.* P., 'Transportation Engineering', Scitech Publications, Chennai, 2015.
5. Sharma S.K., 'Principles, Practice and Design of Highway Engineering', S. Chand Publishing, 2014.
6. IRC 'Geometric Design Standards for Rural (Non-urban) Highways' IRC: 73-1980, Indian Roads Congress, New Delhi.
7. IRC 'Geometric Design Standards for Urban Roads in Plains' IRC: 86-1983, Indian Roads Congress, New Delhi.
8. Ministry of Road Transport and Highways, (Government of India), 'Pocket Book for Highway Engineers', Indian Roads Congress, 2002.
9. https://nptel.ac.in/courses/105101087
10. https://www.smartzworld.com/notes/transportation-engineering-pdf-notes-te-pdf-notes/
11. https://jntukucen.ac.in/ebook_files/166.pdf

UNIT 3
CONSTRUCTION OF ROAD PAVEMENTS

UNIT SPECIFICS

This unit discusses the following aspects:

- Types of road construction materials
- Properties of road construction materials and their significance
    - Soil
    - Aggregates
    - Bituminous materials
- Tests on road construction materials
    - Tests on road aggregates
    - Tests on bitumen
- Pavement - types, components and functions
- Flexible pavements - types and construction methods
- Rigid pavements - types and construction methods
- Joints in cement concrete pavements

Multiple-choice questions along with answers, short and long answer type questions including numerical problems and practical works, relevant to the topics covered in the unit, are added. A list of references and suggested readings are also given. It should be noted that dynamic QR codes are provided for additional reading in different sections, which can be scanned for relevant supportive information. A "KNOW MORE" section is also given at the end, which has been carefully designed so that additional information relevant to this unit is provided for the users of the book. This section mainly contains some 'Activities' for the students to make them conversant with the topics he/she had studied, and some interesting facts related with the contents of the unit.

RATIONALE

A well-performing road infrastructure is a great asset to any nation. Many a times roads collapse due to the use of inferior quality materials and with the adoption of unskilled construction techniques, rather than over stressing and adverse environmental factors. The right judgement of material's quality evolves from the broad understanding of the material's behavior, instead of the mere comparison of test results with standard values. For this, a concise knowledge about materials used in highway construction and their applications is a must.

Quality control in highway construction is of paramount importance. The term quality control contains two words, quality which means standards and control which means regulate or monitor. Therefore, quality control may be defined as organized operations viz. inspection, sampling and testing, necessary for regulating and monitoring the construction.

UNIT OUTCOMES

After completing this unit, students will be able

U3-O1: To identify the desirable properties of materials used for construction of roads

U3-O2: To understand the importance and method of testing the qualities of road construction materials

U3-O3: To identify the various types of road pavements, their components and functions

U3-O4: To identify the relative merits and demerits of different types of pavements

U3-O5: To understand the methods of construction of different types of pavements as per IRC recommendations

Unit-3 Outcomes	EXPECTED MAPPING WITH COURSE OUTCOMES (1- Weak Correlation, 2-Medium Correlation, 3- Strong Correlation)				
	CO-1	CO-2	CO-3	CO-4	CO-5
U3-O1	-	1	3	-	-
U3-O2	-	1	3	-	-
U3-O3	1	1	1	-	-
U3-O4	1	1	1	-	-
U3-O5	1	-	1	-	-

3.1 ROAD MATERIALS AND CONSTRUCTION: SIGNIFICANCE

Quality control in selection of road materials as well as construction practices makes superior pavements. The design of thickness of pavement, performance and efficiency of roads are governed by the quality of materials used and construction methods adopted for them. In fact, a series of tests are to be conducted on the road materials used and the works undertaken in a highway project. Most commonly used tests and construction techniques are discussed in the following sections.

3.2 TYPES OF ROAD CONSTRUCTION MATERIALS

Various materials used for road construction are:

i) Soil – for embankment construction and as subgrade (formation bed) material
ii) Aggregates
iii) Bitumen and Road tar
iv) Cement and cement concrete
v) Steel
vi) Geosynthetics (geotextiles, geocells etc.)

3.3 PROPERTIES OF ROAD CONSTRUCTION MATERIALS AND THEIR SIGNIFICANCE

3.3.1 Soil

For the construction of roads, soil is a crucial component. Very often, roads are built on a prepared subgrade. It acts as the essential base that offers vital support to the pavement. For the construction of embankments as well as for stabilized soil base and sub base courses, soil is used. Following are the ideal characteristics of soil to be used as subgrade for construction:

i. Stability - the soil should possess sufficient stability, providing adequate support to the pavement under adverse climatic and loading conditions.
ii. Incompressibility - to avoid differential settlement of the embankment.
iii. Resistance to weathering
iv. Non-susceptibility to volume changes
v. Good drainage characteristics
vi. Ease of compaction

The essential tests conducted on soil used for road design and construction to assess the above mentioned properties are:

In-situ density – Density of prepared subgrade as well as other pavement layers is of importance to check field compaction control.

Plasticity index – This is a numerical index obtained as liquid limit minus plastic limit. It gives some idea about the plasticity characteristics of the soil.

Compaction - Soil is compacted to get desired degree of compaction or densification. The amount of compaction energy to attain maximum dry density and the respective water content called optimum moisture content of soil are the parameters deciding the degree of compaction.

California Bearing Ratio – It is a penetration test carried out to evaluate strength of soil under impact loads, directly or indirectly, the value being primarily used in the structural design of flexible pavements.

Moisture content: The test for determining the moisture content of the soil is vital for assessing the existing natural state of the soil.

3.3.2 Aggregates

Aggregates constitute the major component of the pavement structure. They primarily bear wheel load stresses as well as resist wear due to abrasive action and impact of moving wheel loads. The desirable properties of aggregates are:

i. Strength - Resistance to crushing due to wheel loads
ii. Hardness - Resistance to abrasion and attrition
iii. Toughness - Resistance to impact due to hammering action by moving loads
iv. Durability - Resistance to disintegration due to weathering action
v. Good shapes - Not too flaky or elongated, but angular shapes are better
vi. Good adhesion with bitumen - to avoid stripping of aggregates.

Aggregates are of two types based on their size - coarse aggregates and fine aggregates. Coarse aggregates are obtained by crushing parent rock masses (granite, sand stone, etc.). Fine aggregates are obtained from natural sources (Natural sand) and by crushing and screening rock pieces (M Sand).

3.3.3 Bituminous Materials

Bituminous materials used in road (flexible pavement)construction works include bitumen and tar, both having same colour (black), but have different characteristics. While bitumen is a petroleum byproduct obtained by the destructive distillation of crude petroleum, road tar is obtained by the destructive distillation of coal or organic materials.

Various terms related to bituminous materials are defined below:

a) Bitumen —Bitumen is a viscous, non-crystalline adhesive material and is black or dark brown in colour. It is obtained by natural or refinery distillation of petroleum, and is highly soluble in carbon disulphide.

b) Cutback Bitumen — It is manufactured by reducing the viscosity of bitumen using a suitable volatile dilutent, usually a petroleum distillate. Cutback bitumen is classified into the following three types.

i) Rapid Curing Cutback Bitumen (RC)

It is prepared by blending bitumen with a distillate similar to naphtha. It is further divided into four grades based on its initial kinematic viscosity at 60°C (in Centi Stokes, cSt = $10^{-6}m^2s^{-1}$)and shall be used with aggregates that include almost no fine particles and pass through a 2.36 mm sieve as under:

a) RC 70 — RC having kinematic viscosity between 70 to 140 cSt.

b) RC 250— RC having kinematic viscosity between 250 to 500 cSt.

c) RC 800— RC having kinematic viscosity between 800 to 1600 cSt.

d) RC 3000— RC having kinematic viscosity between 3000 to 6000 cSt.

ii) Medium Curing Cutback Bitumen (MC)

It is prepared by blending of bitumen with a kerosene type distillate. It shall be used with aggregates containing less than 40 percent of fine aggregates passing through 2.36 mm sieve and is again classified into five grades according to their initial kinematic viscosity at 60°C as under:

a) MC 30— MC having kinematic viscosity between 30 to 60 cSt

b) MC 70— MC having kinematic viscosity between 70 to 140 cSt.

c) MC 250— MC having kinematic viscosity between 250 to 500 cSt.

d) MC 800— MC having kinematic viscosity between 800 to 1600 cSt.

e) MC 3000— MC having kinematic viscosity between 3000 to 6000 cSt.

iii) *Slow Curing Cutback Bitumen (SC)*

It shall be used with aggregates containing more than 20 percent of fine aggregates passing through 2.36 mm sieve and shall be classified into four grades according their initial kinematic viscosity at 60°C as under:

a) SC 70— SC having kinematic viscosity between 70 to 140 cSt.
b) SC 250— SC having kinematic viscosity between 250 to 500 cSt.
c) SC 800— SC having kinematic viscosity between 800 to 1 600 cSt
d) SC 3000— SC having kinematic viscosity between 3 000 to 6 000 cSt.

c) Bitumen Emulsion— A liquid product that contains a significant quantity of bitumen that has been mixed with emulsifiers and stabilizers to form finely divided droplets in an aqueous medium. Depending on the type of emulsion, it is further divided into slow setting, medium setting, and quick setting.

d) Rubberized Bitumen — A straight run bitumen that has had its properties altered by the addition of crumb or natural rubber is known as rubberized bitumen.

e) Straight Run Bitumen — Bitumen produced as a byproduct or residue of the direct distillation process used to refine crude oil.

f) Road Tar — A product created by mixing pitch, anthracene oil, and creosote oil according to a proportion that is suitable for usage on roads.

g) Prime Coat- It is a low viscosity bitumen application over a granular base or base course for laying a bituminous mixture over it.

h) Tack Coat — It is an application of bitumen, road tar or an emulsion as a thin film on an intermediate layerso as to achieve the adhesion with superimposed course preventing slippage.

i) Seal Coat - It is placed on top of the pavements. It increases the life span of the road and also provide friction to the vehicles which is moving on the road.

The desirable properties of bitumen are:

i. **Viscosity** - bitumen should have adequate viscosity during mixing as well as compacting, so that the bituminous layer can gain stability and resist deformation under wheel loads.

ii. **Ductility** - bitumen should possess sufficient ductility so that better interlocking of aggregates can be achieved.

iii. **Temperature susceptibility** - bitumen should be durable against weathering, and not highly temperature susceptible.

iv. **Adhesion with aggregates** - bitumen should possess adequate affinity and adhesion with aggregate surface in the presence of water.

3.4 TESTS ON ROAD CONSTRUCTION MATERIALS

Several tests are performed on road construction materials to evaluate the properties listed above. Most important ones only are discussed here.

3.4.1 California Bearing Ratio (CBR) Test on Subgrade Soil

The apparatus consists of a cylindrical mould of 150 mm diameter with a base plate and collar, a loading frame with a cylindrical plunger of 50 mm diameter, and dial gauges for monitoring the expansion on soaking and the penetration values on loading. The test specimen is prepared by the compacting the soil that has passed through a 20 mm sieve. Both soaked and unsoaked conditions are considered for test. The test involves inserting the plunger into the compacted specimen, at a rate of 1.25 mm per minute. The loads related to 2.5mm and 5mm penetration values are determined after applying the correction, if required, on the graph drawn between load and penetration. To get the CBR value, this load is represented in terms of percentage of the standard load at the relevant penetration level. The standard loads corresponding to 2.5 mm and 5 mm penetrations are 1370 kg and 2055 kg respectively.

3.4.2 Tests on Road Aggregates

The essential tests conducted on aggregates used in road construction to check their quality are given in Table 3.1.

Table 3.1 List of tests on road aggregates and the properties measured

Sl. No.	Name of test	Property measured
1	Aggregate crushing test	Resistance to crushing
2	Ten percent fines value	Resistance to crushing
3	Abrasion test	Resistance to wear or abrasion
4	Aggregate impact test	Resistance to impact under moving loads
5	Soundness test	Resistance to weathering action
6	Shape tests: Combined Flakiness & Elongation index and Angularity number	Shape and angularity for interlocking
7	Stripping value test	Adhesion of bitumen to aggregate in the presence of water.

The Combined Flakiness and Elongation Index test, and Angularity Number tests are described below and the detailed tests are given at the end of the chapter in practical section.

Combined Flakiness and Elongation Index: Flakiness is the percentage of particles in an aggregate (measured by weight) whose thickness is less than three-fifths of their mean dimension. The elongation index is the proportion of weighted particles in an aggregate whose maximum dimension (length) is more than or equal to one and four-fifths times or nine-fifths of the mean dimension. After determining the flakiness index, the remaining non-flaky aggregates are put through an elongation index test to get the property of Combined Flakiness and Elongation index of aggregates.

To perform the test, initially, the representative aggregate sample is washed, dried and weighed. Each particle's thickness is examined individually by inserting them through the thickness gauge shown in Fig. 3.1(a). The cumulative total weight of particles that travel through slots in a width-wise direction is calculated for each fraction. The sum of these totals expressed as a percentage of the total weight is then used to calculate the flakiness index. Following that, the length of the remaining non-flaky stone aggregates is examined using the length gauge shown in Fig. 3.1(b), and elongated particles are separated. The elongation index is obtained as the total weight of particles held on slots lengthwise in each fraction divided by the total weight of non-flaky aggregate. Then, the sum of flakiness index and elongation index is reported as the Combined Flakiness and Elongation index of aggregates.

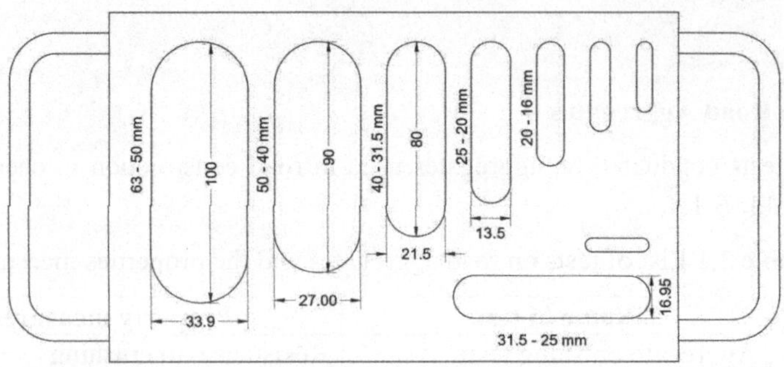

(a) Thickness Gauge

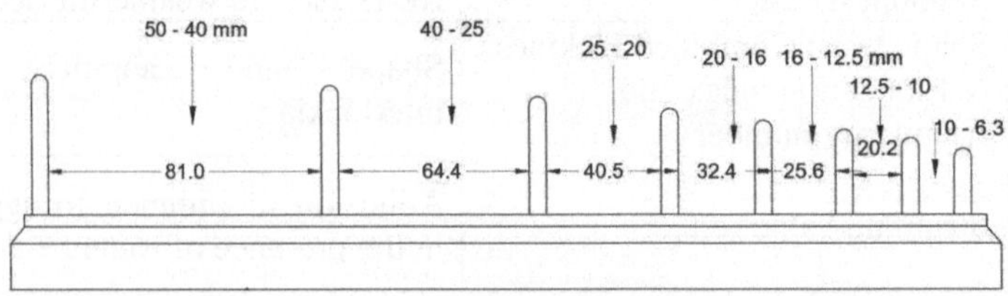

(b) Length Gauge

Fig. 3.1 Metallic Gauges for Testing Flakiness Index and Elongation Index

Angularity Number Test: The Angularity gives some idea regarding absence of roundness of the aggregate specimen. A well compacted single sized rounded (all pieces are of almost same size e.g. 16mm -20mm range) aggregate sample is found to have a solid volume of 67 per cent and void volume 33 per cent. Angularity number measures the voids in excess of 33 per cent. Higher the angularity number, the more angular is the aggregates. In cement concrete (Rigid pavements) roads aggregate with lesser angularity number is preferred because of better workability and higher strength, whereas, in bituminous or water bound macadam (Flexible pavements)

SCAN ME for Tests on Road Aggregates

roads, aggregates having higher angularity number is preferred because of increased stability due to higher degree of interlocking and friction between aggregates. For flexible pavement construction, angularity number between 7 and 10 is generally preferred.

The representative sample of aggregates is sieved, filled and tamped in layers in the metal cylinder of capacity 3 litres, and weighed. Then the cylinder is emptied, filled with water, and weighed. Specific gravity of aggregate, G_a is also determined. Then, Angularity Number is found from the equation:

$$AN = 67 - \frac{100W}{C.G_a} \qquad \text{Eq. 3.1}$$

where 'W' is the weight of aggregates filling the cylinder in kg and 'C' is the weight of water filling the cylinder in kg.

3.4.3 Tests on Bitumen

Out of various tests conducted on bituminous materials to evaluate the qualities for being used as binder in road construction and hence to find the suitability for its intended use, the most important ones are briefly described here.

i) Penetration: The penetration of a bituminous material is the distance in tenths of a millimeter that a standard loaded needle of 3mm diameter will penetrate vertically in 5 seconds into a sample of the material under standard conditions of temperature. It indicates the consistency of bitumen. It is used to classify bitumen into different grades (Grade 25- penetration value between 20 and 30, Grade 35- penetration value between 30and 40, Grade 45- penetration value between 40 and 50, Grade 65- penetration value between 60 and 70, Grade 90- penetration value between 80 and 100 and Grade 200 - penetration value between 175 and 200).

ii) Ductility: The ability of a substance to be drawn into fine thread without breaking is known as ductility. When two ends of a briquette specimen made of bitumen with the prescribed shape and cross-section are dragged apart at a certain speed (50±2.5 mm per minute) and temperature (27±0.5°C), ductility is measured by the distance in cm to which it will stretch without breaking.

iii) Softening point: It is measured as the temperature in degree Celsius at which a standard ball of diameter 9.5mm and weight 2.50±5g, when heated under water or glycerine under specific test conditions, passes through a bitumen sample in a mould and falls over a distance of 2.5 cm. Ring and Ball apparatus is used for this test.

SCAN ME
for
Tests on Bitumen

iv) Viscosity: The coefficient of viscosity of a liquid is the property that determines how well it resists flow caused by internal friction and it is the inverse of fluidity of the liquid. It is the ratio of shearing stress to the rate of shear. Absolute or dynamic viscosity is the tangential force necessary to maintain a velocity between two layers spaced one unit apart, whereas kinematic viscosity is the ratio of absolute viscosity to liquid density, which measures the resistance to flow of a liquid under gravity. It affects the strength properties of bituminous paving mixtures. Either a float test or an orifice viscometer is used to determine it.

v) Flash Point and Fire Point

The Flash point is the lowest temperature at which, under the required test conditions, a flame may momentarily ignite the material's vapour.

The term "Fire point" refers to the lowest temperature at which a substance ignites and burns continuously under specified test conditions. Always, the fire point exceeds the flash point. These are indicative temperatures to prevent fire hazards during construction.

vi) Stripping

It is said to be the peeling off of coated bituminous film from the surface of road aggregates in presence of water. The ratio of the visually observable exposed area to the total surface area of aggregates, is adopted as the stripping value of aggregates, expressed in percentage.

3.5 PAVEMENT

The structure intended to carry vehicular traffic is known as pavement. The pavement consists of one or more layers of selected and desirable materials. Its main function is to distribute safely the applied load of vehicles to the subgrade (prepared ground) through different layers. Essentially, the pavement should provide sufficient skid resistance, proper riding quality, good drainage, favorable light-reflecting characteristics, and low noise pollution.

3.5.1 Functions of Pavements

i. Primary function of a pavement is to transfer vehicular loads to the sub-base and the soil underneath.
ii. Provide a strong and smooth surface with adequate riding quality to withstand traffic loads.
iii. Distribute the loads safely on to a larger area of the foundation soil through the intermediate layers/courses.
iv. Bear repeated application of traffic loads during the projected design life, without developing excessive or harmful deformations/strains.

3.5.2 Requirements of Pavements

i. It should be strong enough to withstand the stresses imposed by the vehicles.
ii. Its thickness should be adequate to transmit the applied loads and distribute them on to a larger area of the soil below.
iii. It should provide a hard wearing surface so as to resist the abrasion caused by vehicle tyres.
iv. It should be smooth enough to provide riding comfort, yet provide enough friction for tractive effort and to prevent skidding.

v. It should be impervious to water so as to prevent its deteriorating effect on the layers below.
vi. It should have adequate durability to serve through its design period.
vii. Its initial cost and maintenance cost during its design life should be a minimum.

3.5.3 Types of Pavements

Pavements can be classified in many ways. Structurally pavements are classified into three types as follows:

a) ***Flexible pavements:*** A flexible pavement is a multi-layered structure with low flexural strength. The intermediate layers viz. the base and the subbase allows the pavement to transmit the load to the subgrade. The most common example of the flexible pavement is the bituminous roads..

b) ***Rigid Pavements:*** In contrast to flexible pavement, rigid pavement resists loads because of its flexural strength and they can bridge over minor irregularities or weak localized locations in the subgrade. The main factor in resisting the tyre loads is the strength of the concrete slab itself. E.g. Cement concrete roads.

c) ***Composite Pavements:*** A composite pavement comprises of multiple, structurally different layers of heterogeneous nature. A typical example is a concrete pavement of two layers, sandwiching a brick layer. A base of roller compacted concrete and surface course of bitumen is another example. Pavements of bricks, stone blocks, and precast cement concrete blocks laid over granular bases also belong to this category. It is rarely constructed in India.

3.5.4 Comparison between Flexible pavements and Rigid Pavements

Major differences between flexible pavements and rigid pavements are summarized in Table 3.2.

3.5.5 Components of Pavement Structure and their Functions

As mentioned in the section 3.5 pavement is a multi-layer system that distributes the vehicular load to the subgrade soil. The various components of pavement structure are Surface course or wearing course, base course, Sub base course and Subgrade. Typical cross sections of Flexible pavement and Rigid pavement are shown in Fig 3.2(a) & (b).

Surface Course or Wearing Course

- This is the topmost layer which comes in immediate contact with traffic.
- It provides a smooth and skid-resistant riding surface.
- It resists the pressure exerted by tires and takes up the abrasion due to traffic.

- It acts as an impervious layer to protect the bottom layers from the weakening effect of water.

Table 3.2 Comparison between Flexible pavements and Rigid Pavements

Flexible Pavement	Rigid Pavement
1. It has a layered structure with highest quality materials at or near the surface.	1. It consists of a thick concrete slab having high flexural (bending) strength.
2. The strength of sub grade primarily influences the design thickness.	2. Rigidity and high modulus of concrete influences the design.
3. Stability of pavement is through aggregate interlocking, friction and cohesion.	3. Its structural capacity of the pavement slab is by beam action.
4. Load distribution is from the contact area of wheels through the component layers.	4. Load distribution is from the entire width of slab irrespective of the wheel position, to a wider area, due to rigidity and high modulus of elasticity of concrete.
5. Design is less precise.	5. Design is more abstract.
6. Design life - 10 to 15 years.	6. Design life - 20 to 30 years.
7. Less capital cost & more life cycle cost.	7. High capital cost & less life cycle cost.
8. Stage construction is possible.	8. Stage construction is difficult.

Base Course

- The base course is provided immediately beneath the surface course.
- It distributes the loads from top layer to the underneath sub-base and sub-grade layers.
- It is constructed with hard and durable aggregates, generally consisting of two layers- bottom one, a non-bituminous base like Water Bound Macadam (WBM) or Wet Mix Macadam (WMM), over which a bituminous base layer like Dense Bituminous Macadam (DBM).
- Thickness of base course must be adequate enough to reduce the stresses on sub-grade and sub-base courses.

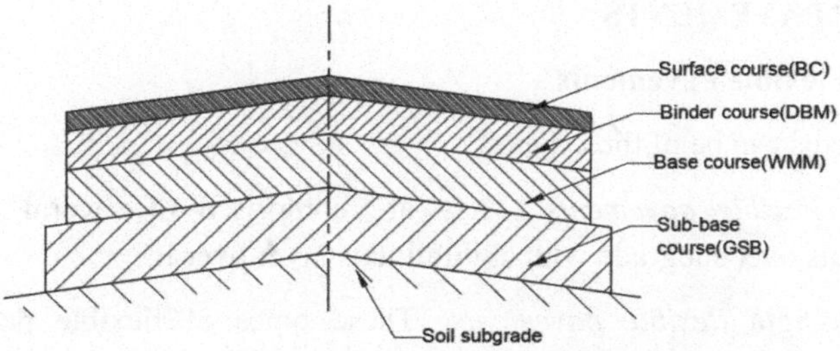

(a) Flexible Pavement

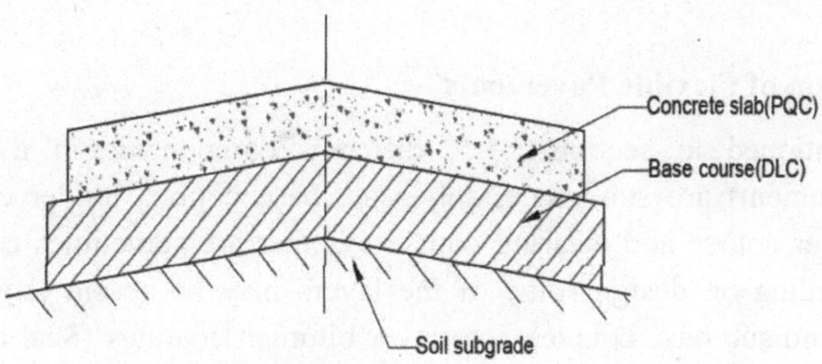

(b) Rigid Pavement

Fig. 3.2 Structure of Flexible and Rigid Pavements

Sub base Course

- The sub-base course is granular layer made up of natural gravel, aggregates or brick bats, between the base course and the subgrade.
- It acts as a separating layer between base and subgrade and prevents the intrusion of fines from the sub-grade into the pavement structure.
- It is extended beyond the pavement edge to enhance lateral support and uniform subgrade loading.
- It reduces the wheel load stress on subgrade and acts as a drainage layer and prevents subgrade from wetting up.

Sub grade

- The layer of natural soil beneath the pavement prepared to take care of the stresses from the layers above.
- Subgrade bearing capacity, uniformity, and permeability are key factors in determining various pavement layers' thickness.
- Apart from the natural material on which the road is built, imported fill material is used to create an embankment which should be compacted well to the desired density at optimum moisture content.

3.6 FLEXIBLE PAVEMENTS

3.6.1 Types of Flexible Pavements

Flexible pavements can be of three types:

a) *Layered flexible pavements:* They are comprised of several layers of granular materials over subgrade with abituminous layer over it.

b) *Deep strength flexible pavements:* These types of flexible pavements have full thickness bituminous construction over sub grade.

c) *Composite flexible pavements:* These pavements make use of stabilized layer with bituminous surfacing.

3.6.2 Construction of Flexible Pavements

As already mentioned in section 3.5.5, different components in a flexible pavement (bituminous pavement) are sub grade, sub base, base course, binder course and wearing course. The binder course and wearing course together are sometimes called as bituminous surfacing. Depending on design some of the layers may be absent (e.g. only base course instead of base and sub base course). Interlayer bitumen coatings (Seal coat, Tack coat and Prime coat) are provided in between layers to have adequate bonding between them. Construction of each component layer is briefly explained here under.

Sub grade: After the vegetation is removed from the ground surface, compaction is done with smooth wheeled rollers. If the subgrade is too weak, the soft soil is removed from the top and good soil is spread uniformly in layers of thickness 200mm and compacted to get the required density.

Granular Base / Sub base Course: Construction of granular base or sub base course involves laying and compacting appropriately chosen material over the formed sub grade. There might be more layers with varying materials, amounts of compaction, and thickness. Commonly used materials include slag, natural sand, crushed stone, and crushed concrete. The sub base material for bituminous pavement must have CBR values of 10% and 20% for traffic up to and beyond 2 million standard axles (msa) respectively(IRC). Water Bound Macadam (WBM) and Wet Mix Macadam (WMM) are two types of most commonly constructed sub bases.

Water Bound Macadam (WBM): WBM road is constructed with mechanically compacted layers of crushed aggregate. The compacted layer is bound with filler material called screening. Soil having plasticity index less than 20 is used as binding material (IRC). Screenings are spread over it and compacted in dry condition. Binder soil is then spread along with watering and compaction. This is allowed to dry overnight and if required grouting is done on the next day. Next layer of WBM if needed can be made after the first layer is completely dry and depressions and voids are visible.

Wet Mix Macadam (WMM): Wet mix macadam is constructed by laying and spreading crushed graded aggregates pre-mixed with water. WMM is prepared in mixing plants where water and aggregates of various sizes are thoroughly mixed in the appropriate ratios. The mix is then applied in the required depths to the subgrade that has been prepared and compacted according to meet the specifications. Laying of WMM requires lateral confinement.

Bituminous Penetration Macadam: Bituminous penetration macadam consists of one or more layers of aggregates with application of bitumen binder in between. Dry, clean aggregates are spread over the prepared base and compacted with smooth-wheeled rollers. Specified quantity of binder is then applied using a mechanical sprayer and key aggregates spread over it immediately. Then compaction using rollers is done to make a smooth finished surface.

Bituminous Binder Course: Two types of bituminous binder courses are commonly used, Bituminous Macadam (BM) and Dense Graded Bituminous Macadam (DBM). The bituminous mixes are designed previously by any standard mix design procedure. The mix is prepared by mixing graded aggregate with optimum bitumen content. Mix is produced in bitumen mixing plants either batch mixing plants or continuous plants. Dump trucks are used to transport the mix. After laying the mix in required thickness, it is compacted to get achieve density and finish. Automated paving machines are nowadays used in major projects.

Bituminous Wearing Course: The commonly used wearing courses are bituminous concrete (BC), Semi Dense Bituminous Concrete (SDBC), surface dressing, premix surfacing etc. The construction of bituminous concrete and semi dense bituminous concrete are same as that of bituminous macadam or dense bituminous macadam. The size and gradation of aggregates are different in this case.

3.7 RIGID PAVEMENTS

As explained in section 3.5.3 rigid pavements have sufficient rigidity and high modulus of elasticity. Rigid pavements are mostly made of cement concrete, however pre-stressed concrete and composite pavements are sometimes used. Concrete pavements are built directly over subgrade soil, with a base layer of stabilized soil, dry lean concrete, or some gravely material. Steel reinforcements are only provided when temperature stresses are taken into account.

3.7.1 Types of Rigid (Concrete) Pavements

***Plain cement concrete pavement*:** Plain cement concrete pavements are constructed without reinforcements (except for temperature).The load is transferred at the joints using interlocking properties of the aggregate. Steel tie bars are provided to form a longitudinal warping joint between two lanes.

***Plain dowelled concrete pavement*:** This pavement is made of simple cement concrete. To transmit weight, reinforcements (dowel bars) are added at transverse joints. Tie bars are provided at longitudinal junctions..

***Continuously reinforced cement concrete pavement* :** This type of concrete road is reinforced throughout with no expansion or contraction joints. The reinforcements acts as load transfer device to prevent transverse cracks, if formed.

***Prestressed Concrete Pavement*:** These types of pavements require lesser thickness compared to ordinary concrete pavement. Though prestressed concrete pavements are not very common for highways, it is being used for airport pavements.

3.7.2 Construction of Concrete Pavements

Mechanized construction using machines for spreading, compacting and finishing is currently used for the construction of important roads. It can be:

a) Fixed form type: The equipment itself consists of many components forming a train. The main components are spreader, vibrator, dowel inserter, diagonal finisher, texturing unit and curing membrane sprayer. This type of construction is being replaced by slip-form technique.

b) Slip form Paving Technique: A slip form paver moves on its own tracks and does not need any side forms. The concrete slab is extruded to the desired dimension as the paver moves forward. The paver is guided by sensors and guiding string lines fixed along the alignment outside the paving area controls the alignment, thickness and profile. The paver consists of slip form unit (for spreading and laying), finisher (vibration and finishing), dowel bar inserter, texturing unit and spraying and curing unit.

Methods of Construction: The construction of concrete roads is carried out in either of the following two ways:

i) Alternate Bay Method: In this method, the concrete slabs are constructed in alternate bays. The next bay is constructed after a time gap depending on the type of cement used. It provides additional working space for laying adjacent bays as also easy in joint construction. Large number of transverse joints increases the construction and maintenance cost and may reduce riding comfort.

***ii) Continuous Construction*:** In this method full traffic lane width is laid continuously without any break. However, at the end of day's work, construction joints are provided. The difficulty in providing joints is the main disadvantage. The method is still preferred because of speedy of construction and easy of diverting traffic through the other traffic lane during construction.

Construction Procedure: In cement pavement construction, concrete layer is laid directly over the subgrade or on prepared base/sub base course. The sub grade is leveled and compacted. It is ensured that the sub grade is moist at the time of laying of concrete.

Sometimes a water proof polyethylene sheet is spread over the subgrade and then concreting is done over it. This sheet acts as capillary cut off layer in the sub base. Base/ Subbase for concrete pavement are selected based on the availability of material in the locality. As per IRC, the subbase can be any one type:

i. Granular material, consisting of brick soling with one layer of sand beneath it (WBM, well graded granular materials, etc.)

ii. Stabilized soil

iii. Semi-rigid material, such as, lime burnt clay pozzolana concrete, lime fly ash concrete, lean cement concrete, etc.

Concrete surfacing: The proportion of concrete is determined using a standard mix design procedure. In order to avoid direct contact of rigid slab with subbase or subgrade, a separation membrane made up of impermeable polyethylene sheet is placed before concreting. A slip form machine will do the stages of spreading, compacting and finishing. Texture of the surface is made by brooming over the laid surface of the pavement in transverse direction. Curing compound having high water retentivity is spread over the surface. For final curing, continuous ponding is adopted. After curing the joints are filled with sealants. Finally the road is opened for traffic.

SCAN ME
for
Road Construction
Techniques

3.7.3 Joint Fillers and Sealants

Fillers and sealants are used to minimize infiltration of surface water and ingress of stone grits into the joints. This will also help in reducing corrosion of dowel bars. Fillers are materials used to fill the joints in concrete, whereas sealants are poured/placed above the joint fillers to prevent water percolation. Joint fillers are rigid materials protecting joint edges from impact but sealants are flexible materials, deflecting under traffic loads.

Three common categories of materials in use are:

i) *Liquid fillers:* These can be hot poured (polymerized or rubberised asphalt material) or cold poured (silicon).

ii) *Performed elastomeric type*: These are mainly of neoprene materials.

iii) *Rigid type:* Cork or sponge rubber, impregnated fibre board, soft wood, etc.

The essential properties of filler/sealant materials are elasticity, stiffness, adhesion, compressibility and durability.The filler material should be compressible and elastic because, during summer, when the pavement expands, the gap provided reduces, resulting in the compression of filler. Whereas during winter, the pavement edges contracts and if the filler is inelastic, it would leave gap at the joint as shown in Fig. 3.3.

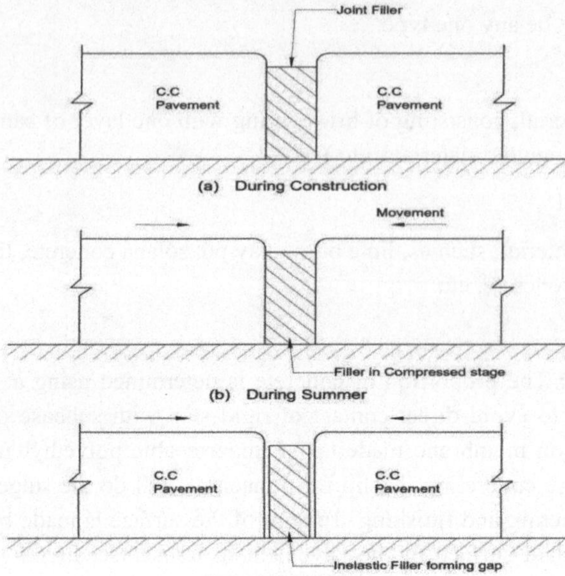

Fig. 3.3 Functioning of Joint Filler

Similarly, if the sealers used are not good quality, then during winter, when the pavement contracts, the sealer breaks. Whereas in summer, if the flow characteristic of sealer is not good, it flows and spreads around the joints, spoiling the appearance and riding quality of the pavement. See Fig. 3.4.

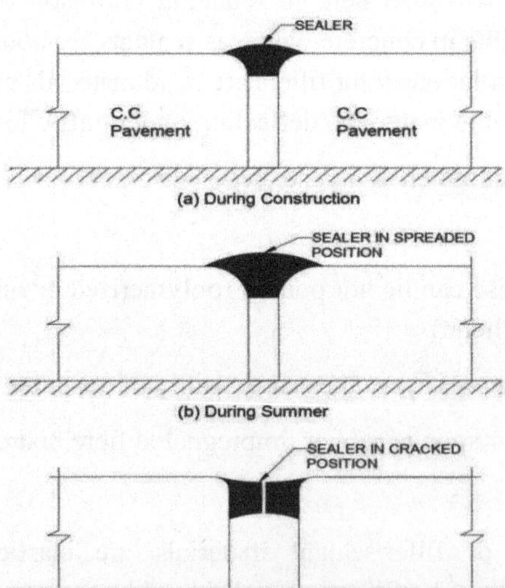

Fig. 3.4 Functioning of Joint Sealer

3.7.4 Joints in Cement Concrete Pavements

In concrete pavements, joints are provided to:

i) Release stresses (warping and curling) due to temperature variation

ii) Permit expansion and contraction of concrete under adverse environmental conditions

iii) Provide proper bonding between two phases of construction (breaking at the end of day's work).

iv) Allow pavement to be constructed in lanes of convenient width.

3.7.4.1 Types of Joints in Pavements

Joints are classified based on its function and location. Based on location it can be longitudinal joint and transverse joint. Based on function it can be expansion joint, contraction joint, warping joint and construction joint. Fig. 3.5 shows the lay-out of longitudinal joint and transverse joints in a two-lane concrete pavement. Brief description of different joints is given below.

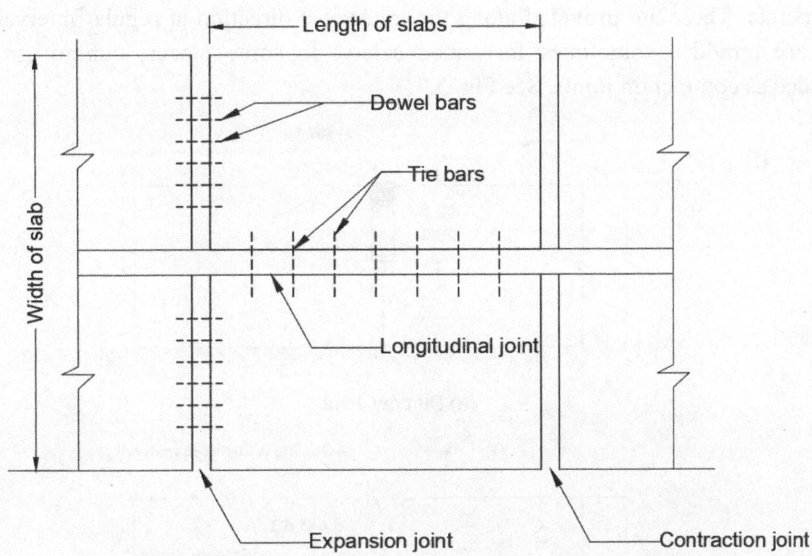

Fig. 3.5 Lay-out of Joints in Cement concrete pavements

Expansion Joint: Concrete expands due to increase in temperature. Unless some provisions are made for expansion, the concrete slab may bend outward and ultimately break. These types of joints are full depth joints and are provided at specified regular intervals along the transverse direction of the pavement. Dowel bars (steel rods) are provided across the expansion joint to take care of load transfer. A typical expansion joint is shown in Fig. 3.6.

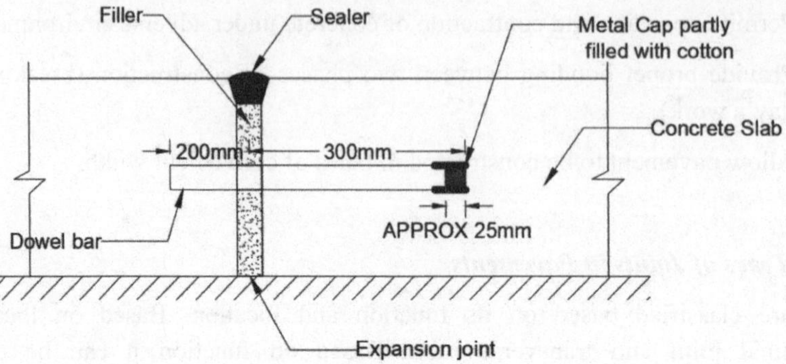

Fig. 3.6 Expansion Joint

***Contraction Joint*:** These types of joints are provided to resist the ill effects of shrinkage of concrete. These are provided along the transverse direction at regular intervals. Dowel rods are provided sometimes for added safety. In some places, dummy grooves are provided as contraction joints. See Fig. 3.7.

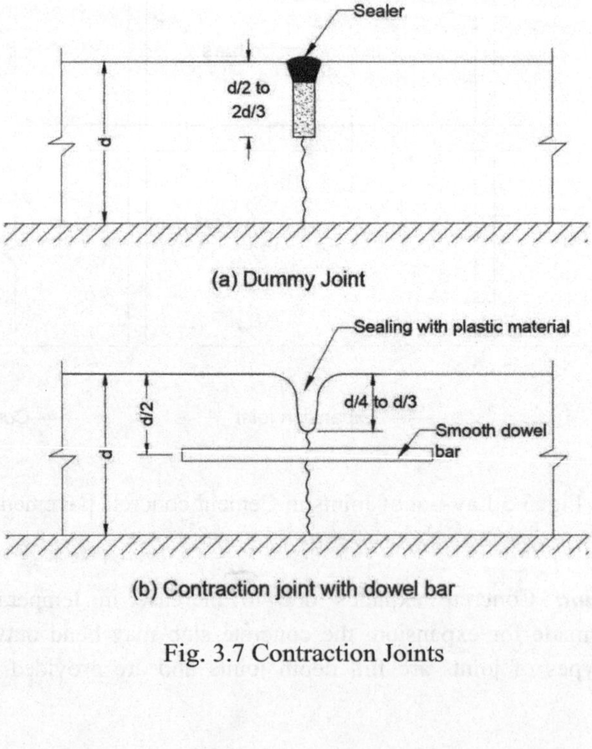

Fig. 3.7 Contraction Joints

***Warping Joints*:** Warping joints are provided to release stresses due to warping effect. These joints are rarely needed, if properly designed expansion and contraction joints are provided. A typical warping joint is shown in Fig.3.8.

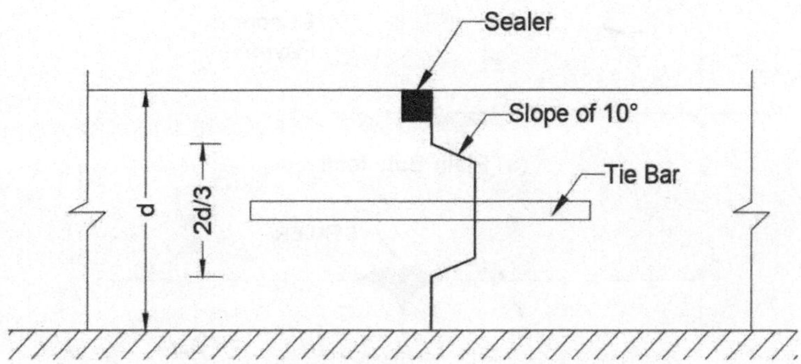

Fig. 3.8 Tongue and groove warping joint

***Construction joints*:** Construction joints are the joints between pavement sections constructed at a time lag (breaking after a day's work, etc.). It can be a longitudinal joint or transverse joint. See Fig.3.9.

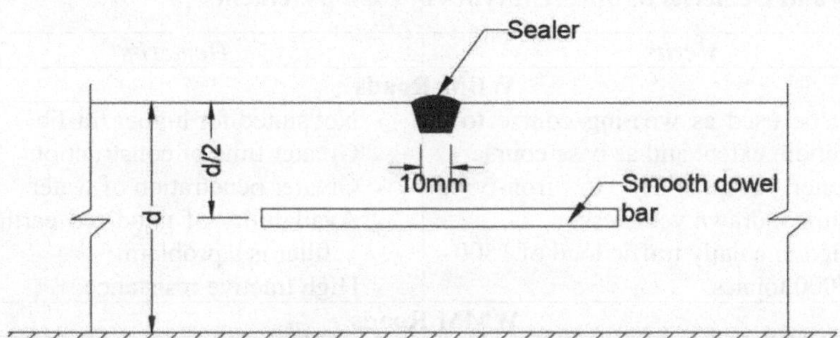

Fig. 3.9 Dowelled Construction Joint

Longitudinal Joints: They are provided to prevent the formation of longitudinal cracks in the slab as a result of differential shrinkage and swelling of clayey subgrade soil below due to rapid variations of moisture content, at the edges of the slab than at the centre. These joints are required only if the width of pavement exceeds 4.5m. They are either plain butt joint or butt joint with tie bar. See Fig.3.10.

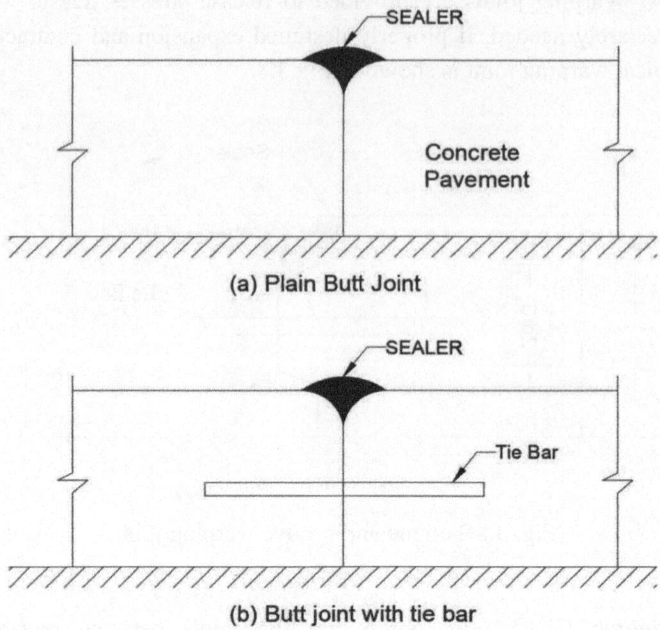

Fig. 3.10 Longitudinal Joints

3.7.5 Merits and Demerits of different types of road pavements

Merits	*Demerits*
WBM Roads	
• Can be used as wearing course to a certain extent and as base course • Greater adaptability to iron-tyred animal drawn vehicles • Suited to a daily traffic load of 1500 - 2000 tonnes.	• Not suited for higher traffic • Greater time of construction • Greater penetration of water • Availability of good red earth as a filler is a problem • High tractive resistance
WMM Roads	
• Can be used as a good base course • Red earth is not required • Better stability and strength, hence carries greater loads • Less time for construction	• Cannot be used as wearing course • Requires skill in construction
Bituminous Roads	
• Less initial cost • Less time for construction and opening to traffic • Fit for stage construction • Less glare under sunlight	• Less design life • High maintenance and life cycle cost • Greater penetration of water • Poor night time visibility • High tractive resistance • Good subgrade is essential.

Concrete Roads	
• Provides good riding surface • Greater life (30 to 40 years), hence lesser life-cycle cost • Low maintenance cost and vehicle operating cost • Low rolling resistance to vehicles • High night time visibility	• High capital cost • Requires skill in construction • Greater time of construction and opening to traffic • Not possible to lay underground cables and sewers after construction of pavement • Higher noise during traffic

UNIT SUMMARY

Types of Road Construction Materials

- Soil
- Aggregates
- Bitumen and Road tar
- Cement and cement concrete
- Steel
- Geosynthetics (geotextiles, geocells etc.)

Desirable properties of soil to be used as sub grade

- Stability
- Incompressibility
- Resistance to weathering
- Non-susceptibility to volume changes
- Good drainage characteristics
- Ease of compaction

Tests conducted on soil used for road construction

- *In-situ density*
- Plasticity index
- Compaction .
- California Bearing Ratio

Desirable properties of aggregates

- Strength
- Hardness
- Toughness

- Durability
- Good shapes
- Good adhesion with bitumen

Bituminous materials used in flexible pavement construction

- Bitumen
- Cutback bitumen
- Bitumen Emulsion
- Rubberized bitumen
- Straight run bitumen
- Road tar

Bituminous Coatings provided

- Prime coat
- Tack coat
- Seal coat

Desirable properties of bitumen

- Viscosity
- Ductility
- Temperature susceptibility
- Adhesion with aggregates

Tests on Road Aggregates

- Aggregate crushing test
- Ten percent fines value
- Abrasion test
- Aggregate impact test
- Soundness test
- Shape factors- Combined Flakiness & Elongation index and Angularity number.
- Stripping value test

Tests on Bitumen

- *Penetration*
- Ductility
- Softening point
- Viscosity

- Flash Point and Fire Point
- Stripping

Types of Pavements

- Flexible pavements
- Rigid Pavements
- Composite Pavements

Comparison between Flexible pavements and Rigid Pavements

Flexible Pavement	Rigid Pavement
a. It has a layered structure with highest quality materials at or near the surface.	a. It consists of a thick concrete slab having high flexural (bending) strength.
b. The strength of sub grade primarily influences the design thickness.	b. Rigidity and high modulus of concrete influences the design.
c. Stability of pavement is through aggregate interlocking, friction and cohesion.	c. Its structural capacity of the pavement slab is by beam action.
d. Load distribution is from the contact area of wheels through the component layers.	d. Load distribution is from the entire width of slab irrespective of the wheel position, to a wider area, due to rigidity and high modulus of elasticity of concrete.
e. Design is less precise.	e. Design is more abstract.
f. Design life - 10 to 15 years.	f. Design life - 20 to 30 years.
g. Less capital cost & more life cycle cost.	g. High capital cost & less life cycle cost.
h. Stage construction is possible.	h. Stage construction is difficult.

Components of pavement structure

- Surface course or wearing course
- Base course
- Sub base course
- Subgrade.

Types of Flexible Pavements

- Layered flexible pavements
- Deep strength flexible pavements
- Composite flexible pavements

Methods of construction of concrete roads

- Alternate Bay Method
- ii) Continuous Construction

Essential properties of filler/sealant materials

- Elasticity
- Stiffness
- Adhesion
- Compressibility
- Durability

Type of Joints in Pavements

- Expansion Joint
- Contraction Joint
- Warping Joints
- Construction joints

Merits & Demerits of different types of road pavements

Merits	*Demerits*
WBM Roads	
• Can be used as wearing course to a certain extent and as base course • Greater adaptability to iron-tyred animal drawn vehicles • Suited to a daily traffic load of 1500 - 2000 tonnes.	• Not suited for higher traffic • Greater time of construction • Greater penetration of water • Availability of good red earth as a filler is a problem • High tractive resistance
WMM Roads	
• Can be used as a good base course • Red earth is not required • Better stability and strength, hence carries greater loads • Less time for construction	• Cannot be used as wearing course • Requires skill in construction
Bituminous Roads	
• Less initial cost • Less time for construction and opening to traffic • Fit for stage construction • Less glare under sunlight	• Less design life • High maintenance and life cycle cost • Greater penetration of water • Poor night time visibility • High tractive resistance • Good subgrade is essential.
Concrete Roads	
• Provides good riding surface • Greater life (30 to 40 years), hence lesser life-cycle cost • Low maintenance cost and vehicle operating cost • Low rolling resistance to vehicles • High night-time visibility	• High capital cost • Requires skill in construction • Greater time of construction and opening to traffic • Not possible to lay underground cables and sewers after construction of pavement • Higher noise during traffic

EXERCISES

Multiple Choice Questions

3.1 CBR test is carried out in

b) Aggregates b) soil c) bitumen d) Cement concrete

3.2 CBR test is a type of

a) shear test b) bearing test c) penetration test d) none of these

3.3 CBR test is widely used in the design of

a) flexible pavement b) rigid pavement c) composite pavement d) all of the above

3.4 Abrasion test is carried out on aggregates to find

a) hardness b) toughness c) crushing strength d) water absorption

3.5 As per IRC, Los Angeles abrasion value of stone aggregates for bituminous concrete construction is limited to

a) 16% b) 30% c) 40% d) 50%

3.6 The residual product obtained by destructive distillation of coal is known as

a) Asphalt b) Bitumen c) tar d) cutbacks

3.7 The solution of bituminous material in a volatile solvent is known as

a) Asphalt b) bitumen c) cutbacks d) tar

3.8 A liquid product obtained by vigorously stirring up a mixture of bituminous material and water in presence of an emulsifying agent is known as

a) Asphalt b) emulsion c) cutbacks d) tar

3.9 Flashpoint test is a test for

a) soil b) aggregates c) bituminous material d) none of these

3.10 The test which is carried out to find out the temperature at which a bituminous material attains a particular degree of softening is known as

a) softening point test b) flash point test c) viscosity test d) solubility test

3.11 The test which is carried out to find out the temperature at which a bituminous material catches fire is

a) softening point test b) viscosity test c) ductility test d) flash point test

3.12 The lowest temperature at which the vapour of a bituminous material momentarily catches fire is known as

a) softening point b) fire point c) flash point d) none of these

3.13 Penetration test on bitumen is conducted to know its

a) Viscosity b) consistency c) ductility d) softening

3.14 Los Angeles abrasion test of stone aggregates is to find

a) strength b) hardness c) toughness d) soundness

3.15 Aggregate impact value of aggregates represents the property of

a) strength b) hardness c) toughness d) soundness

3.16 Aggregate impact value of aggregates used for bituminous bases is limited to

a) 15% b)30% c) 40% d) 50%

3.17 The layer which is in direct contact with traffic is

a) Base course b) sub base c) sub grade d) wearing course

3.18 Sub base course is placed immediately above

a) Base course b) sub grade c) wearing course d) none of the above

3.19 Design life of flexible pavements is generally in the range of

a) 20 - 30 years b) 20 - 40 years c) 10 - 15years d) 5 - 10 years

3.20 Joint parallel to the centre line of road is called

a) Longitudinal joint b) transverse joint c) expansion joint d) contraction joint

Answers to Multiple Choice Questions

3.1 b), 3.2 c), 3.3 a), 3.4 a), 3.5 b), 3.6 c), 3.7 c), 3.8 b), 3.9 c), 3.10 a), 3.11 d), 3.12 c), 3.13 b), 3.14 b), 3.15 c), 3.16 b), 3.17 d), 3.18 b), 3.19 c), 3.20 a).

Short and Long Answer Type Questions

Category I

3.1. List the commonly used materials for road construction.

3.2. What are the desirable properties of sub grade soil?

3.3. List the functions of sub grade.

3.4. What are the tests conducted on soil used for road construction?

3.5. What is a CBR test? What is its use?

3.6. Name the different tests carried out on road aggregates.

3.7. What are the different laboratory tests conducted on bitumen?

3.8. Explain the terms : softening point, flash point and fire point related to bitumen.

3.9. Why penetration test is carried out on bitumen?

3.10. What is a cutback bitumen?

3.11. Differentiate Cutbacks and Emulsions.

3.12. What do you understand by specifying the grade of bitumen as 80/100?

3.13. Differentiate Road tar and bitumen.

3.14. What is the significance of ductility test on bitumen?

3.15. Give the classification of pavements in view of structural design.

3.16. Sketch typical cross sections of flexible and rigid pavements.

3.17. Compare flexible and rigid pavements.

3.18. What are WBM roads? Explain its construction procedure.

3.19. What are WMM roads? Compare WMM and WBM roads.

3.20. Explain the procedure of constructing Bituminous macadam.

3.21. How joints are classified in rigid pavement construction?

3.22. What are the merits and demerits of Bituminous roads?

3.23. List the merits and demerits of concrete roads.

Category II

3.1. What are the desirable properties of road aggregates? Explain how impact teston aggregates is conducted. What is its significance?

3.2. Explain how Los Angeles abrasion test is conducted. What is its importance?

3.3. Differentiate the various bituminous coatings provided in flexible pavement construction.

3.4. What are the different shape tests conducted on road aggregates? Explain their importance in road construction.

3.5. What are the components of a flexible pavement? Explain their functions.

3.6. What are the methods of constructing cement concrete roads?

3.7. What are Joint fillers and sealants in rigid pavements? Give their classification and significance.

PRACTICAL

TESTS ON AGGREGATES

3P1 Flakiness Index test

Theory: Flaky particles are the particles whose thicknesses are less than 0.6 times of their mean size (e.g. mean size of 14–10mm fraction is 12mm and therefore, thickness of flaky particle is less than 0.6 x 12 = 7.2mm).

The Flakiness Index of aggregates is the percentage by weight of particles whose thickness is less than 0.6 times their mean dimension. The test is carried out on the aggregate samples having size 6.3mm to 63mm (particles of size below 6.3mm and greater than 63mm are discarded). The flakiness is checked using the thickness gauge having specific slot sizes. [Fig. 3.1(a)].

Test procedure:

i. Obtain the test sample passing 63mm sieve and retained on 6.3mm sieve.

ii. Weigh and record the weight of the test sample.

iii. Sieve the sample on 63mm, 50mm, 40mm, 31.5mm, 25mm, 20mm, 16mm, 12.5mm, 10mm and 6.3 mm sieves.

iv. Determine the weight of particles retained on each sieve.

v. Pass each fraction through the specified slot on the thickness gauge.

vi. Determine the weight of particles passing through each slot.

vii. Flakiness Index is calculated as:

$$Flakiness\ Index\ (in\ \%) = \frac{Sum\ of\ weights\ of\ particles\ passing\ through\ the\ slots}{Weight\ of\ sample\ taken\ for\ the\ test} x100$$

Example:

Aggregate Fraction (mm)	Weight of fraction (g)	Weight retained on the slot (g)	Weight passing on the slot(g)
Passing 63mm and Retained on 50mm	2131.3	1971.5	159.8
Passing 50mm and retained on 40mm	2045.6	1840.5	205.1
Passing 40mm and Retained on 31.5mm	1987.1	1748.6	238.5
Passing on 31.5mm and Retained on 20mm	1875.6	1688.0	187.
Passing on 20mm and Retained on 12.5mm	1563.9	1345.0	218.9
Passing on 12.5mm and Retained on 10mm	1245.2	1033.5	211.7
Passing on 10mm and Retained on 6.3mm	856.0	624.9	231.1
Total	11704.7		1452.7
$FI = \frac{1452.7}{11704.7} \times 100 = 12.40\%$			

3P2 Elongation Index Test

Theory: Elongated particles are the particles whose lengths are more than 1.8 times their mean size (e.g. mean size of 14–10mm fraction is 12mm and therefore, elongation of particle is more than 1.8 x 12 = 21.6mm).

The Elongation Index of aggregates is the percentage by weight of particles whose length is more than 1.8 times their mean dimension. The test is carried out on the aggregate samples having size 6.3mm to 50mm (particles of size below 6.3mm and greater than 50mm are discarded). The elongation is checked using the elongation gauge having specific gaps. [Fig. 3.1(b)].

Test procedure:

i. Obtain the test sample passing 63mm sieve and retained on 6.3mm sieve.

ii. Weigh and record the weight of the test sample.

iii. Sieve the sample on 50mm, 40mm, 25mm, 20mm, 16mm, 12.5mm, 10mm and 6.3 mm sieves

iv. Determine the weight of particles retained on each sieve.

v. Pass each fraction,with its longest dimension, through the specified gap on the elongation gauge.

vi. Determine the weight of particles that does not pass through the designated gaps.

vii. Elongation Index is calculated as

$$Elongation\ Index\ (in\ \%) = \frac{Sum\ of\ weights\ of\ retained\ particles\ in\ the\ gaps}{Weight\ of\ sample\ taken\ for\ the\ test} \times 100$$

Example:

Aggregate Fraction (mm)	Weight of fraction (g)	Weight retained on the gap (g)
Passing 50mm and retained on 40mm	1988.6	488.9
Passing 40mm and Retained on 25mm	1869.7	198.5
Passing on 25mm and Retained on 20mm	1754.6	221.9
Passing on 20mm and Retained on 12.5mm	1331.1	111.4
Passing on 12.5mm and Retained on 10mm	1051.6	317.2
Passing on 10mm and Retained on 6.3mm	961.7	105.1
Total	8957.3	1443.0
EI $= \frac{1443.0}{8957.3} \times 100 = 16.10\%$		

***Note:** To get the combined flakiness and elongation index (CI) of aggregates, the Flakiness Index (FI) is first determined on the sample and then Elongation Index (EI) is found out on the remaining non-flaky stone particles. Then, CI = (FI + EI).*

3P3 Angularity Number Test

Theory: The Angularity gives some idea regarding absence of roundness or angularity of the aggregate specimen. The Angularity number of a single sized (all pieces are of almost same size e.g. 16mm -20mm range) aggregate sample is defined as the amount by which the percentage voids in the sample exceed 33 after being compacted in a specified manner. The percentage voids will be 33% when all the particles are truly spherical, an ideal case.

Higher the angularity number, the more angular is the aggregates. In cement concrete (Rigid pavements) roads aggregate with lesser angularity number is preferred because of better workability and higher strength whereas in bituminous or water bound macadam (Flexible pavements) roads aggregates having higher angularity number is preferred because of high stability due to better interlocking and friction.

For flexible pavement construction, angularity number between 7 and 10 is generally preferred.

The sample used for testing must be single sized(retained on 20mm and retained on 16mm, 16mm and 12.5mm, 12.5mm and 10mm, 10mm and 6.3mm or 6.3mm and 4.75mm). A cylindrical container of 3 litres capacity opened at one end (diameter 156.4mm and height 156.4mm) is used. Tamping rod is of 16mm diameter and 600mm long.

Test Procedure

1. Oven dried single sized aggregate more than required to fill the container of 3L capacity is taken
2. The sample is put in three layers and each layer is compacted by tamping 100 times at a rate of 2 blows per second by the standard tamping rod.
3. The cylinder is then filled to overflowing and then trimmed with tamping rod as a straight edge.
4. The aggregate with cylinder is weighed. Knowing weight of empty cylinder, weight of compacted aggregate (W_a) is found out.
5. Volume of water to fill the cylinder is measured to get correct volume of cylinder (V_c)
6. Specific gravity of aggregate (G_s) is determined using any standard procedure
7. Three separate measurements are made and then average is taken.
8. Angularity number is calculated as

$$Angularity\ Number = 67 - \left(\frac{W_a}{V_c \times G_s}\right) \times 100$$

Expressed as next higher whole number.

Example

Weight of empty cylinder = 5083.7g

Weight of cylinder + Aggregate = 9897.6g

Weight of aggregate = 9897.6 – 5083.7 = 4813.9g

Volume of water filling cylinder = 3004.5cc

Specific gravity of aggregate = 2.67

$$Angularity\ Number = 67 - \left(\frac{4813.9}{3004.5 \times 2.67}\right) \times 100 = 7$$

3P4 Aggregate Impact Test

The aggregate impact testing machine consists of a metal base and a cylindrical steel cup of internal diameter 10.2 cm and depth 5cm in which the aggregate specimen is placed. A cylindrical metal hammer weighing 13.5 to 14 kg having a free fall from a height of 38 cm is arranged to drop through vertical guides. The test sample consists of aggregates passing 12.5 mm sieve and retained on 10mm sieve. It is filled in the cylindrical measure provided, in three layers by tamping using a tamping rod, each layer subjected to 25 blows. The weight of this sample is taken and then transferred to the cup placed at the base of the aggregate impact testing machine, and again compacted by tamping 25 times. Then the hammer of the machine is raised to the specified height of 38cm and allowed to fall freely on the specimen. Likewise 15 blows are applied on the specimen and then the crushed aggregate is sieved through 2.36mm sieve. The aggregate impact value is expressed as percentage of fines passing 2.36mm sieve formed in terms of the total weight of the sample taken.

The aggregate impact value should not normally exceed 30 per cent for aggregates to be used in wearing course of pavements, and should not exceed 35% for bituminous macadam and 40 % for water bound macadam.

3P5 Los Angeles Abrasion Test

The machine consists of a hollow cylinder closed at both ends having inside diameter 700 mm and length 500 mm and mounted so as to rotate about its horizontal axis. The abrasive charge consists of cast iron spheres of approximate diameter 48mm and each of weight 390 - 445 gram. The number of spheres to be used as abrasive charge and their total weight have been specified based on the grading of the selected aggregate sample. The specified weight of aggregate specimen of desired grading along with the specified abrasive charge are placed in the machine and it is rotated at a speed of 30 - 33 rpm for the specified number of revolutions depending on the grading of specimen. The abraded aggregate is then sieved through 1.7 mm sieve and the weight of powdered aggregate passing is found out. Los Angeles abrasion value is taken as the percentage wear or the percentage passing 1.7 mm sieve in terms of the original weight of the sample.

Los Angeles abrasion value should be less than 30% for high quality pavement like bituminous concrete, and and it should be less than 35% for dense bituminous macadam and up to 40% for granular base courses like wet mix macadam and a water bound macadam.

3P6 Aggregate Crushing Test

The apparatus consists of a steel cylinder 152 mm diameter with a base plate and a plunger, compression testing machine, cylindrical measure of diameter 115 mm and height 180mm, tamping rod and sieves. Dry aggregate passing 12.5 mm sieve and retained on 10 mm sieve is filled in the cylindrical measure in three equal layers, each layer being tamped 25 times by the tamping rod. The test sample is weighed and placed in the test cylinder in three equal layers, each layer being tamped 25 times. The plunger is placed on the top of the specimen and using the compression testing machine, a load of 40 tonnes is applied at a rate of 4tonnes per minute. After crushing, the sample is taken out and sieved on 2.36 mm sieve. The crushed material which passed the sieve is weighed.The percentage of crushed material passing 2.36 mm sieve in terms of original weight of the specimen is represented as the aggregate crushing value.

Aggregate crushing value shall not exceed 45% for base course materials and 30 % for surface course.

TESTS ON BITUMEN

3P7 Penetration Test

Apparatus

i) A metal or glass cylindrical container with flat bottom having the following dimensions are used:

For penetrations below 225: Diameter 55mm and Internal depth 35mm

For penetrations between 225 and 350: Diameter 70mm and Internal depth 45mm.

ii) A straight, highly polished, cylindrical, stainless steel rod with conical and parallel portions

iii) Penetration Apparatus – An apparatus which will allow the needle to penetrate without appreciable friction, and which is accurately calibrated to yield results in tenths of millimetre is used.

Test Procedure

i) Soften the bitumen to pouring consistency and fill the container to a depth at least 10mm excess of expected penetration. Allow it to cool in atmosphere at a temperature between 15 to 30°C for 1 to 2 hours and then in water bath at testing temperature of 25.0 ± 0.1°C for another 1 to 2 hours.

ii) Keep the sample container on the stand of the apparatus and adjust the needle so that it just touches the sample. Load the needle holder with the weight required to make a total moving weight of100± 0.25 g.

iii) Bring the pointer to zero. Release the needle and measure the distance penetrated. Since the dial is calibrated so as to read penetration in one tenth of a millimeter, the penetration value can be directly read out from the dial.

iv) Average of three test results on separate identical samples are reported as the final answer.

3P8 Ductility Test

Apparatus

i) Mould made of brass with the shape, dimensions and tolerances

ii) Testing Machine - For pulling the briquette of bituminous material apart, any apparatus may be used which is so constructed that the specimen will be continuously immersed in water while the two clips are pulled apart horizontally.

iii) Water bath.

Procedure

i) Melt the bitumen at temperature of 75 to 100°C above the approximate softening point until it becomes fluid. Assemble the mould on a brass plate and coat the surface of the plate and interior surfaces of the sides of the mould with a mixture of glycerine and dextrin to avoid sticking.

ii) Place the brass plate and mould with briquette specimen in the water bath at test temperature of 25.0 ± 0.5°C for 85 to 95 minutes. Then remove the briquette from the plate, detach the side pieces immediately before testing.

iii) Attach the rings at each end of the clips to the pins or hooks in the testing machine and pull the two clips apart horizontally at a uniform speed until the briquette ruptures.

iv) Measure the distance in centimeters through which the clips have been pulled to produce rupture which is reported as ductility.

3P9 Softening point test

Apparatus

i) Ring and Ball Apparatus - It consists of

a) Two Steel Balls each 9.5 mm in diameter and weight 3.50 ± 0.05 g.

b) Two Brass Rings– The rings are be tapered having Depth 6.4 ± 0.1 mm, Inside diameter at bottom 15.9 ± 0.1 mm, Inside diameter at top 17.5 ± 0.1 mm and Outside diameter 20.6 ± 0.1 mm

c) Ball centering guide

d) Ring Holder

ii) Water bath

iii) Stirrer

Procedure

i) Melt the bitumen at temperature of 75 to 100°C above the approximate softening point until it becomes fluid. Assemble the mould on a brass plate and coat the surface of the plate and interior surfaces of the sides of the mould with a mixture of glycerine and dextrin to avoid sticking.

ii) Place the rings, previously heated to a temperature approximating to that of the molten material, on a metal plate which has been coated with a mixture of glycerin and dextrin, and fill with sufficient molten bitumen. Cool the specimen for 30 minutes in air and excess is trimmed off.

iii) Assemble the apparatus with the rings, thermometer and ball guides in position, and fill the bath to a height of 50 mm above the upper surface of the rings with freshly boiled distilled water at a temperature of 5°C.

iv) Maintain the bath at a temperature of 5°C for 15 minutes after which place the balls in position.

v) Apply heat to the bath and stir the liquid so that the temperature rises at a uniform rate of 5.0 ± 0.5°C per minute until the material softens and allows the ball to pass through the ring.

vi) The temperature at the instant the sample surrounding the ball touches the bottom plate of the support is recorded as Softening point.

3P10 Flash point and Fire point test

Determination of flash point and fire point of bitumen using Pensky- Martens apparatus closed type is described.

Apparatus

i) Pensky-Martens Closed type apparatus. It consists of a cup made of brass having inside diameter 50.8 mm and inside height 55.9 mm. The inside of the cup may be turned to a slightly larger diameter above the filling mark and the outside may be tapered. The flange is approximately 12 mm width and 3 mm thick. It shall be equipped with devices for locating the position of the lid on the cup and the cup itself in the stove.

ii) Lid- The lid includes stirring device, cover proper, shutter, and flame-exposure device.

Procedure

i) Fill the cup with the bitumen to be tested up to the level indicated by the filling mark. Place the lid on the cup and set the latter in the stove. Insert the thermometer in place.

ii) Bitumen is heated and adjust the test-flame so that it is of the size of a bead of 4 mm in diameter. Heating is done at the rate of 5^0C to 6^0C per minute. Turn the stirrer at a rate of approximately 60 revolutions per minute.

iii) Apply the test-flame by operating the device controlling the shutter and test-flame burner.

iv) Flash point is recorded as the temperature read on the thermometer at the time of the flame application that causes a distinct flash in the interior of the cup.

v) The heating is continued until the volatile ignites and the bitumen continues to burn for 5 seconds. The temperature at this instant is recorded as the Fire point.

3P11 Study on distress in road pavements and remedial measures

A. Visit a major road having an age more than 5 years in your locality and identify the defects or distresses by visual inspection, and prepare a detailed report with the support of photographs.

B. After studying the nature and causes of the distresses in the above road, prepare a detailed report giving suggestions for remedial measures for each of the defect.

3P12 Study on features of Hill Roads

A. Visit a hill road in your locality and understand its special features and their necessities.

B. Prepare a detailed report covering the photographs of the components of the hill road visited.

3P13 Study on features of drainage system of Roads

A. Visit a major road (flexible or rigid) in your locality and understand the drainage facilities given and check their sufficiency.

B. Prepare a detailed report with photographs of the drainage measures provided in the above road and suggest remedial measures for repair / improvement / maintenance.

KNOW MORE

Activity:

3.1 Visit a new road being constructed in your locality and take photographs of the works going on at different stages and prepare a report on it.

3.2 Visit a Highway Quality Control lab of your nearby major road and understand the procedure of sampling the specimens to be tested and how they are conducting the quality tests. Prepare a report of the same.

3.3 Identify the pavement maintenance management system being followed in your highway division and prepare a report.

3.4 Consult any three highway engineers / contractors and collect data regarding the problems/issues they are facing in the field for the proper execution/ implementation of the highway project. Make a report of the same, giving suggestions for remedial measures.

Interesting Facts:

Smart / Innovative Technologies and Products in Road Construction

Smart Technologies

The way we build roads will change as a result of a number of smart technologies viz. *robotics, artificial intelligence, big data, cloud computing,* etc. which would result in more safer, more comfortable, and more energy-efficient roads. Some examples are given below:

- ***In-transit material management systems:*** The Internet of Things (IoT) improves quality control of the material mix while it is in transit, which cuts down the labour costs. Sensors attached on the sides of trucks automatically detect the consistency and properties of the aggregates, bitumen, or ready-mix concrete. These sensors enable the required adjustments while the material is being moved from the plant to the job site. Big data from the sensors is sent to the cloud for analysis by which changes in job mix, logistic operations and cost reduction could be achieved.

- ***Solar-powered roadways:*** They are solar-powered, energy-efficient road surfaces that enhance visibility and safety. To melt accumulating ice and snow, heat is produced on the pavement during the day. At night, the surface is lighted by embedded LED lights. To warn drivers of potential dangers, warning signs that are integrated into the surface of the road are triggered. There are three layers to the road: a base plate that distributes energy to the integrated safety components, a layer of photo-voltaic solar cells that collects solar energy, and a top layer of sturdy, resilient, and highly textured glass that supports traction of vehicles.

- ***Interactive lights:*** They are solar-powered lights that automatically illuminate the roadway as vehicles pass by. Each light is connected to a small windmill-like device that senses the movement of air. This activates the beam for a fraction of a second.
- ***Smart pavement:*** They are pavements provided with buit-in sensors which monitor the road and weather conditions, a control station where this data will be disseminated, Wi-Fi transmitters to deliver broad-band services to nearby structures and moving traffic, and charging mechanism for recharging electric cars while they move.

Innovative Products

- ***Noise-reducing Bitumen:***It is developed to minimize road traffic noise generated during the running of vehicles, satisfying all the requirements for hot-mix asphalt, making it an ideal material to use particularly in residential areas.
- ***Eco-friendly Bituminous mixes:*** Warm mixes that have less environmental impact are being developed to replace traditional hot-mix asphalt construction. Because it is produced at a lower temperature, odour, smoke, fuel consumption and emissions are reduced during manufacturing. It can reduce carbon emissions by as much as 20%.
- ***Eco-friendly ingredients:*** Recycling materials can be added to the road mix to make road construction more environment-friendly. For instance, Vegecol, a mix provided by Canadian Road Builders Inc., can be used on both main roads and other pathways, and is fully composed of renewable, plant-based materials. Vegecol's carbon footprint is smaller because it is produced at a colder temperature. Additionally, there aren't any petrochemical ingredients that could taint run-off water.
- ***Computer modelling:*** It is frequently employed in structural design, which benefits taxpayers, and produces more efficient roads. Engineers can quickly assess the effects of proposed changes, including price variations with the aid of computer modelling.
- ***Water-saving pavement:*** They are constructed using pervious concrete or porous asphalt to allow rainwater to flow through the surface and into a catchment area below. They are useful in parking lots because they let owners collect runoff and store it for gardening.
- ***Perpetual pavements:*** They are intended to serve about 50 years instead of the 20 years that conventional pavements last, and they are expected to gain popularity for use on major highways. The components of high-performance asphalt mixtures, such as Superpave, which resist rutting, cracking, and wear, are responsible for their durability.

SCAN ME
for
Amazing Techniques of
Road Construction

- ***Full-depth reclamation:*** Full-depth reclamation is a method of repairing where the old asphalt is combined with the gravel beneath it and used to create a new road base. It results in base material of higher quality, avoids the expense and environmental problems of removing the old asphalt from the site, and uses minimum of virgin aggregates.

- ***Collaboration***: Although it isn't a product or a method of developing roads, it has an impact on the calibre of roads. Industry partners are exchanging information and best practices, and adopting a far more cooperative approach to develop a solution. These partners may include the road builder group, transportation experts, and consulting engineers. In the future, this will lead to better products and greater innovation.

REFERENCES AND SUGGESTED READINGS

1. *Arora N.* L., 'Transportation Engineering', New India Pub., 1977.
2. Chakraborthy Partha, Das Animesh,'Principles of Transportation Engineering', Prentice-Hall of India Pvt.Ltd., New Delhi, 2003.
3. Duggal Ajay K. and Puri V P., 'Laboratory Manual for Highway Engineering', New Age International (P) Ltd. Publishers, New Delhi, 2017.
4. *Kadiyali L.* R., 'Transportation Engineering', Khanna Book Publishing Co., 2018.
5. *Khanna S.* K., Justo C. E. G., Veeraraghavan A., 'Highway Engineering', Nem Chand & Bros., Roorkee, 2014.
6. *Subramanian K.* P., 'Transportation Engineering', Scitech Publications, Chennai, 2015.
7. Sharma S.K., 'Principles, Practice and Design of Highway Engineering', S. Chand Publishing, 2014.
8. IRC 'Guidelines for the design of Flexible pavements' IRC: 37-2018, Indian Roads Congress, New Delhi.
9. IRC 'Guidelines for the design of plain jointed rigid pavements' IRC: 58-2015, Indian Roads Congress, New Delhi.
10. Ministry of Road Transport and Highways, (Government of India), 'Pocket Book for Highway Engineers', Indian Roads Congress, 2002.
11. Ministry of Road Transport and Highways, (Government of India), Specifications for Road and bridge works', Fifth Rev., Indian Roads Congress, New Delhi, 2013.
12. https://nptel.ac.in/courses/105101087
13. https://www.smartzworld.com/notes/transportation-engineering-pdf-notes-te-pdf-notes/
14. https://jntukucen.ac.in/ebook_files/166.pdf

UNIT 4
BASICS OF RAILWAY ENGINEERING

UNIT SPECIFICS

This unit discusses the following aspects:

- Classification of Indian Railways
- Zones of Indian Railways
- Permanent way - Requirements, Components
- Rail Gauge - Types, Factors affecting and Selection of gauge
- Rails, Rail Joints- Requirements and Types
- Creep of Rails - Causes and Prevention
- Sleepers - Functions, Requirements and Types
- Ballast - Functions, Types, and Suitability
- Rail Fixtures and Fastenings - Fish plates, Spikes, Bolts, Bearing plates, Chairs and Keys, Creep Anchors

Multiple-choice questions along with answers, short and long answer type questions including numerical problems and a practical work, relevant to the topics covered in the unit, are added. A list of references and suggested readings are also given. It should be noted that dynamic QR codes are provided for additional reading in different sections, which can be scanned for relevant supportive information. A "KNOW MORE" section is also given at the end, which has been carefully designed so that additional information relevant to this unit is provided for the users of the book. This section mainly contains some 'Activities' for the students to make them conversant with the topics he/she had studied, and some interesting facts related with the contents of the unit.

RATIONALE

Railways play a vital role in the transportation sector of the country, helping her in national production, social and industrial development and elevation of economic status. Apart from conventional railways, other modes of rail transport like Metro railway, High speed railway, semi high speed railway, light gauge railway mono railway, etc. are also gaining importance now a days due to their efficiency and safety in handling mass transportation and also due to the reduced environmental impacts.

In general, the railway engineering comprises of different phases like understanding of the components of the railway track, design of various geometrics of the track, its construction, traffic control and maintenance. This unit discusses the basics of railway engineering i.e. the components the railway track, their functions, requirements, types and suitability, the understanding of which are the essential pre-requisites for a railway engineer.

UNIT OUTCOMES

After completing this unit, student will be able

U4-O1: To identify the classification of Indian Railway lines and Railway Zones.

U4-O2: To identify the components of permanent way, Rail gauge, types and factors affecting selection of gauge.

U4-O3: To identify the different types and requirements of rails, rail joints, also rail creep, its causes and prevention.

U4-O4: To identify the functions, requirements, and suitability of different types of sleepers and ballast.

U4-O5: To identify the functions, requirements, and suitability of different types of rail fixtures and fastenings.

Unit-4 Outcomes	EXPECTED MAPPING WITH COURSE OUTCOMES (1- Weak Correlation, 2-Medium Correlation, 3- Strong Correlation)				
	CO-1	CO-2	CO-3	CO-4	CO-5
U4-O1	-	-	-	1	-
U4-O2	-	-	-	3	2
U4-O3	-	-	-	3	3
U4-O4	-	-	-	3	3
U4-O5	-	-	-	3	3

4.1 INTRODUCTION

In India, Railways form the principal mode of transportation due to its versatility not only in the passenger and freight movement, but also in activities like business, sightseeing and pilgrimage. The Indian Railway network, comprising more than 68,000 km presently, is the fourth largest in the world after the US, China and Russia. Railways were first introduced in India in 1853 by the British, running the first passenger train from Bombay's Bori Bunder station to Thane, using steam locomotives. During the year of independence, 1947, there were 42 rail systems in the country which were nationalized as one unit in 1951.

4.1.1 Necessity of Railways

The roles played by railways listed below depict their necessity towards the contribution in economic, social and industrial development of our nation:

a. Unite the people of different cross sections including, religion, custom, tradition, etc. across the entire country.

b. Help in mass transportation of passengers and freight with speed, safety and comfort.

c. Provide employment to millions of people and help in increasing the standard of living.

d. Help in industrial development through efficient means of transporting raw materials as well as finished products, and also in the price stabilization of commodities.

e. Help in maintaining law and order.

f. Help in reducing air pollution through electric traction of vehicles.

4.2 CLASSIFICATION OF INDIAN RAILWAYS

Depending on the significance of route traffic carried and the permissible speed limit, Railway Board has classified the Indian Railway lines as given in Table 4.1.

Table 4.1 Classification of Indian Railways

(Source: Ministry of Indian Railways)

Sl. No.	Main Classification	Sub Classification	Meant for
1	Broad Gauge Routes	Group A lines	Sanctioned speed of 160kmph
		Group B lines	Sanctioned speed of 130kmph
		Group C lines	Suburban sections of Mumbai, Kolkata & Delhi
		Group D & DSpecial lines	Sanctioned speed of 100kmph
		Group E & ESpecial lines	Other sections & branch lines
2	Metre Gauge Routes	Q Routes	Max.permissible speed of >75kmph & Traffic density >2.5 GMT*

Sl. No.	Main Classification	Sub Classification	Meant for
	• Trunk Routes • Main lines • Branch lines (Earlier classification)	R Routes	Max.permissible speed of 75kmph & Traffic density >1.5 GMT
		R1	Traffic density >5 GMT
		R2	Traffic density 2.5-5.0 GMT
		R3	Traffic density 1.5-2.5 GMT
		S Routes	Max. permissible speed of <75kmph & Traffic density <1.5 GMT
		S1	Through movement of freight traffic
		S2	Routes which are neither S1 *nor* S3
		S3	Uneconomical branch lines

*GMT - Gross Million Tonne per km per annum

4.3 ZONES OF INDIAN RAILWAYS

For administrative purpose Indian Railways are presently divided into 19 divisions as listed in Table 4.2.

Table 4.2 List of Indian Railway Zones, their Head Quarters and Divisions

(Source: Ministry of Indian Railways)

Sl. No.	Railway Zone	Head Quarters	Railway Divisions
1	Central Railway	Mumbai CSMT	Mumbai, Bhusaval, Nagpur, Solapur, Pune.
2	Eastern Railway	Kolkata	Asansol, Howrah, Malda, Sealdah.
3	East Central Railway	Hazipur	Sonpur, Samastipur, Danapur, Dhanbad, Pt. Deen Dayal Upadhyaya
4	East Coast Railway	Bhubaneshwar	Khurda Road, Sambalpur, Waltair.

Sl. No.	Railway Zone	Head Quarters	Railway Divisions
5	Northern Railway	New Delhi	Ambala, Delhi, Lucknow, Moradabad, Ferozpur.
6	North Central Railway	Prayagraj, Allahabad	Prayagraj, Agra, Jhansi
7	North Eastern Railway	Gorakhpur	Lucknow, Izzatnagar, Varanasi
8	Northeast Frontier Railway	Maligaon, Guwahati	Alipurduar, Katihar, Lumding, Rangiya, Tinsukia.
9	North Western Railway	Jaipur	Ajmer, Bikaner, Jaipur , Jodhpur
10	Southern Railway	Chennai Central	Chennai, Madurai, Palakkad, Tiruchchirappalli, Thiruvananthapuram, Salem.
11	South Central Railway	Secunderabad	Guntakal, Guntur, Hyderabad, Nanded, Secunderabad, Vijayawada.
12	South Eastern Railway	Garden Reach, Kolkata	Adra, Chakradharpur, Kharagpur, Ranchi.
13	South East Central Railway	Bilaspur	Raipur, Nagpur, Bilaspur.
14	South Western Railway	Hubli	Bengaluru, Hubballi, Mysuru.
15	Western Railway:	Church Gate, Mumbai	Mumbai Central, Vadodara, Ratlam , Ahmedabad, Rajkot, Bhavnagar.
16	West Central Railway :	Jabalpur	Bhopal, Jabalpur, Kota.
17	Metro Railway, Kolkata	Kolkata	-
18	Southern Coast Railway	Visakhapatnam	Waltair, Vijayawada, Guntur, Guntakal
19	Konkan Railway	Navi Mumbai	Karwar, Ratnagiri

4.4 PERMANENT WAY

Permanent way is the completed railway track consisting of rails fitted on sleepers which are resting on ballast and subgrade. The term permanent way is used to distinguish it from a temporary track which is initially laid to transport the materials for construction of the proposed track. Temporary tracks are removed immediately after the completion of the permanent way.

SCAN ME for Classification of Indian Railways

4.4.1 Components of a permanent way: A typical cross section of a permanent way constructed on embankment illustrating its components is shown in Fig.4.1.

The components of a permanent way include the following:

i. Subgrade
ii. Ballast
iii. Sleepers
iv. Rails
v. Fixtures and fastenings.

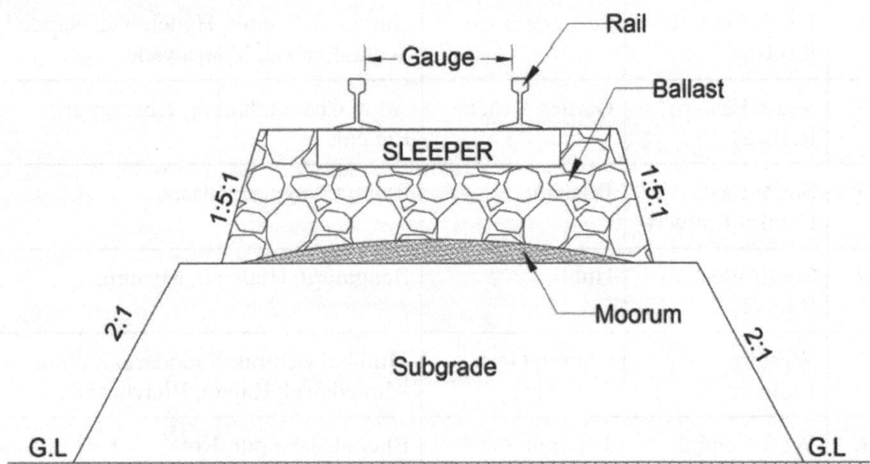

Fig.4.1. Cross section of a permanent way showing its components

In a permanent way the rails are joined by using 'fishplates' or by welding, and are fixed to the 'sleepers' using appropriate 'fastenings. Sleepers are properly spaced and boxed in the 'ballast', which is laid over the subgrade called 'formation'.

The wheel load of rail is transmitted to the sleepers. The sleepers hold the rails in proper position and then transmits load from rails to ballast. The ballast distributes the load over the formation and holds the sleepers in position.

4.4.2 Requirements of a Permanent Way: The basic requirements of a permanent way are listed below:

a) Gauge should be even, uniform and correct.

b) On straight track, both rails should be at the same level.

c) At curves, radii and superelevation should be properly designed.

d) The design of the track should be such that the load is distributed uniformly over the two rails.

e) Sufficient elasticity should be there for the track such that the impact of moving loads on rails is less.

f) Tracks should be strong enough to resist lateral forces.

g) Components (rails, sleepers, fixtures and fastenings) as well as points and crossings should be properly designed.

h) Tractive resistance should be least.

i) Proper drainage system should be provided.

j) Repairs and renewals should be easy.

4.5 GAUGE

Gauge is the transverse width or clear minimum horizontal distance between inner or running faces of two rails of the track. See Fig. 4.1.

4.5.1 Types of gauges: The gauges followed in India are as follows:

i.	Broad Gauge (BG)	-	1.676m
ii.	Metre Gauge (MG)	-	1.000m
iii.	Narrow Gauge (NG)	-	0.762m & 0.610m
iv.	Standard gauge for Metro railways	-	1.435m

4.5.2 Factors affecting selection of gauge: Selection of gauge depends on the following factors:

a) *Availability of funds* - wider gauge is more expensive than narrower gauges because of increased land acquisition and increased earthwork.

b) *Volume and nature of traffic* - wider gauges are preferred for heavier loads and high speed traffic.

c) *Future development of area* - wider gauges are generally preferred in areas having greater potential of traffic.

d) *Topography* -In hilly or steep terrains, narrow gauges may be preferred.

e) *Speed of train* -Speed of a train is proportional to diameter of its wheel. Also, diameter of wheel is proportional to the gauge of the track. Hence for higher speed, wider gauges are preferred.

4.6 RAILS

Rails are the rolled steel sections laid along two parallel lines over sleepers to act as girders to carry axle loads. They provide a hard, smooth and good riding surface for the movement of trains. They are strong enough to bear the stresses due to wheel loads, lateral and other forces, as well as due to temperature variation. Rails should distribute the traffic load to sleepers which in turn reduces pressure on ballast and formation. They are made of high carbon steel to withstand wear and tear. The composition of the high carbon steel used for the manufacture of rails is given in Table 4.3.

Table 4.3 Composition of Rail Steel

Element	Quantity in % for	
	Ordinary rails	Rails on points & crossings (Junctions)
Carbon	0.55 - 0.68	0.50 -0.60
Manganese	0.65 - 0.90	0.95 - 1.25
Silicon	0.05 -0.30	0.05 -0.20
Sulphur	≤0.05	≤0.06
Phosphorus	≤0.05	≤0.06

4.6.1 Types of Rail Sections: There are three types of rail sections used in the construction of a railway track which are as follows:

i. Dumb-bell or double headed (DH) rails

ii. Bull headed (BH) rails

iii. Flat footed (FF) rails

The foot and head of *Double Headed (DH) rails* are made of same dimensions on the idea that when the head has become worn out, it could be inverted and re-used, see Fig.4.2(a).It was observed that due to the impact of heavy wheel loads, the bottom surface of rail-foot became corrugated and hence could not be used for smooth riding. Subsequently, the rail head which is in direct contact with the wheel is made thicker and stronger by adding more metal. These rail sections are popularly called *Bull Headed rails or BH rails.* See Fig.4.2(b). These rails require iron chairs for fixing to sleepers and are mainly used in points and crossings. During the same time, Charles Vignole (1836) invented a *Flat Footed (FF) rail* section. See Fig 4.2(c). These rails can be fixed directly on wooden sleepers with small fastenings, eliminating the chairs and keys required for BH rails. Though FF rails possesses higher lateral rigidity, it was observed that under heavy train loads, the foot of the rail section sink into wooden sleepers,resulting in the loosening of spikes.To avoid this defect, steel bearing plates were introduced between sleepers and rails. FF rails are commonly used in India. Table 4.4 gives a comparison between BH and FF rails.

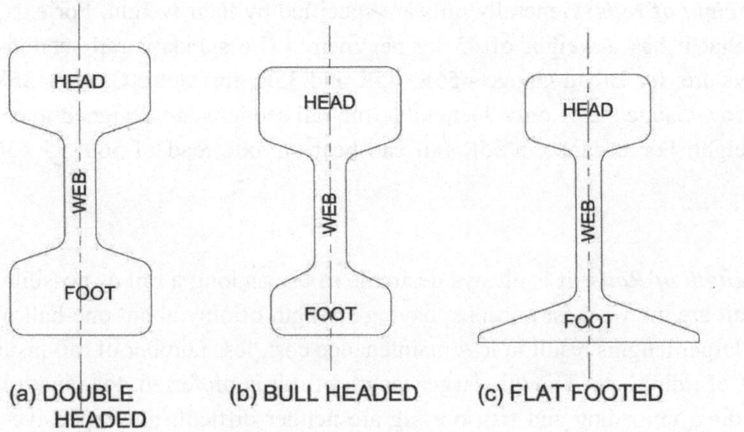

Fig 4.2. Types of Rails

Table 4.4 BH Rails vs. FF rails

Sl. No.	Feature	BH Rails	FF Rails
1	Strength & Stiffness	Less	More
2	Initial cost	More	Less
3	Maintenance cost	More	Less
4	Ease of laying	Difficult	Simple
5	Requirement of fastenings / chairs	Chairs & costly fastenings required	No chairs, less & cheaper fastenings required
6	Alignment & stability of track	Better	Lesser
7	Rigidity	Less	More
8	Arrangements at points and crossings	Complicated	Simpler
9	Daily Inspection	Compulsory	Not necessary
10	Suitability	More suitable at curves	Suitable at straight & curves

4.6.2 Selection of Rail Sections: It depends on the following factors:

i. Gauge of track

ii. Sleeper spacing

iii. Type of rail

iv. Speed of train

v. **Axle load and nature of traffic**

vi. **Maximum permissible wear on top of rail**

4.6.3 Weight of rails: Generally rails are specified by their weight. For e.g., 45R rail section means that it has a weight of 45 kg per metre. The standard rail sections used in Indian Railways are: for Broad Gauge - 55R, 45R and 35R, for Metre Gauge - 35R, 30R, 25R and for Narrow Gauge - 25R only. Generally, the rail sections are designed to carry 560 times its own weight. For instance, a 55R rail can bear an axle load of 560×55 =30800 kg or 30.8 tonnes.

4.6.4 Length of Rails: It is always desirable to use as long a rail as possible, since the joints in the rail are the weakest portions, having strength of only about one-half of the rails. Also, rails of larger lengths result in less maintenance cost, less number of rail fastenings, increased comfort of riding, etc. Though, larger length of rail is preferred, the length is restricted such that loading, unloading and transporting are neither difficult nor expensive. The length of a rail also depends on the length at which it can be manufactured at a reasonable cost. Further, very long rails cannot be handled manually for laying, for which special cranes are required. If a defect is detected in a rail, a much longer length has to be wasted in renewal than in the case of short rails. The permissible expansion gap may also be considered in deciding the length of rail. Indian Railways has standardized a rail length as 13m (previously 12.8m) for BG, and 12m (previously 11.8m) for MG and NG tracks. Although there is no restriction on the shortest length of rail that can be used on a track with through traffic, it is preferable to avoid having any pieces that are shorter than the wheel base (length between adjacent axles) of the longest wagon.

4.7 RAIL JOINTS

Rail joints are places where two adjoining ends of rail are joined together, holding the rails in correct position with respect to both horizontal and vertical planes. These joints are made of either by using fish plates and bolts or by welding. If fish plates are used, an expansion gap of 6 - 8 mm is provided between rail ends to allow expansion of rails due to rise in temperature. Rail joints are the weakest portion of a track having only 50% strength of rails. Sleepers near the rail joints are placed closer for giving more strength. Fig 4.3. is an isometric view of a rail joint.

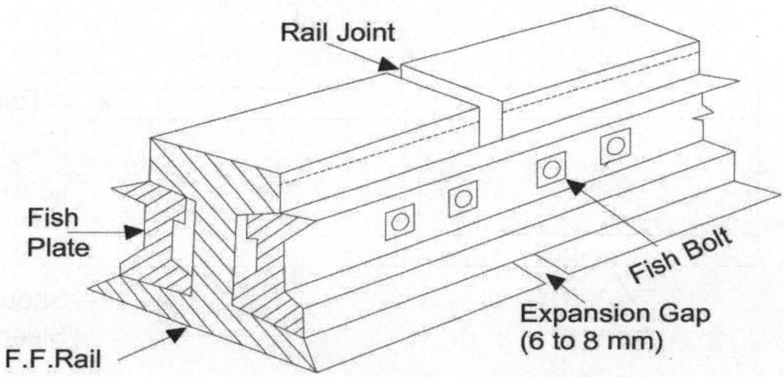

Fig 4.3. Isometric view of a rail joint

4.7.1 Types of rail joints: There are different types of 'rail joints', depending on the location of joint or sleepers provided, or the nature of function it serves. They are:

a) *Supported rail joint* - Rail ends rest on a single sleeper [See Fig. 4.4 (a)].

b) *Suspended rail joint* - Rail ends are projected beyond sleepers [See Fig. 4.4 (b)].

c) *Bridge rail joint* - Rail ends are projected beyond sleepers and are supported by a bridge plate [See Fig. 4.4 (c)].

d) *Welded rail joint* - Rail ends are welded together [See Fig. 4.4 (d)].

e) *Square or even rail joint*- Joints in the two rails of the track are directly opposite to each other; usually provided in straight track only. [See Fig. 4.4 (e)].

f) *Staggered or broken rail joint* - Joints in the two rails of the track are staggered; usually provided in curved track only.[See Fig. 4.4 (f)].

g) *Compromise rail joint* - Joints where two different rail sections are joined together using special fish plates [See Fig. 4.4 (g)].

h) *Insulated rail joint*- Insulating material is inserted in the joint to arrest the flow of current beyond the circuited portion of the track.

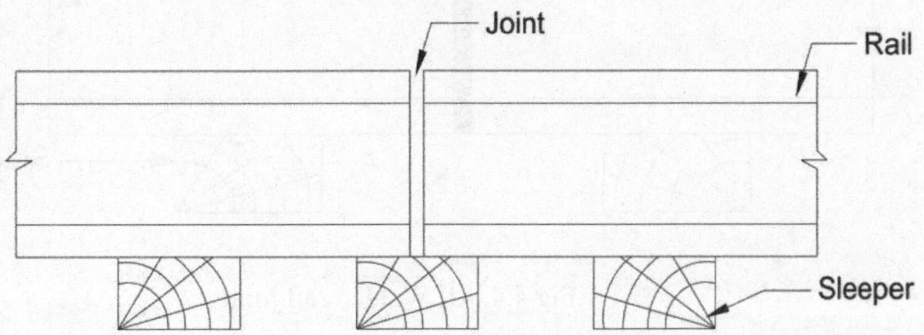

Fig 4.4. (a) Supported rail joint

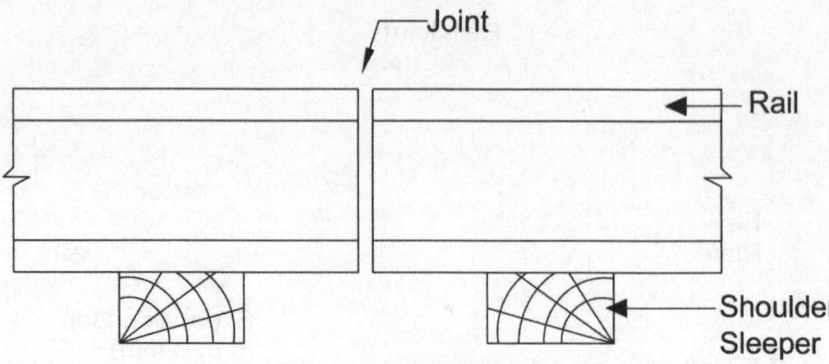

Fig 4.4. (b) Suspended rail joint

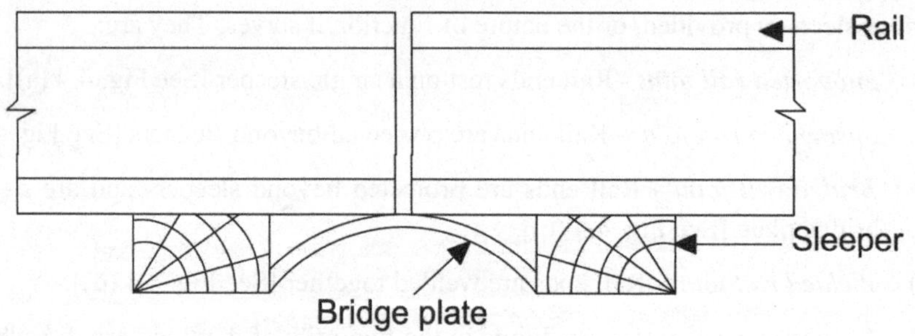

Fig 4.4. (c) Bridge rail joint

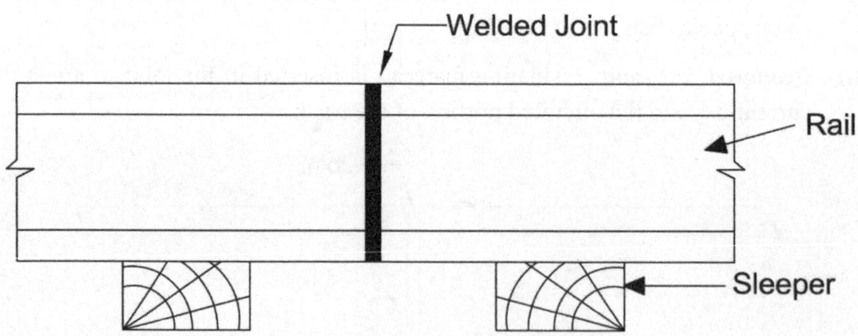

Fig 4.4. (d) Welded rail joint

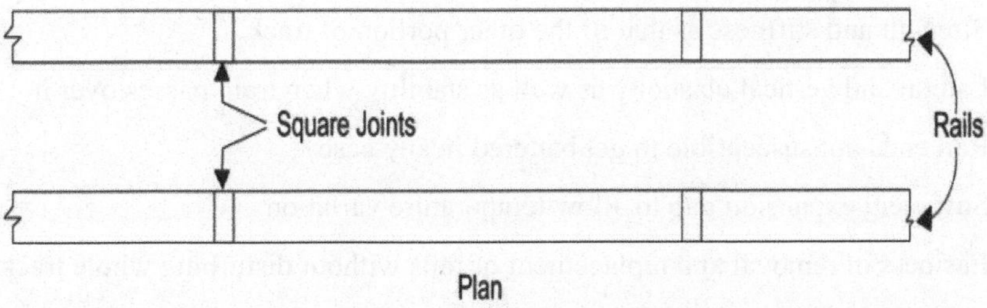

Fig 4.4. (e) Square or Even rail joint

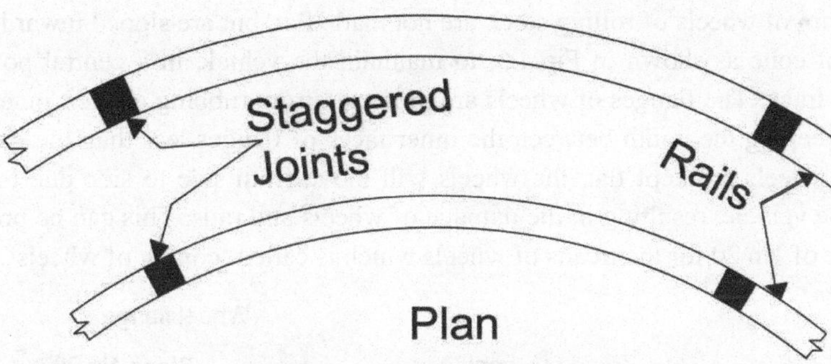

Fig 4.4. (f) Staggered rail joint

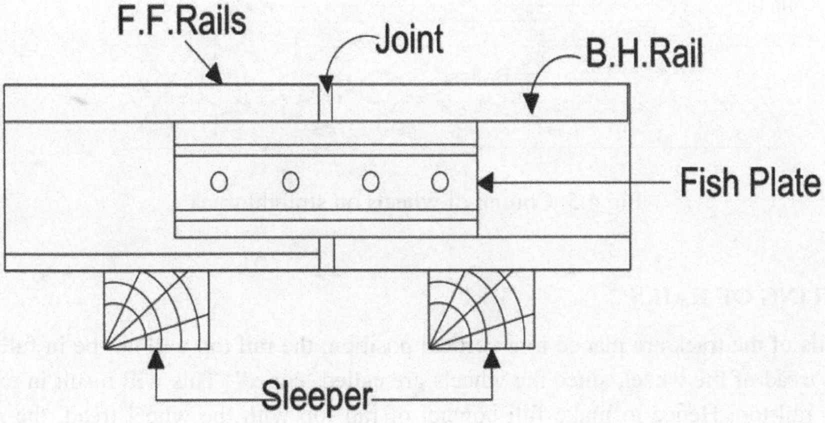

Fig 4.4. (g) Compromise rail joint

4.7.2 Requirements of a good rail joint: Following requirements are to be met by a good rail joint:

a) Strength and stiffness as that of the other portion of track
b) Lateral and vertical elasticity as well as stability when train passes over it
c) Rail ends not susceptible to get battered in any case
d) Sufficient expansion gap to allow temperature variation
e) Easiness in removal and replacement of rails without disturbing whole track
f) Minimum initial and maintenance cost.

4.8 CONING OF WHEELS

The tread or rim of wheels of rolling stock are not made flat, but are sloped inward at 1:20, to form a part of cone as shown in Fig.4.5, to maintain the vehicle in a central position with respect to the track. The flanges of wheels are protected from rubbing of their inner face with the rails, by keeping the width between the inner faces of flanges less than the gauge. If the treads of the wheels are kept flat, the wheels will move from side to side due to the slight swaying of the vehicle, resulting in the damage of wheels and rails. This can be prevented by giving a slope of 1in 20 for the treads of wheels which is called 'coning of wheels'.

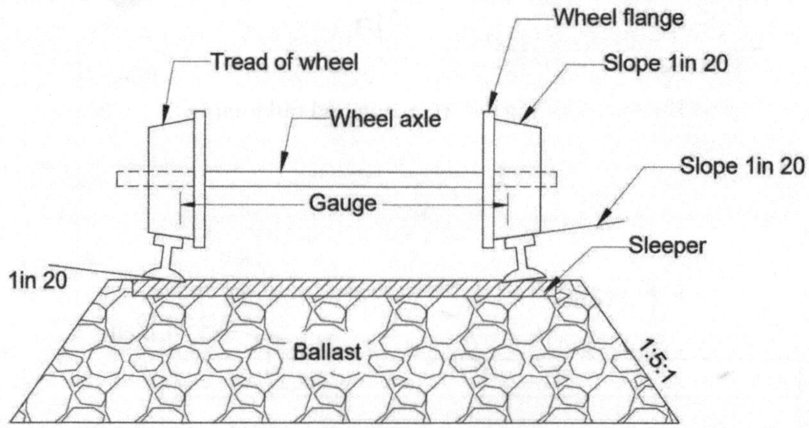

Fig 4.5. Coning of wheels on straight track

4.9 TILTING OF RAILS

If the rails of the track are placed in a vertical position, the rail top will not be in full contact with the tread of the wheel, since the wheels are called 'coned'. This will result in excessive wear on rail top. Hence to make full contact of rail top with the wheel tread, the rails are placed at a slope of 1 in 20 which is called 'tilting of rails'. Thus, by tilting of rails, the wheel load will be distributed equally on both the rails, maintaining the proper gauge, and increases the life of rails and sleepers.

4.10 DEFICIENCIES IN RAILS

4.10.1 Corrugated or Roaring Rails

At certain places, especially at places of application of brakes, the rail heads are found to be corrugated by forming minute depressions on the surface of rails.When train passes over such sections a roaring sound is produced.These rails are called 'roaring rails'.

4.10.2 Hogging of Rails

Due to the loose fish plates and loose packing under the joints of rails, there are chances getting the rail ends bent down and deflected at ends. This phenomenon is called 'hogging of rails'.

4.10.3 Kinks in Rails

They are formed when the ends of the adjoining rails move slightly out of their position because of many reasons like, defective gauge and alignment, loose packing at joints, defective transverse level at joints, wear of rail head, etc. Kinks in rails may cause discomfort in riding and risk in turning operations. It can be prevented by proper packing at joints and proper maintenance of alignment and gauge at joints as well as curves.

4.10.4 Buckling of Rails

Due to inadequate expansion gap provided at joints or extra tightening of fish plates, the rails may get out of their original position. This phenomenon of misalignment is called 'Buckling of rails'. This can be prevented by:

- Proper design of sleeper density and ballast section.
- Reducing the number of welded joints and providing proper anchorages to welded joints.
- Lubricating the the fish plates and rail surface
- Avoiding extra tightening of fish bolts.

4.11 CREEP OF RAILS

It is the longitudinal movement of rails in a track. Creep occurs in almost all railway tracks, but varies considerably in magnitude. At certain places, it might be several centimetres in a month, whereas, it is negligible in other sections.

4.11.1 Causes of Creep

The main causes of creep identified are as follows:

a) *Wave Motion theory:* When trains pass over the rails, the rail portion under the wheel loads get depressed slightly. As the wheels move, the depressions move with them, creating a wave motion in the track.This wave motion tends to move the rail forward along with the movement of the train.See Fig 4.6.

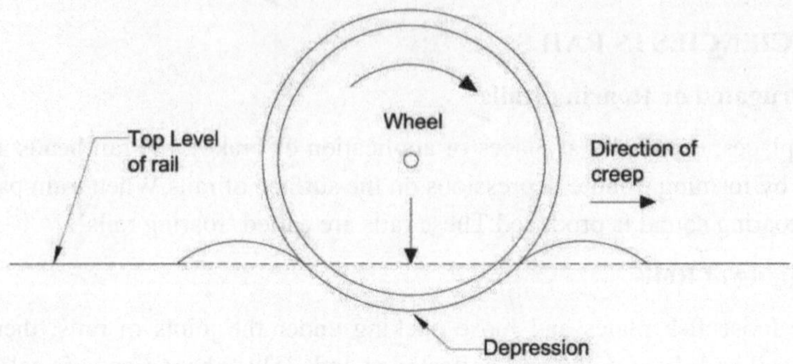

Fig 4.6. Wave theory of creep

b) *Percussion theory:*At rail joints, when trains pass by, the trailing rail make get depressed and the wheel hits the leading rail, resulting in creep in forward direction. See Fig 4.7.

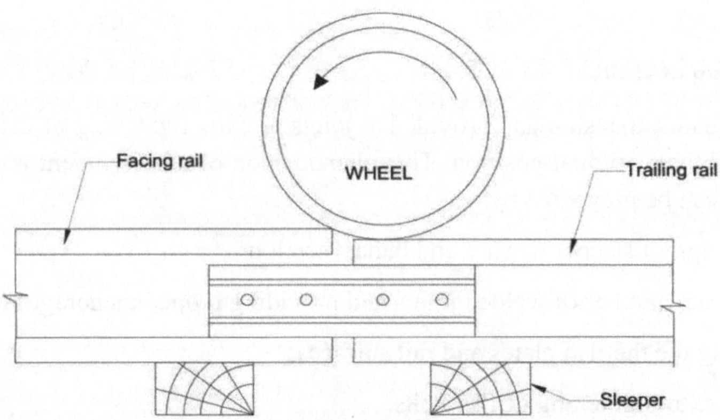

Fig 4.7. Percussion theory of creep

c) Drag Theory: During acceleration or starting of a train, the engine wheels may give a backward thrust tending the rails to push backward. Similarly, during stopping or slowing down of the vehicle, creep in reverse direction may happen.

d) Creep can occur due to unequal expansion or contraction because of the temperature variations.

e) Creep can also occur in the direction of heavy traffic, if the traffic is not uniform in both directions of a track.

f) Creep is more in tracks with steep gradients and also on curves.

Apart from the above reasons, the following factors may also cause creep in rails:

a. Improper compaction of formation bed of track
b. Improper packing of ballast
c. Improper spacing of sleepers
d. Improper width of gauge
e. Poor maintenance of rail joints
f. Use of inferior quality of rails or sleepers
g. Insufficient expansion gap

4.11.2 Prevention of Creep

To prevent creep the following measures may be adopted:

a) By pulling back the rail to the original position with the help of crow-bars or hooks
b) By using anti-creepers (Fig. 4.8)
c) By proper boxing of sleepers in angular ballast
d) By providing Steel sleepers
e) By proper maintenance of rail joints and gauge
f) By increasing the number of sleepers per rail length

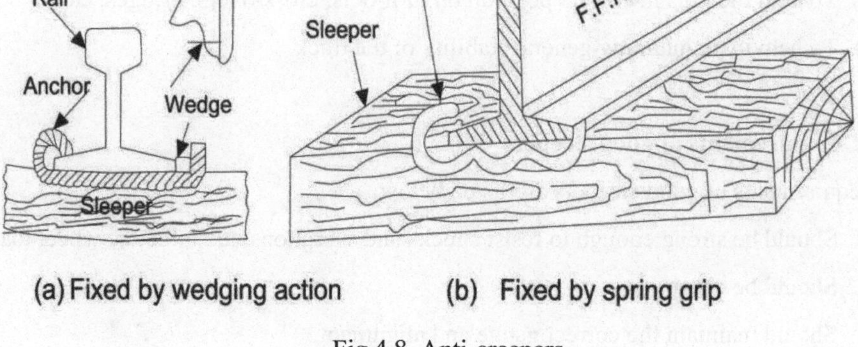

Fig 4.8. Anti-creepers

4.12 WEAR OF RAILS

Wear on rails is due to the metal flow caused by abnormally heavy loads which results in battered ends near the joint. It may also occur due to curve skidding, slipping the striking of wheel flanges with rails. Wear can occur on the head or top of the rail or at the ends of rails or on the side of the rail head. Wear can be reduced by adopting the following methods:

- Use of long welded rails.
- Use of special alloy steel for rails.
- Lubricating the rails
- Correct maintenance of gauge, joints, fish plates, etc.
- Use of check rails at curves.
- Interchanging inner and outer rails and changing faces at curves.

4.13 SLEEPERS

Rails in a track are to be supported properly, and the greater the support, the lower the stresses induced in the rails. Sleepers are the transverse members fixed to the rails to support and transfer the loads from rails to the ballast and sub grade below.

4.13.1 Functions of sleepers

The main functions of sleepers are as follows:

a) To hold the rails maintaining correct gauge.

b) To distribute the loads from rails to ballast and formation below.

c) To provide an elastic medium between rails and ballast by absorbing shocks and vibrations of moving loads.

d) To support and fix the rails in proper position in straight tracks and at curves providing the required super elevation.

e) To hold the rails in correct position on turn-outs, cross-overs, bridges, etc.

f) To help in maintaining general stability of the track.

4.13.2 Requirements of good sleepers

The requirements of good sleepers are listed below:

a. Should be strong enough to resist shocks and vibrations due to heavy wheel loads.

b. Should be cheap.

c. Should maintain the correct gauge and alignment.

d. Should provide sufficient bearing area for rail.

e. Should have sufficient weight for stability.

f. Should facilitate easy fixing and taking out of rails.

g. Should facilitate easy removal and replacement of ballast.

h. Should not be pushed out easily off its position due to moving train.

i. Should not get damaged during packing and boxing process.

j. Should be possible to insulate for track circuiting.

k. Should be suitable to all types of ballast.

4.13.3 Types of sleepers

The following are the different types of sleepers used in India:

- Wooden sleepers
- Steel sleeper
- Cast iron sleepers
- RCC sleepers
- Pre-stressed concrete sleepers

The selection of a particular type of sleeper depends upon their availability, suitability and design.

(i) Wooden sleepers: These sleepers are regarded as the best as they fulfill almost all the requirements of a good sleeper. The life of wooden sleepers depends upon their ability to resist wear, termite attack and quality of timber used. Normally its life is 12 years. Sal, Teak, Deodar and Chir wood are commonly used in India for making wooden sleepers. The standard sizes of wooden sleepers used are for:

BG - 2740mm x 250mm x 130mm

MG - 1830mm x 203mm x 114mm

NG - 1520mm x 150mm x 100mm

(ii) Steel sleepers: They are in the form of inverted channels made of 6mm thick steel sheets with both ends bend down to prevent the running out of ballast. Also, an inward slope of 1 in 20 on either end of the sleeper is provided to achieve required tilt of rails as shown in Fig. 4.9.

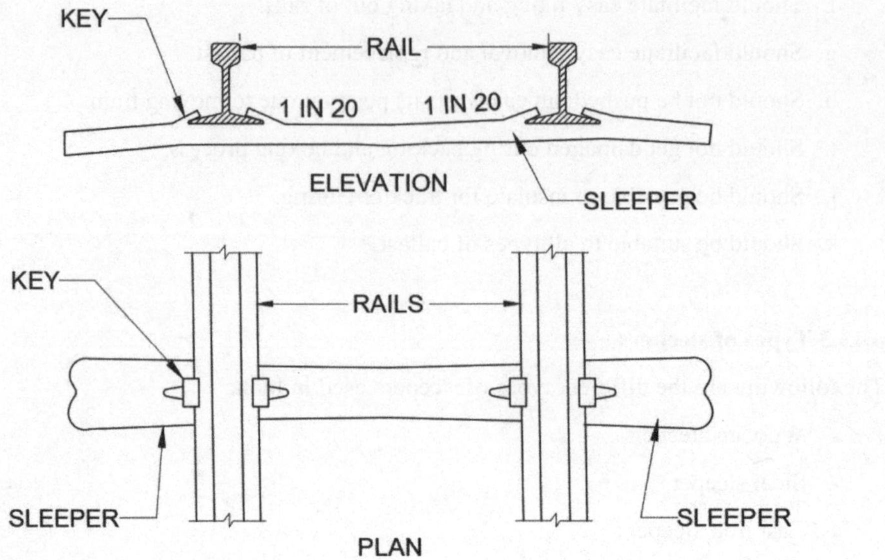

Fig 4.9. Steel Sleepers

There are three types of steel sleepers generally used:

a. Key type Steel sleepers

b. Clip and bolt type sleepers

c. Saddle type sleepers.

(a) Key type steel sleepers: In this type lugs or jaws are pressed out of metal and the rails are held using keys. These are of two types : (i) Lug type and (ii) Loose jaw type

Key type steel sleepers [Fig. 4.10 (a)] are found to crack at the corner of the hole which is left by the pressing up of lugs. Hence these sleepers have been improved as 'loose jaw type', where holes are drilled in the plate to accommodate loose jaw [Fig. 4.10 (b)].

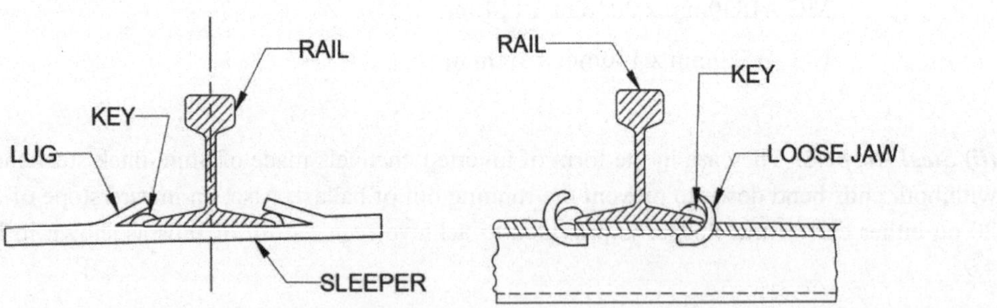

(a) Pressed lug type (b) Loose jaw type

Fig 4.10 Key type steel sleepers

(b) Clip and bolt type of sleepers: In this type of sleepers the rails are held in position by means of the built-in clips and bolts. See Fig. 4.11.Since the bolt holes are small and round, the chances of developing cracks in the sleepers are less. Each rail must be held in place using four pairs of clips and bolts.

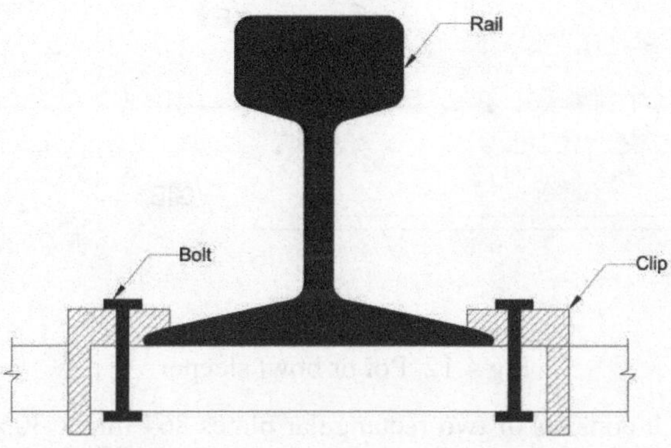

Fig 4.11. Clip and Bolt type steel sleepers

(c) Saddle type: In saddle type of sleepers the rail seat is strengthened by a saddle plate.

(iii) Cast iron sleepers: These are quite popular in India compared to other countries. They are of the following types:

a) Pot or Bowl sleeper
b) Plate sleepers
c) Box sleepers
d) CST-9 sleepers
e) Duplex sleepers

a) *Pot or Bowl Sleeper:* They are in the form of two bowls or pots placed inverted on the ballast under each rail and connected together by a tie bar with various fittings, such as keys, gibs and cotters. The effective bearing area of a pot sleeper is 0.232 m^2. For inspection and packing of ballast, each pot is provided with two holes. A rail seat to hold the rail is provided on the top of sleeper at the inward slope of 1 in 20. See Fig. 4.12.

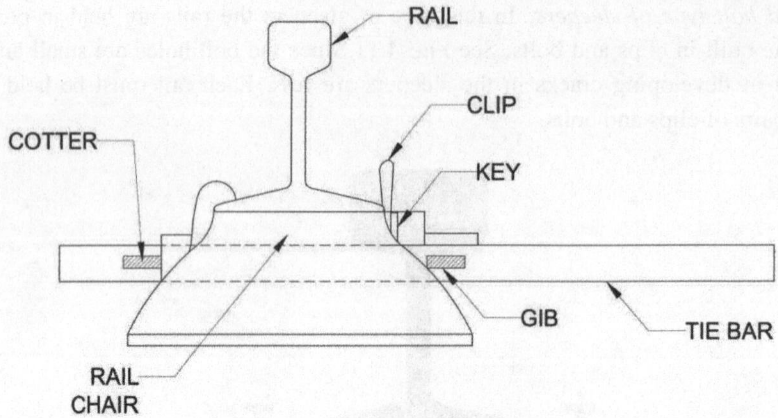

Fig 4.12. Pot or bowl sleeper

b) *Plate Sleeper:* It consists of two rectangular plates 864 mm x 305 mm size with short side parallel to rail. Projecting ribs are provided in the bottom for lateral stability. Stiffeners are provided at the top of the plate to increase the strength. The plates are held in position with tie bar, the connections being similar to that with pots. See Fig. 4.13. Both pot and plate sleepers can be used with FF and BH rails.

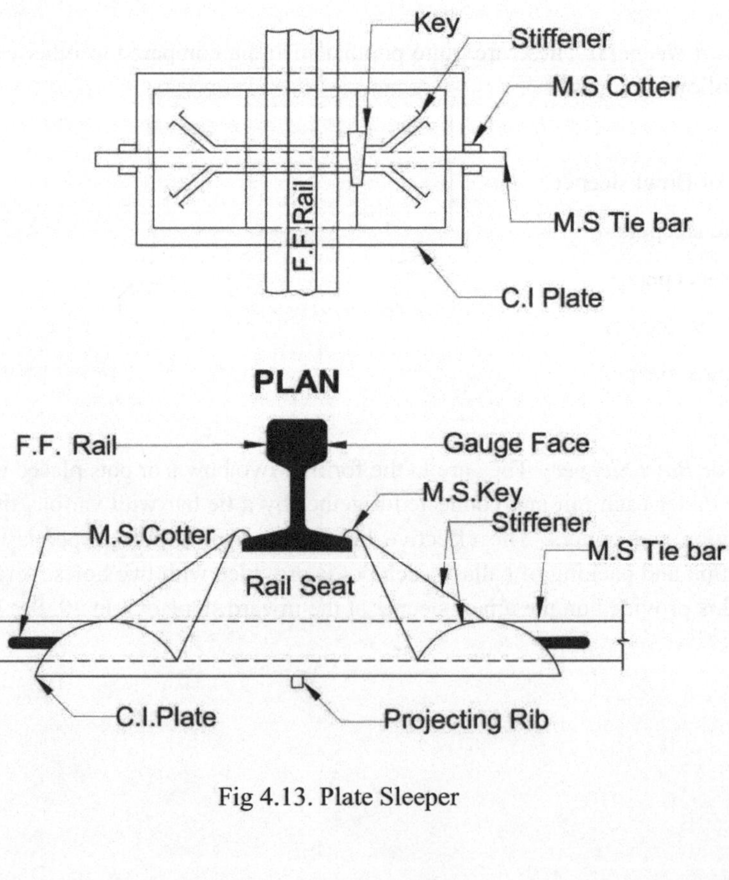

Fig 4.13. Plate Sleeper

c) *Box Sleepers:* These sleepers are outdated now. They are similar to plate sleepers. A box is provided at the top of each plate to hold the rails.

d) *CST-9 Sleepers:* This is a combination of plate, pot and box sleepers and is more satisfactory than other cast iron sleepers and is widely used in Indian Railways. It consists of a triangular inverted pot on either of the rail seat, a rib under a plate, and the rail is supported on a box. Rail seat is provided at the top to hold the rails at 1in 20 inward slope. The pots are connected together by means of a tie rod. See Fig. 4.14. For speeds greater than 100 km per hour, these sleepers are not suitable, because, packing becomes loose under vibrations, key tends to loose and drop out, and plates are liable to crack and break.

e) Duplex sleepers: They are used at rail joints in conjunction with CST-9 sleepers to prevent cantilever action between two supports of the CST-9 sleepers. These consist of two plates 850 mm x 750 mm which are placed with the longer side parallel to the rails and are connected with a tie bar. Since it is found that the rail ends on these sleepers get severely battered, the use of these sleepers is being discarded.

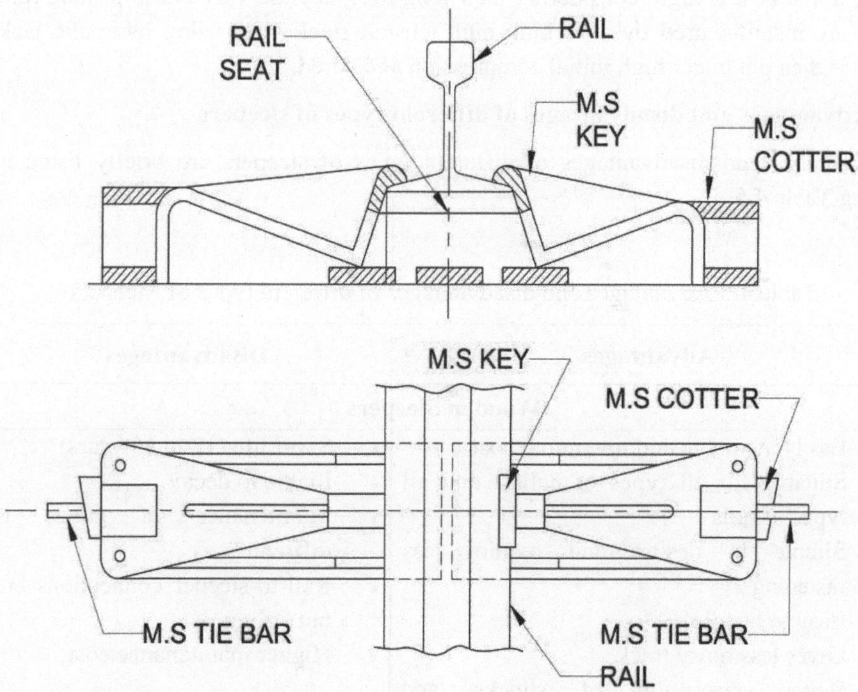

Fig 4.14. CST-9 Sleepers

iv) RCC sleepers: Two types are there: (a) Through type (b) Block and Tie type

(a) Through type - They are also called one-piece or mono-block sleepers. These sleepers when subjected to repeated impact loading are susceptible to tension cracks gradually causing their failure.

(b) Block and tie type - It consists of two RCC blocks connected by a metal tie of inverted T-section. See Fig. 4.15. These are not affected by any tensile stresses as that of through type.

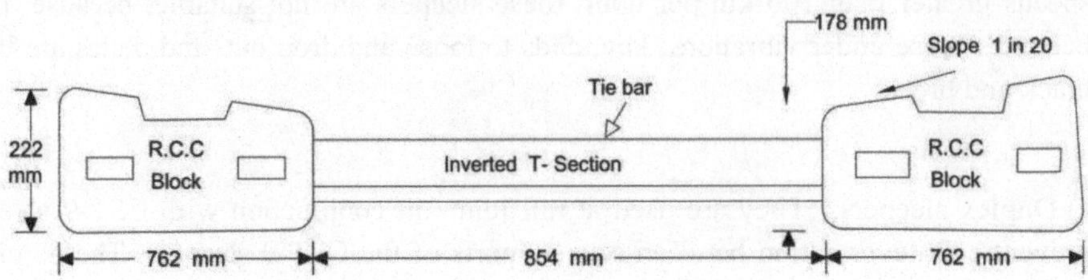

Fig 4.15. Block and tie type RCC sleepers

v) Prestressed concrete sleepers: Nowadays, they are extensively used in Indian Railways. Though, initial cost is high, considering their long life, they are very cheap in long run. The sleepers are manufactured by stretching high tension steel wires using hydraulic jack and concrete is then put under high initial compression and cured.

4.13.4 Advantages and disadvantages of different types of sleepers

The advantages and disadvantages of different types of sleepers are briefly listed in the following Table 4.5.

Table 4.5 Advantages and disadvantages of different types of sleepers

Advantages	Disadvantages
Wooden Sleepers	
• Easily available and low initial cost • Suitable for all types of ballast and all types of rails • Simple in design and require less fastening • Easy to handle • Gives less noisy track • Better absorption of shocks and vibrations than any other sleeper • Best suited for track circuiting • Less damage during accident.	• Short life (12 to 15 years) • Liable to decay • Maintenance of gauge is difficult • Rail-to-sleeper connections are not strong • Higher maintenance cost

<table>
<tr><th colspan="2">Steel Sleepers</th></tr>
<tr><td>• Light in weight and can be easily handled
• Require less fastenings
• More life than wooden sleepers
• Ease in maintenance of gauge
• More scrap value than wooden sleepers
• Give track better lateral and longitudinal rigidity
• Creep of rails can be checked easily</td><td>• More initial cost than wooden sleepers
• Cracks developed at the rail seat of the sleeper
• Not suitable for track circuiting
• Not suitable for all types of ballast
• Liable to corrosion</td></tr>
<tr><th colspan="2">Cast Iron Sleepers</th></tr>
<tr><td>• More life
• Low maintenance cost
• Easy maintenance of gauge
• More durability
• Easy checking of rail creep</td><td>• More ballast required than any other sleeper
• More number of fastenings
• Liable to break
• Not suitable for track circuiting
• Not suitable for all types of ballast</td></tr>
<tr><th colspan="2">RCC Sleepers</th></tr>
<tr><td>• Long life (40 to 60 years)
• Free from natural decay and insect attack
• Less number of fittings
• Track circuiting is possible
• Higher lateral and longitudinal rigidity
• Low maintenance cost
• Withstand stresses due to fast moving trains due to higher elastic modulus.</td><td>• Handling and transportation are difficult due to heavy self-weight
• More chances of breaking during handling
• Renewal of track is difficult
• Scrap value is nil.</td></tr>
<tr><th colspan="2">Pre-stressed Concrete Sleepers</th></tr>
<tr><td>• Long life (40 to 60 years)
• Free from natural decay and insect attack
• Less number of fittings
• Track circuiting is possible
• Higher lateral and longitudinal rigidity
• Low maintenance cost
• Less self weight compared to RCC sleepers.</td><td>• High initial cost
• Chances of heavy damage during accidents of trains.</td></tr>
</table>

4.13.5 Sleeper Density

It is the number of sleepers used per length of rail on a track. It depends on the following factors:

- Axle load of train
- Speed of train
- Type of ballast and ballast cushion

- Type of sleeper and rails
- Methods of providing rail joints

As sleepers provide lateral rigidity to the track, higher the number of sleepers, the more will be the lateral stability. However, number of sleepers cannot be increased beyond a limit, since a minimum spacing of sleepers is essential for proper packing of ballast. Generally, sleeper density is expressed in terms of (n + x), where n is the length of rail in metres, that is, if rail length = 12.8 m, n= 13, and x is a number varying from 3 to 6.In India sleeper density varies between (n + 3) to (n + 6) for main track. Thus, if the sleeper density for a Broad Gauge track is (n+ 5), the number of sleepers per rail having a length of 13.0 m is 13 + 5= 18 nos.

4.14 BALLAST

Ballast is the granular material packed under and around the sleepers to distribute the load from the sleepers to the formation bed.

4.14.1 Functions of Railway Ballast

The ballast has the following functions:

- To distribute uniformly the load from the sleepers to a larger area of formation.
- To hold the sleepers in position, preventing lateral and longitudinal movement due to moving loads.
- To provide elasticity to the track.
- To help in maintaining level and alignment of track.
- To drain easily the water from track.
- To prevent growth of weeds inside the track

4.14.2 Characteristics of a good ballast

To be a good ballast, the following requirements are to be met:

- Sufficient crushing strength against crushing under dynamic loads
- Permit easy drainage
- Durable
- Good workability
- Rough and angular surface to provide good lateral and longitudinal stability
- Cheaply available
- Easy to clean
- No chemical attack on rails and metal sleepers.

4.14.3 Types of ballast

Following are the different types of ballast normally used in India:

- *Broken stone*: It is the best type of the ballast meeting almost all the requirements of a good ballast. Igneous rocks such as granite, quartzite, and trap belong to this category.
- *Gravel*:It is the second best one and is obtained from river beds or sea beaches.
- *Sand*: Coarse sand is preferred. It is suitable for packing pot sleepers and also for unimportant or temporary tracks.
- *Ashes or Cinders:* They are waste products from steam locomotives, and are preferred to use in station yards, sidings, etc.
- *Kankars:* They are lime agglomerate found in certain clayey soil and are suitable in light traffic conditions like MG or NG.
- *Moorum:* They are soft aggregates red or yellow in colour obtained from the decomposition of laterite and are used in unimportant lines or sidings.
- *Blast furnace slag*: It is a waste product from the smelting of iron ore in steel manufacturing industry.
- *Brick ballast*: They are over-burnt broken bricks.
- *Selected Earth*: It consists of hardened clay or decomposed rock. They are used while laying track on a new formation. It gets consolidated after two or three monsoons, and when the surface becomes hard, normal types of ballast may be laid over it.

4.14.4 Advantages and Disadvantages of Different Types of Ballast

The advantages and disadvantages of different types of ballast used in India are briefly listed in the following Table 4.6.

Table 4.6 Advantages and disadvantages of different types of Ballast

Advantages	Disadvantages
Broken Stone	
• Resists crushing under heavy loads. • Gives more stability to sleepers due to its angular and rough surface. • Excellent drainage property.	• Greater cost. • Less availability.
Gravel	
• Cheaper than stone ballast. • Excellent drainage property. • Holds the track to correct gauge and alignment. • Better for unstable formation.	• Due to their round faces packing below the sleepers gets loosen and rolls down from the ballast bed under vibrations. • Due to large variation in size, requires screening before use . • Requires washing before use, if taken from pits.

<table>
<tr><td colspan="2">Sand</td></tr>
<tr><td>• Cheap.
• Possesses good drainage property.
• Produces silent track.
• Suited for packing pot sleepers.</td><td>• Causes heavy wear of vehicles as well as track as it is easily blown and gets into moving parts of vehicles resulting in costly maintenance.
• Packing gets disturbed due to vibrations.
• Use restricted to temporary or unimportant tracks.</td></tr>
<tr><td colspan="2">Ashes or Cinders</td></tr>
<tr><td>• Cheap.
• Possesses good drainage property.
• Easy availability and easy to handle and transport, and hence can be used in emergency.</td><td>• As it is very soft, gets crumbled to powder under heavy loads, and makes the track dusty.
• Causes corrosion of rails and sleepers, hence use restricted to station yards and sidings.</td></tr>
<tr><td colspan="2">Kankar</td></tr>
<tr><td>• Cheap.
• Possesses good drainage property.</td><td>• As it is very soft, gets crumbled to powder under traffic loads, and makes the track dusty, hence used in light traffic tracks only.
• Causes corrosion of rails and sleepers, hence difficult to maintain.</td></tr>
<tr><td colspan="2">Moorum</td></tr>
<tr><td>• Easily available.
• Possesses good drainage property.
• Used as blanket for new embankment.</td><td>• As it is soft, gets crumbled to powder under traffic loads, and makes the track dusty.
• Maintenance of track is difficult.
• Use restricted to unimportant tracks and sidings.</td></tr>
<tr><td colspan="2">Blast Furnace Slag</td></tr>
<tr><td>• Cheap.
• Possesses good drainage property.
• Strong ballast.
• Holds the track in correct position.</td><td>• Not available in large quantity.
• Spreading on the formation bed is difficult.
• Maintenance of track is difficult.</td></tr>
<tr><td colspan="2">Brick Ballast</td></tr>
<tr><td>• Cheap.
• Possesses good drainage property.
• Prevents growth of vegetation.</td><td>• As it is soft, gets crumbled to powder under traffic loads, and makes the track dusty.
• Causes corrugation of rails.</td></tr>
<tr><td colspan="2">Selected Earth</td></tr>
<tr><td>• Cheap.
• Can be used as blanket for new embankment.
• After consolidation and setting, provides a hard surface,preventing the sinking of ballast into the formation.</td><td>• Restricted to use only as a sub ballast material, stabilizing the formation bed.
• Consumes greater time for getting consolidated and stabilized.</td></tr>
</table>

4.14.5 Size and Section of Ballast

The size of ballast depends on the type of sleepers used and location of track. It varies from 19 mm to 51 mm.

For Wooden sleepers - 51mm

Steel sleepers - 38 mm

Points and Crossings - 25.4 mm

Ballast section is defined by the depth of ballast provided under the sleepers and the width of ballast section at the foot level of rails. Depth of ballast section depends upon the mode of load dispersion and bearing capacity of formation. The lateral strength of the track increases with the increase in width of the ballast section. Generally, maximum limit of width is 380 to 430 mm from the ends of the sleeper used in the track. The size of ballast section followed in India is given in Table 4.7.

Table 4.7 Size of Ballast Section

Description	Gauge of Tracks		
	BG	MG	NG
Width (m)	3.35	2.35	1.83
Depth (cm)	20 -25	15 - 20	15
Quantity of stone ballast (m^3/m length of track)	1.036	0.71	0.53

Note: Additional quantity of ballast is required on tracks sections with super elevation (curves).

4.15 RAIL FIXTURES AND FASTENINGS

They are the fittings required for connecting rail ends to ends, and for fixing the rails to sleepers.

4.15.1 Functions of Rail Fixtures and Fastenings

Their functions are as follows:

- To keep the rail in correct position and alignment.
- To connect rail to rail forming full length of track.
- To set points and crossings properly.
- To allow expansion and contraction of rails due to temperature variations.
- To maintain the required tilt of rails.

4.15.2 Types of Fixtures and Fastenings

Fish plates: They are used to maintain continuity and alignment of track and also to accommodate expansion or contraction of rails occur due to temperature fluctuations. Generally, they are made of mild steel plates 20 mm thick, 457 mm long and provided with four holes 32 mm diameter at 114 mm centre-to-centre. See Fig. 4.16 (a).

Two types of fish plates are commonly used in Indian Railways:

(i) Bone shaped fish plate for FF rails and

(ii) Increased depth fish plate for BH rails. See Fig. 4.16 (b).

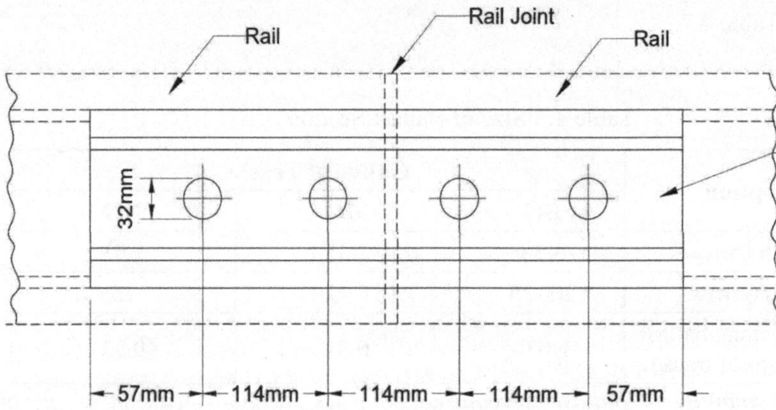

Fig. 4.16 (a) Fish Plates with Rails

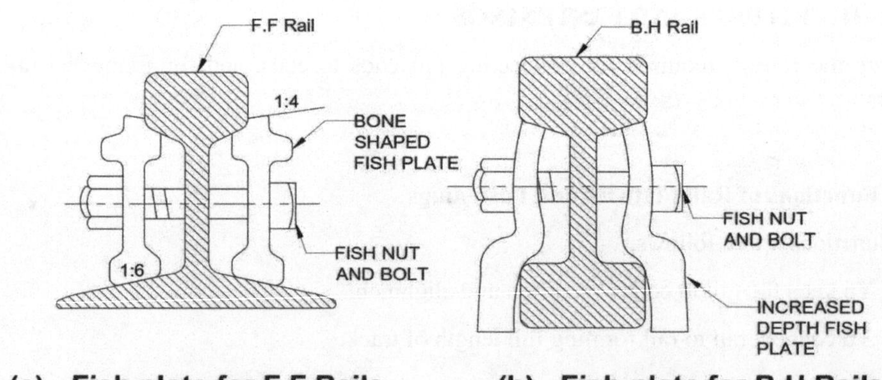

Fig. 4.16 (b) Fish Plates (Bone shaped and Increased depth types)

Requirements of fish plates:

- Should hold the adjoining rail ends in correct alignment with respect to horizontal and vertical planes.
- Should properly fit between head and foot of rails, and should not touch the web of rail so that free movement of rail under the temperature variation is facilitated.
- Should be able to withstand vertical and lateral stresses without any distortion.
- Should resist all types of wear.
- Should be easy for replacement, when needed.

Bearing plates: They are made of cast iron or steel plates, placed between FF rails and wooden sleepers to serve as chairs for the rails. If FF rails are fixed directly over the wooden sleepers, the rails sink in the sleeper under heavy loads, thus loosening the spikes. This effect can be avoided if the load is distributed over a wider area with the help of bearing plates. See Fig. 4.17.

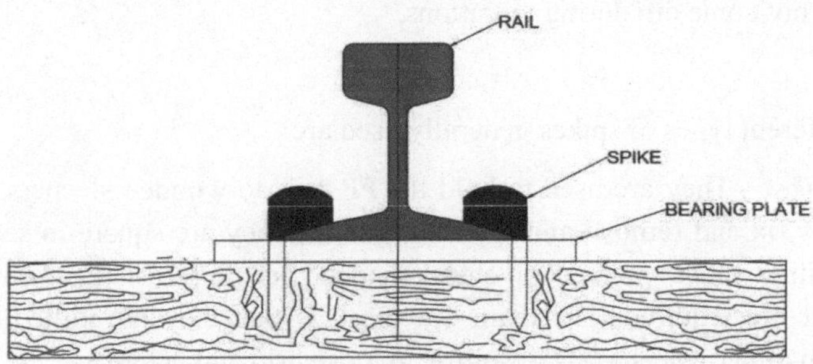

Fig. 4.17 Bearing Plate

Two types of bearing plates are available:

(i) Flat bearing plates - for fitting rails in a flat condition (eg: under points and crossings)

(ii) Canted bearing plates - for fitting rails in a tilted (1:20) condition.

Merits:

- Distribute the load to a wider area avoiding sinking of rail to the sleeper.
- Avoid adzing* of sleepers
- Increase the life of sleepers
- Help spikes to remain in tight position
- Maintain gauge on curves
- Increase overall stability of track.

**Adzing of sleepers is the process of cutting wooden sleepers to match the tilted rails (i.e., providing an inward slope of 1:20) at the rail seat.*

Demerits:

- Loose bearing plates produce rattling noise, and also admit moisture between sleepers and plates, causing sleepers to wear.
- Provision of new hole while changing the damaged spike, requires the removal of bearing plate, which reduces the holding power of spikes for sleepers.

Spikes: They are used to fix rails to wooden sleepers.

Requirements of good spikes:

- Should have sufficient strength to hold the rails in required alignment.
- Should help in maintaining proper gauge.
- Should be easy to fix and take out from sleepers
- Should be cheap in initial as well as maintenance costs
- Should not come out during vibrations.

Types: The different types of spikes generally used are:

a) *Dog spikes* - They are used to hold the FF rails to wooden sleepers. They are cheap, easy to fix and remove and maintain gauge. They are square in section, with lower end either blunt, pointed or chisel-shaped. See Fig.4.18 (a). Four dog spikes per sleeper are required. The main drawback is that they are pulled out due to wave motion under wheel loads, resulting in loose grip and creep.

b) *Round spikes* - They are used to fix chairs of BH rails to wooden sleepers and also to fix slide chairs of points and crossings. They have cylindrical or hemispherical head and blunt end. See Fig. 4.18(b).

c) *Screw spikes* - They are tapered screws with V-threads, and have circular head with square projection, and are used to fasten BH rails with wooden sleepers. The holding power of these spikes is much higher than dog spikes and can resist lateral thrust in a better way. However, these spikes are costlier and provide difficulty in gauge maintenance. (Fig. 4.18(c).

d) *Elastic Spikes* - They are used for fixing FF rails to wooden sleepers. These can withstand effectively the wave motion of rails under wheel loads and provide better grip, resulting in reduced wear and tear of rail. See Fig. 4.18(d).

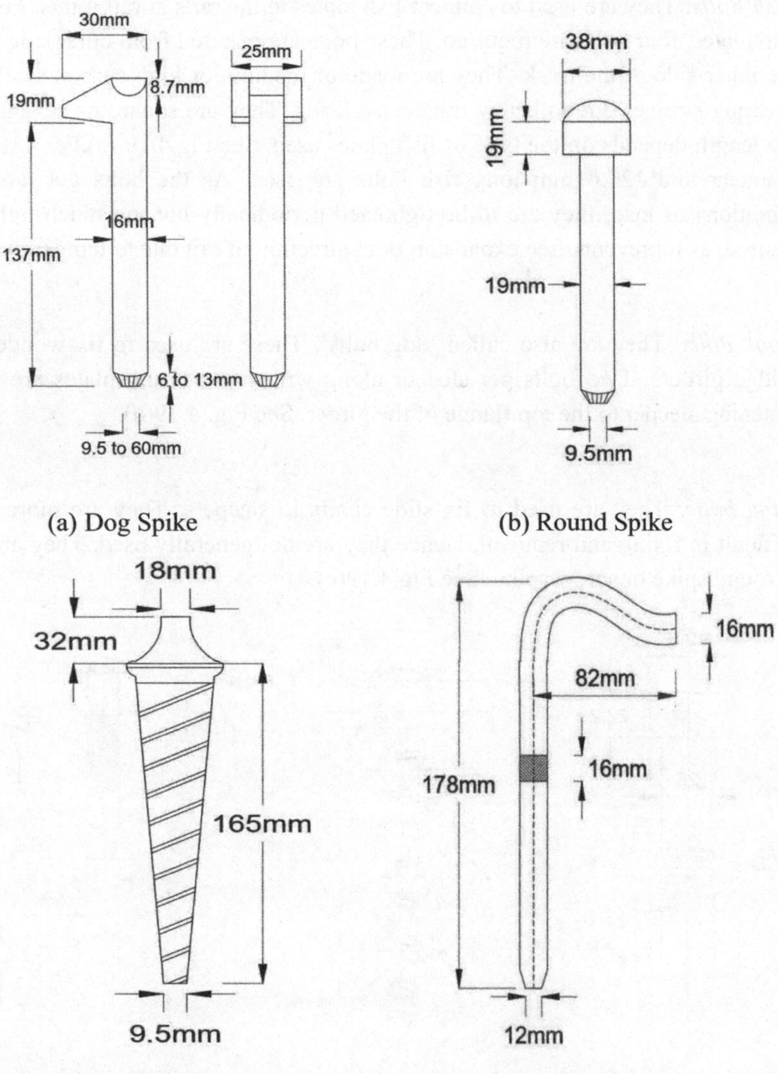

(a) Dog Spike (b) Round Spike

(c) Screw Spike (d) Elastic Spike

Fig. 4.18 Different types of Spikes

Bolts: They are used for connecting:

i. Fish plates to rails at each rail joint.

ii. Chairs or bearing plates to wooden sleepers.

iii. Sleepers to bridge girders, etc.

Types: The different types of bolts used in Indian Railways are:

Fish Bolts: They are used to connect fish plates to the rails at rail joints. For each pair of fish plates, four bolts are required. These bolts are inserted from outer side and bolted on the inner side of the track. They are made of medium or high carbon steel to withstand shearing stresses due to heavy transverse loads. They are square or hexagonal in shape, the length depends on the type of fish plates used. See Fig.4.19 (a).For 45R rails, 25mm diameter and 127.6 mm long fish bolts are used. As the bolts get loosened due to vibrations of load, they are to be tightened periodically but too much tightening is not desired, as it prevents free expansion or contraction of rail due to temperature variations.

Hook Bolts: They are also called 'dog bolts'. These are used to fix wooden sleepers to bridge girders. Two bolts per sleeper along with two bearing plates are sufficient for fastening sleeper to the top flange of the girder. See Fig. 4.19(b).

Fang bolts: They are used to fix slide chairs to sleepers. They are more effective but difficult in fixing and removal. Hence they are not generally used. They are alternatives to round spike or screw spike. See Fig.4.19(c).

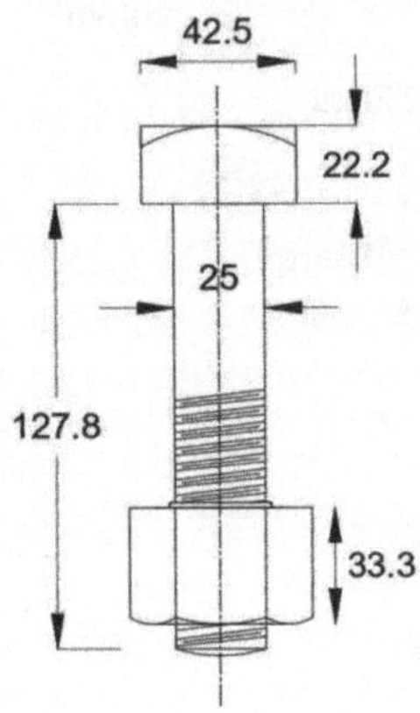

Fig. 4.19 (a) Fish Bolt

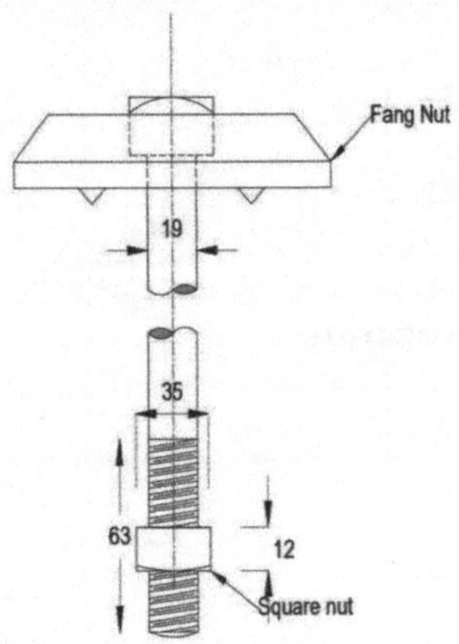

Fig. 4.19 (b) Hook Bolt

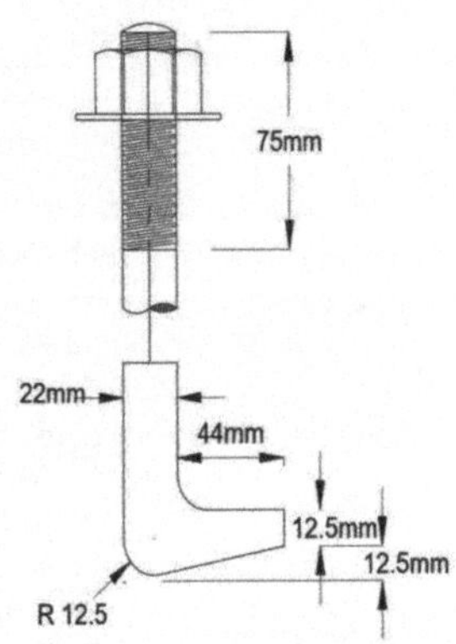

Fig. 4.19 (c) Fang Bolt

Chairs and Keys: They are used to hold the DH and BH rails in the required position. They are made of cast iron,and have two jaws and a rail seat provided with an inward slope of 1 in 20. These chairs distribute the load from the rails to a wider area on sleepers. Each chair weighs 20.4 kg approximately. In the case of wooden sleepers, chairs are fixed to the sleeper using two or four round spikes, whereas, in the case of cast iron sleepers, they are cast together, and in the case of steel sleepers, the chairs are welded to them. See Fig. 4.20.In order to fix rails to chairs 'keys' are used. They can be made of either timber or metal.

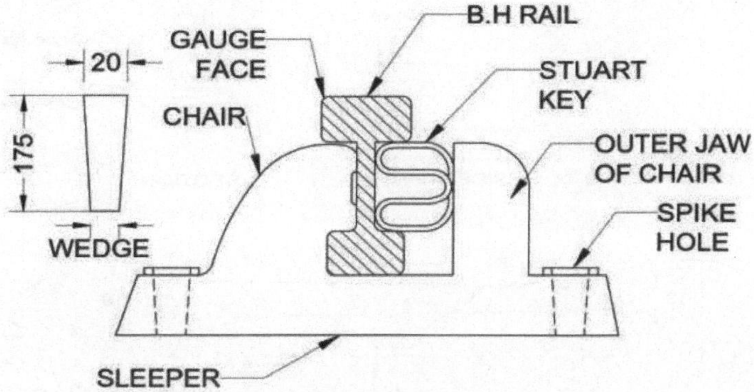

Chair with spring key

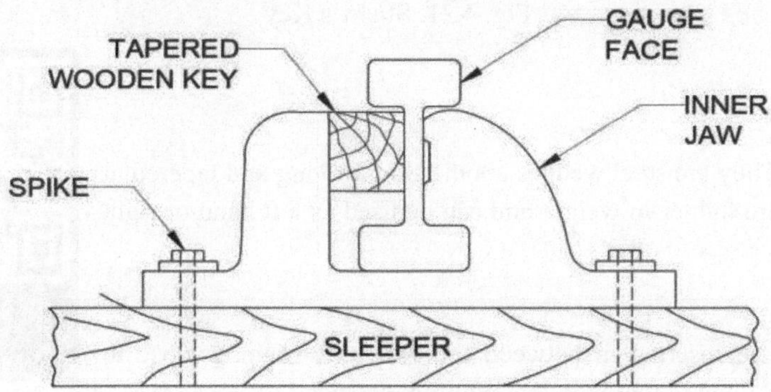

Chair with Wooden keys

Fig. 4.20 Rails fixed to Sleepers using Chairs and Keys

Timber keys: They are small tapered pieces of timber and are cheap. As they are susceptible to termite attack, they are not popular.

Metal keys: They are tapered or spring type steel pieces. They are costlier, but more durable than timber keys. The two popular types of metal keys are: Stuart's key and Morgan keys.

Stuart's key: This is an E-shaped steel plate. A steel wedge is introduced at the ends to keep the keys tight against the rail web and the outer jaw of the chair.See Fig. 4.21.

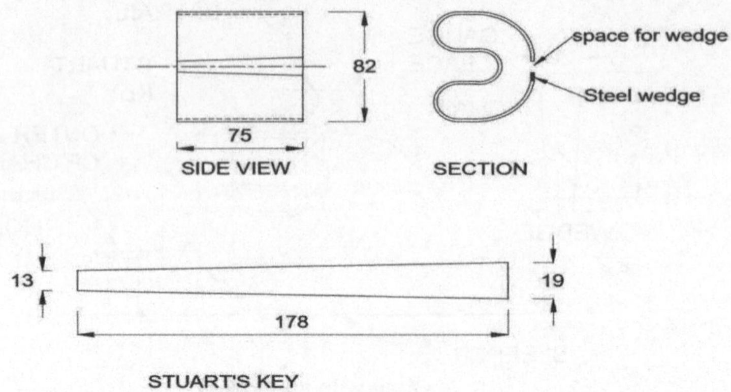

Fig. 4.21. Stuart's Key

SCAN ME
for
Rail Fixtures & Fastenings

Morgan keys: They are steel wedges about 180 mm long and tapered at 1 in 32. They are lighter in weight and can be used as left hand or right hand keys.

Blocks: They are inserted in between the two rails running close to each other and bolted to maintain the required distance.

Anchors or Anti-creepers: They are used to prevent creep occurring in the railway track. Different types of anchors are available and are fixed to the foot of the rail as discussed in Section 4.11.2. See Fig. 4.8 also.

UNIT SUMMARY

Classification of Indian Railways

Sl. No.	Main Classification	Sub Classification	Meant for
1	Broad Gauge Routes	Group A lines	Sanctioned speed of 160kmph
		Group B lines	Sanctioned speed of 130kmph
		Group C lines	Suburban sections of Mumbai, Kolkata & Delhi
		Group D & DSpecial lines	Sanctioned speed of 100kmph
		Group E & ESpecial lines	Other sections & branch lines
2	Metre Gauge Routes • Trunk Routes • Main lines • Branch lines (Earlier classification)	Q Routes	Max. permissible speed of >75kmph & Traffic density >2.5 GMT*
		R Routes	Max.permissible speed of 75kmph & Traffic density >1.5 GMT
		R1	Traffic density >5 GMT
		R2	Traffic density 2.5-5.0 GMT
		R3	Traffic density 1.5-2.5 GMT
		S Routes	Max. permissible speed of <75kmph & Traffic density <1.5 GMT
		S1	Through movement of freight traffic
		S2	Routes which are neither S1 nor S3
		S3	Uneconomical branch lines

*GMT - Gross Million Tonne per km per annum

List of Indian Railway Zones, their Head Quarters and Divisions

Sl. No.	Railway Zone	Head Quarters	Railway Divisions
1	Central Railway	Mumbai CSMT	Mumbai, Bhusaval,Nagpur, Solapur, Pune.
2	Eastern Railway	Kolkata	Asansol, Howrah, Malda, Sealdah.
3	East Central Railway	Hazipur	Sonpur, Samastipur, Danapur, Dhanbad, Pt. Deen Dayal Upadhyaya
4	East Coast Railway	Bhubaneshwar	Khurda Road, Sambalpur, Waltair.
5	Northern Railway	New Delhi	Ambala, Delhi, Lucknow, Moradabad, Ferozpur.
6	North Central Railway	Prayagraj, Allahabad	Prayagraj, Agra, Jhansi
7	North Eastern Railway	Gorakhpur	Lucknow, Izzatnagar, Varanasi
8	Northeast Frontier Railway	Maligaon, Guwahati	Alipurduar, Katihar, Lumding, Rangiya, Tinsukia.
9	North Western Railway	Jaipur	Ajmer, Bikaner, Jaipur , Jodhpur
10	Southern Railway	Chennai Central	Chennai, Madurai, Palakkad, Tiruchchirappalli, Thiruvananthapuram, Salem.
11	South Central Railway	Secunderabad	Guntakal, Guntur, Hyderabad, Nanded, Secunderabad, Vijayawada.
12	South Eastern Railway	Garden Reach, Kolkata	Adra,Chakradharpur, Kharagpur, Ranchi.
13	South East Central Railway	Bilaspur	Raipur, Nagpur, Bilaspur.
14	South Western Railway	Hubli	Bengaluru, Hubballi, Mysuru.
15	Western Railway:	Church Gate, Mumbai	Mumbai Central, Vadodara, Ratlam , Ahmedabad , Rajkot , Bhavnagar.
16	West Central Railway :	Jabalpur	Bhopal, Jabalpur, Kota.

17	Metro Railway, Kolkata	Kolkata	-
18	Southern Coast Railway	Visakhapatnam	Waltair, Vijayawada, Guntur, Guntakal
19	Konkan Railway	Navi Mumbai	Karwar, Ratnagiri

Components of a permanent way:

- Subgrade
- Ballast
- Sleepers
- Rails
- Fixtures and fastenings.

Requirements of a permanent way:

- Gauge should be even, uniform and correct.
- Both rails should be at the same level on straight track.
- At the curves, radii and superelevation should be properly designed.
- The track should be properly designed so that the load is distributed uniformly over the two rails.
- Track should be elastic enough to reduce impact between rails and moving wheels.
- Tracks should be strong enough to resist lateral forces.
- Components (rails, sleepers, fixtures and fastenings) as well as points and crossings should be properly designed.
- Tractive resistance should be least.
- Proper drainage system should be provided.
- Repairs and renewals should be easy.

Types of gauges followed in India:

- Broad gauge - 1.676m
- Metre gauge - 1.000m
- Narrow gauge - 0.762m & 0.610m
- Standard gauge for Metro railways - 1.435m

Factors affecting selection of gauge:

- Availability of funds
- Volume and nature of traffic

- Future development of area
- Topography
- Speed of train

Types of rail sections:

- Dumb-bell or double headed (DH) rail
- Bull headed (BH) rails
- Flat footed (FF) rails

Comparison of BH Rails and FF Rails

Sl. No.	Feature	BH Rails	FF Rails
1	Strength & Stiffness	Less	More
2	Initial cost	More	Less
3	Maintenance cost	More	Less
4	Ease of laying	Difficult	Simple
5	Requirement of fastenings / chairs	Chairs & costly fastenings required	No chairs, less & cheaper fastenings required
6	Alignment & stability of track	Better	Lesser
7	Rigidity	Less	More
8	Arrangements at points and crossings	Complicated	Simpler
9	Daily Inspection	Compulsory	Not necessary
10	Suitability	More suitable at curves	Suitable at straight & curves

Selection of Rail Sections depends on:

a. Gauge of track

b. Sleeper spacing

c. Type of rail

d. Speed of train

e. Axle load and nature of traffic

f. Maximum permissible wear on top of rail

Weight of rails: is specified by weight per metre.45R - refers to 45kg/m.

Rails used for BG - 55R, 45R and 35R

MG- 35R, 30R, 25R

NG - 25R only.

Generally, the rail sections are designed to carry 560 times its own weight.

Length of Rails: For BG - 13m

For MG & NG - 12m

Types of rail joints: Depending on the position of joint or sleepers provided, or the nature of function it serves:

a. *Supported*
b. *Suspended*
c. *Bridge*
d. *Welded*
e. *Square or even*
f. *Staggered or broken*
g. *Compromise*
h. *Insulated*

Requirements of a good rail joint:

a. Strength and stiffness as that of the other portion of track
b. Lateral and vertical elasticity as well as stability when train passes over it
c. Rail ends not susceptible to get battered in any case
d. Sufficient expansion gap to allow temperature variation
e. Easiness in removal and replacement of rails without disturbing whole track
f. Minimum initial and maintenance cost.

Coning of Wheels:The tread or rim of wheels of train are sloped inward at 1:20, to form a part of cone to maintain the vehicle in a central position with respect to the track.

Tilting of rails: The rails are placed at a slope of 1 is to 20 to make full contact of rail top with the wheel tread, so that the wheel load will be distributed equally on both the rails, maintaining the proper gauge, and thereby increasing the life of rails and sleepers.

Deficiencies in Rails:

Corrugated or Roaring Rails : Minute depressions on the surface of rails on certain stretches which causes a roaring sound when train passes over.

*Hogging of Rails:*Due to the loose fish plates and loose packing under the joints of rails, there are chances getting the rail ends bent down and deflected at ends.

*Kinks in Rails:*They are formed when the ends of the adjoining rails move slightly out of their position

*Buckling of Rails:*Due to inadequate expansion gap provided at joints or extra tightening of fish plates, the rails may get out of their original position.

Creep of rails : longitudinal movement of rails in a track.

Causes of creep:

a) Wave theory: When trains pass over the rails, the rail portion under the wheel loads get depressed slightly. As the wheels move, the depressions move with them, creating a wave motion in the track.This wave motion tends to move the rail forward with the train.

b) Percussion theory: At rail joints, when trains pass by, the trailing rail make get depressed and the wheel hits the leading rail, resulting in creep in forward direction.

c) Drag theory: During acceleration or starting of a train

d) Non uniform heavy loads in the train

e) Due to unequal expansion or contraction

f) Steep gradients and curves.

Prevention of Creep:

a) By pulling back the rail with the help of crow-bars or hooks

b) By using anti-creepers

c) By proper boxing of sleepers in angular ballast

d) By providing Steel sleepers

e) By proper maintenance of rail joints and gauge

f) By increasing the number of sleepers per rail length

Wear of Rails: Due to the metal flow caused caused by abnormally heavy loads which results in battered ends near the joint. Also occur due to curve skidding, slipping the striking of wheel flanges with rails. Can be reduced by:

- Use of long welded rails.
- Use of special alloy steel for rails.
- Lubricating the rails
- Correct maintenance of gauge, joints, fish plates, etc.
- Use of check rails at curves.
- Interchanging inner and outer rails and changing faces at curves.

Sleepers: The transverse members fixed to the rails to support and transfer the loads from rails to the ballast and sub grade below.

Functions of sleepers :

a) To hold the rails maintaining correct gauge.

b) To distribute the loads from rails to ballast and formation below.

c) To provide an elastic medium between rails and ballast by absorbing shocks and vibrations of moving loads.

d) To support and fix the rails in proper position in straight tracks and at curves providing the required super elevation.

e) To hold the rails in correct position on turn-outs, cross-overs, bridges, etc.

f) To help in maintaining general stability of the track.

Requirements of good sleepers :

a. Strong enough to resist shocks and vibrations due to heavy wheel loads

b. Cheap

c. Maintain the correct gauge and alignment

d. Provide sufficient bearing area for rail

e. Sufficient weight for stability

f. Facilitate easy fixing and taking out of rails

g. Facilitate easy removal and replacement of ballast

h. Not pushed out easily off its position due to moving train

i. Not get damaged during packing and boxing process

j. Possible to insulate for track circuiting

k. Suitable to all types of ballast.

Types of sleepers:

- Wooden sleepers
- Steel sleeper
- Cast iron sleepers
- RCC sleepers
- Pre-stressed concrete sleepers

Advantages and disadvantages of different types of sleepers

Advantages	Disadvantages
Wooden Sleepers	
• Easily available and low initial cost • Suitable for all types of ballast and all types of rails • Simple in design and require less fastening • Easy to handle • Gives less noisy track • Better absorption of shocks and vibrations than any other sleeper • Best suited for track circuiting • Less damage during accident	• Short life (12 to 15 years) • Liable to decay • Maintenance of gauge is difficult • Rail-to-sleeper connections are not strong • Higher maintenance cost
Steel Sleepers	
• Light in weight and can be easily handled • Require less fastenings • More life than wooden sleepers • Ease in maintenance of gauge • More scrap value than wooden sleepers • Give track better lateral and longitudinal rigidity • Creep of rails can be checked easily	• More initial cost than wooden sleepers • Cracks developed at the rail seat of the sleeper • Not suitable for track circuiting • Not suitable for all types of ballast • Liable to corrosion
Cast Iron Sleepers	
• More life • Low maintenance cost • Easy maintenance of gauge • More durability • Easy checking of rail creep	• More ballast required than any other sleeper • More number of fastenings • Liable to break • Not suitable for track circuiting • Not suitable for all types of ballast
RCC Sleepers	
• Long life (40 to 60 years) • Free from natural decay and insect attack • Less number of fittings • Track circuiting is possible	• Handling and transportation are difficult due to heavy self-weight • More chances of breaking during handling • Renewal of track is difficult

Advantages	Disadvantages
• Higher lateral and longitudinal rigidity • Low maintenance cost • Withstand stresses due to fast moving trains due to higher elastic modulus.	• Scrap value is nil.
Pre-stressed Concrete Sleepers	
• Long life (40 to 60 years) • Free from natural decay and insect attack • Less number of fittings • Track circuiting is possible • Higher lateral and longitudinal rigidity • Low maintenance cost • Less self weight compared to RCC sleepers.	• High initial cost • Chances of heavy damage during accidents of trains.

Sleeper Density: Number of sleepers used per length of rail on a track.

Depends on:

- Axle load of train
- Speed of train
- Type of ballast and ballast cushion
- Type of sleeper and rails
- Methods of providing rail joints

Sleeper density is expressed in terms of (n + x), where n is the length of rail in metres, x is a number varying from 3 to 6.

Ballast: The granular material packed under and around the sleepers to distribute the load from the sleepers to the formation bed.

Functions of ballast:

- To distribute uniformly the load from the sleepers to a larger area of formation.
- To hold the sleepers in position, preventing lateral and longitudinal movement due to moving loads.
- To provide elasticity to the track.
- To help in maintaining level and alignment of track.
- To drain easily the water from track.
- To prevent growth of weeds inside the track

Characteristics of a good ballast :

- Sufficient crushing strength against crushing under dynamic loads
- Permit easy drainage

- Durable
- Good workability
- Rough and angular surface to provide good lateral and longitudinal stability
- Cheaply available
- Easy to clean
- No chemical attack on rails and metal sleepers.

Types of ballast :

- Broken stone
- Gravel
- Sand
- Ashes or Cinders
- Kankars
- Moorum
- Blast furnace slag: .
- Brick ballast
- Selected Earth

Advantages and disadvantages of different types of Ballast

Advantages	Disadvantages
Broken Stone	
• Resists crushing under heavy loads. • Gives more stability to sleepers due to its angular and rough surface. • Excellent drainage property.	• Greater cost. • Less availability.
Gravel	
• Cheaper than stone ballast. • Excellent drainage property. • Holds the track to correct gauge and alignment. • Better for unstable formation.	• Due to their round faces packing below the sleepers gets loosen and rolls down from the ballast bed under vibrations. • Due to large variation in size, requires screening before use . • Requires washing before use, if taken from pits.
Sand	
• Cheap. • Possesses good drainage property. • Produces silent track. • Suited for packing pot sleepers.	• Causes heavy wear of vehicles as well as track as it is easily blown and gets into moving parts of vehicles resulting in costly maintenance.

Advantages	Disadvantages
	• Packing gets disturbed due to vibrations. • Use restricted to temporary or unimportant tracks.
Ashes or Cinders	
• Cheap. • Possesses good drainage property. • Easy availability and easy to handle and transport, and hence can be used in emergency.	• As it is very soft, gets crumbled to powder under heavy loads, and makes the track dusty. • Causes corrosion of rails and sleepers, hence use restricted to station yards and sidings.
Kankar	
• Cheap. • Possesses good drainage property.	• As it is very soft, gets crumbled to powder under traffic loads, and makes the track dusty, hence used in light traffic tracks only. • Causes corrosion of rails and sleepers, hence difficult to maintain.
Moorum	
• Easily available. • Possesses good drainage property. • Used as blanket for new embankment.	• As it is soft, gets crumbled to powder under traffic loads, and makes the track dusty. • Maintenance of track is difficult. • Use restricted to unimportant tracks and sidings.
Blast Furnace Slag	
• Cheap. • Possesses good drainage property. • Strong ballast. • Holds the track in correct position.	• Not available in large quantity. • Spreading on the formation bed is difficult. • Maintenance of track is difficult.
Brick Ballast	
• Cheap. • Possesses good drainage property. • Prevents growth of vegetation.	• As it is soft, gets crumbled to powder under traffic loads, and makes the track dusty. • Causes corrugation of rails.
Selected Earth	
• Cheap. • Can be used as blanket for new embankment. • After consolidation and setting, provides a hard surface,preventing the sinking of ballast into the formation.	• Restricted to use only as a sub ballast material, stabilizing the formation bed. • Consumes greater time for getting consolidated and stabilized.

*Size of Ballast:*Depends on the type of sleepers used and location of track. It varies from 19 mm to 51 mm.

For Wooden sleepers - 51mm

Steel sleepers - 38 mm

Points and Crossings - 25.4 mm

Size of Ballast Section

Description	Gauge of Tracks		
	BG	MG	NG
Width (m)	3.35	2.35	1.83
Depth (cm)	20 -25	15 - 20	15
Quantity of stone ballast (m^3/m length of track)	1.036	0.71	0.53

Rail fixtures and fastenings: The fittings required for connecting rails end to end it and for fixing the rails to sleepers.

Functions of Rail Fixtures and Fastenings:

- To keep the rail in correct position and alignment.
- To connect rail to rail forming full length of track.
- To set points and crossings properly.
- To allow expansion and contraction of rails due to temperature variations.
- To maintain the required tilt of rails.

Types of Fixtures and Fastenings:

Fish plates: to fix rail ends together.

- Bone shaped fish plate for FF rails and
- Increased depth fish plate for BH rails.

Bearing plates: placed between FF rails and wooden sleepers to serve as chairs for the rails.

- Flat bearing plates
- Canted bearing plates

Spikes: They are used to fix rails to wooden sleepers.

Types:

- *Dog spikes*
- Round spikes
- Screw spikes
- Elastic spikes

Bolts: They are used for connecting:

- Fish plates to rails at each rail joint.
- Chairs or bearing plates to wooden sleepers.
- Sleepers to bridge girders, etc.

Types:

- *Fish bolts* to connect fish plates to the rails at rail joints.
- *Hook bolts* to fix wooden sleepers to bridge girders.
- *Fang bolts* to fix slide chairs to sleepers.

*Chairs & Keys:*To hold the DH and BH rails in the required position.

Blocks: are inserted in between the two rails running close to each other and bolted to maintain the required distance.

Anchors or Anti-creepers: They are used to prevent creep occurring in the railway track.

EXERCISES

Multiple Choice Questions

4.1 The sanctioned speed of Broad Gauge - group A lines is

a) 130 kmph b) 160 kmph c) 100 kmph d) 75 kmph

4.2 The sanctioned speed of Broad Gauge - group B lines is

a) 130 kmph b) 160 kmph c) 100 kmph d) 75 kmph

4.3 The load carrying capacity for Metre Gauge Q routes is

a) >2.5GMT b) >1.5GMT c) <1.5GMT d) <2.5GMT

4.4 The first train was run in India between Bombay and Thane in the year

a) 1951 b) 1947 c) 1853 d) 1901

4.5 The criteria for classification of Indian Railways are

a) length and location

b) speed and topography

c) speed and traffic intensity

d) none of these

4.6 Which is the head quarters of Konkan Railway?

a) New Delhi b) Navi Mumbai c) Kolkata d) Mangalore

4.7 Gauge of railway track is

a) clear distance between inner faces of two rails

b) distance between outer faces of two rails

c) centre to centre distance between two rails

d) none of these

4.8 In India width of Broad Gauge is

a) 1.00m b) 1.676m c) 0.762m d) 1.435m

4.9 The width of standard gauge used in Metro Railways in India is

a) 1.00m b) 0.762m c) 1.676m d) 1.435m

4.10 Wheels of trains are coned at a slope of

a) 1 in 30 b) 1 in 10 c) 1 in 20 d) 1 in 40

4.11 The type of gauge adopted in hilly and thinly populated area is

a) Metre Gauge b) Broad Gauge c) Narrow Gauge d) Standard Gauge

4.12 The type of rail section presently used in Indian Railways is

a) Bull headed b) Double headed c) Flat footed d) all of the above

4.13 Rail section is designated by its

a) total length in m b) total weight in kg c) weight in kg per rail

d)weight in kg per metre

4.14Generally, the rail section is designed to carry a load is equal to -------times its own weight per metre length

a) 100 b) 300 c) 460 d)560

4.15 The rail section generally used for narrow gauge is

a) 45R b) 25R c) 35R d) 30R

4.16 For metre gauge track in Indian Railways, the standard length of rails used is

a) 10m b) 11m c) 12m d) 13m

4.17 For broad gauge track in Indian Railways, the standard length of rails used is

a) 10m b) 11m c) 12m d) 13m

4.18 The standard length of rail is decided depending on

a) its weight per metre length b) sleeper density c) longest bogie

d) permissible speed limit

4.19 Tilting of rails adopted in India is

a) 1 in 10 b) 1 in 20 c) 1 in 30 d) 1 in 40

4.20 Weight of rail section to be adopted depends on

a) heaviest axle load b)maximum length of bogie

c) nature of locomotive (diesel or electric) d) gauge

4.21 The maximum axle load borne by a 55 kg rail of Broad gauge is

a) 260 x 55 kg b) 320 x 55 kg c) 440 x 55 kg d) 560 x 55 kg

4.22 The type of sleeper that is worst hit due to derailment is

a) wooden b) steel c) cast iron d) concrete

4.23 Sleeper density is

a) no. of sleepers / km length of trackb)no. of sleepers / rail length

c)density of material of sleeper d) c/c spacing of sleepers in the track

4.24 The rail whose head and foot have the same dimension is known as

a) dumbbell b)bull headed c) flat footed d) none of these

4.25 When the rail endsrest on a single sleeper, the type of joint is called

a) suspended b) supported c)bridge d) staggered

4.26 The longitudinal movement of rails in a track is called

a) buckling b) hogging c)wear d) creep

4.27 Joints generally provided on curves are

a) supported b) suspended c)staggered d) square

4.28 Pot or Bowl sleepers are a type of

a) wooden b) steel c) cast iron d) concrete

4.29 CST-9 sleepers are a type of

a) wooden b) steel c) cast iron d) concrete

4.30 Sleeper density is generally expressed as (n+x), where n is

a) no. of sleepers /rail length b) length of rail in m c) wt. of rail in kg /m

d) none of these

4.31 Type of sleepers commonly used in India presently is

a) wooden b) steel c) cast iron d) pre-stressed concrete

4.32 Which of the following is the best ballast material?

a) broken stone b) gravel c) cinders d) sand

4.33 Ballast size used for wooden sleepers is

a) 51mm b) 38mm c) 25.4mm d) 20.8mm

4.34 Width of ballast section adopted for Broad Gauge track is

a) 1.83m b) 2.25m c) 3.35m d) 3.85m

4.35 Depth of ballast section adopted for NG track is

a) 250mm b) 200mm c) 150mm d) 100mm

4.36 The quantity of ballast required per metre length of MG track is

a) 1.036 m^3 b) 0.71m^3 c) 0.53 m^3 d) 0.63 m^3

4.37 Dog spikes are used for

a) wooden sleepers b) Steel sleepers c) C.I. sleepers d) concrete sleepers

4.38 The fixture used to join rail ends

a) fish plate b) bearing plate c) spikes d) chairs

4.39 The fitting used to prevent creep in rails is

a) fish plates b) spikes c)chairs d) anchor

4.40 Bearing plates are used on

a) DH rail b) BH rail c) FF rail d) All rails

4.41 Fang bolt is used to fix

a) Slide chair to sleepers b) sleepers to girder c) rails to chairs d) none of these

4.42 Keys are used to fix

a) chairs to sleepers b) rails to chairs c) sleepers to girders d) none of these

4.43 The ballast which is best suited to steel sleepers is

a) gravel b) brickbat c) ashes and cinders d) quartzite

Answers to Multiple Choice Questions

4.1 b), 4.2 a), 4.3 a), 4.4 c), 4.5 c), 4.6 b), 4.7 a), 4.8 b), 4.9 d), 4.10 c), 4.11 c), 4.12 c), 4.13 d), 4.14 d), 4.15 b), 4.16 c), 4.17 d), 4.18 c), 4.19 b), 4.20 a), 4.21 d), 4.22 d), 4.23 b), 4.24 a), 4.25 b), 4.26 d), 4.27 c), 4.28 c), 4.29 c), 4.30 b), 4.31 d), 4.32 a), 4.33 a), 4.34 c), 4.35 c), 4.36 b), 4.37 a), 4.38 a), 4.39 d), 4.40 c), 4.41 a), 4.42 b), 4.43 d).

Short and Long Answer Type Questions

Category I

4.1 What are the systems of Railways? Explain briefly.

4.2 Name the normal gauges adopted in Indian Railways and write down their sizes.

4.3 What do you understand by the term ‘permanent way’? Why it is called so?

4.4 What are the requirements of an ideal permanent way?

4.5 Under what conditions a narrow gauge is desired?Give any two examples in Indian Railways.

4.6 Compare BH and FF rails.

4.7 Enumerate different types of rail joints.

4.8 Why FF rails are preferred to BH rails?

4.9 What are the requirements of an ideal rail joint?

4.10 Explain with sketches different types of rail joints and their suitability conditions.

4.11 Explain the terms (a) coning of wheels (b) tilting of rails.

4.12 What is creep in rails? Explain their causes and prevention.

4.13 What do you mean by 'adzing of sleepers'?

4.14 Enumerate the functions and requirements of sleepers.

4.15 Compare wooden and concrete sleepers.

4.16 Compare steel and concrete sleepers.

4.17 What are the functions of ballast in railways?

4.18 What are the requirements of a good ballast?

4.19 Enumerate the different types of fixtures used in Indian Railways.

4.20 What are the functions of fixtures and fastenings in railway track?

4.21 What are bearing plates? What are their functions?

4.22 What are Spikes? Which are the different types and explain their specific uses?

4.23 What are the different types of bolts used in Indian Railways? Where are they specifically used?

4.24 What are the functions of chairs and keys used in Indian Railways? Which are the different types of keys used? What are their specialties?

4.25 What are anti-creepers? Sketch and explain their functions.

Category II

4.1 Draw a typical cross section of a permanent way and mark its components. Discuss briefly the basic functions of each component.

4.2 Discuss the factors affecting selection of gauge.

4.3 Sketch and explain different types of rail sections used. What are their relative merits and demerits?

4.4 What do you mean by coning of wheels? Explain with sketches coning of wheels. What are the advantages of it?

4.5 What are the different types of sleepers used in Indian Railways? Give their relative merits and demerits.

4.6 What are the different types of ballast used in Indian Railways? Give their advantages and limitations.

4.7 Explain the functions and requirements of fish plates. Sketch different types used in Indian Railways. Give their suitability in usage.

KNOW MORE

Activity:

4.1 Visit a Broad Gauge and a Metre Gauge railway lines going through your locality and take photographs at different sections having different types of fittings and lay outs. Prepare a detailed report on it.

4.2 Visit a railway bridge and understand the different types of fastenings and fixtures used there. Prepare a report of the same with photographs.

4.3 Visit a railway loco shed and understand how coning of wheels are done. Take photographs and prepare a report.

Interesting Facts About Indian Railways (IR):

- An elephant dressed like a railway guard, and named Bholu, created in 2002 on the 150th anniversary of railways, is considered as the mascot of Indian Railways.

- IR provides the longest train ride from Kanyakumari to Dibrugarh by Vivek Express, covering a distance of 4189 km with 56 stops in 82.5 hours, and the shortest train ride from Nagpur to Ajni, covering only 3 km.

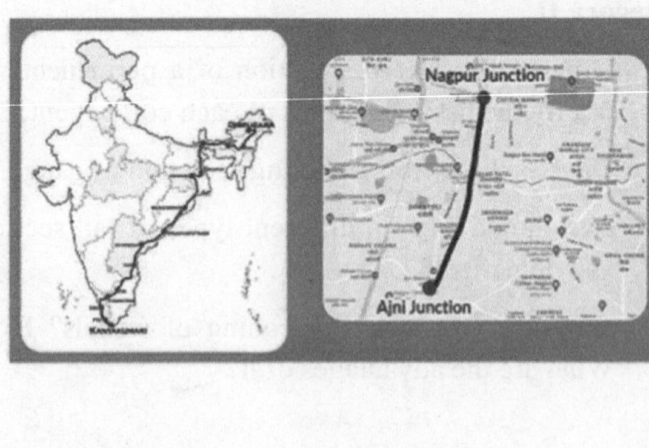

- Indian Railways has four UNESCO recognized World Heritage Sites so far:
    - Darjeeling Himalayan Railway (1999)
    - Chatrapati Shivaji Terminus, Mumbai (2004)
    - Nilgiri Mountain Railway (2005)
    - Kalka Shimla Railway (2008).

- IR provide luxurious rides through its 5 royal trains
    - Royal Rajasthan on Wheels
    - Palace on Wheels
    - The Golden Chariot
    - The Maharaja's Express
    - The Deccan Odyssey.

- IR still uses its oldest working steam locomotive, 'Fairy Queen', for tourist ride between Delhi and Alwar. The train was built in 1885 and retired in 1909. In 1997, it was relaunched and presently, it travels at a speed of 40kmph.

- While 'Mettupalayam-Ooty Nilgiri' passenger train is the slowest one in IR, running at an average speed of 10 kmph, the fastest one is 'Vande Bharat Express' (also called 'Train 18') which runs at a speed of 160 -180 kmph.

- The rail coaches are designed in such a manner that the resonance frequency of their suspension matches the human body's frequency of 1.2 Hz or 72 bpm, helping the train passengers to get sleep on a running train.

- IR is the largest employer in India employing about 1.4 million people. In addition to direct employment, very many others too earn a livelihood through IR by selling goods and services at the stations and trains.

- In Indian Railway coaches, electric appliances like bulbs, fans, and sockets are designed to function at 110 volts, instead of the normal 220 volts of the household appliances, to avoid theft.

REFERENCES AND SUGGESTED READINGS

1. *Arora N.* L., '*Transportation Engineering*', New India Pub., 1977.
2. *Subramanian K.* P., 'Transportation Engineering', Scitech Publications, Chennai, 2015.
3. Saxena S. C. and Arora S. P., 'A Text Book of Railway Engineering', Dhanpat Rai Publications, New Delhi.
4. Rangwala, 'Railway Engineering', Charotar Publishing house Pvt.Ltd., Anand, Gujarat, 2017.
5. Birdi, Ahuja, 'Roads, Railways, Bridges and Tunnel Engineering', Standard Book House, New Delhi.
6. Bindra S.P. and Bindra K.,'Elements of Bridges, Tunnel and Railway Engineering', Dhanpat Rai Publications, New Delhi.
7. Antia K. F.,'Railway track', The New Book Co.Pvt. Ltd., Bombay, 1960.
8. Mundrey J. S., 'Railway Track Engineering', Mc Graw Hill India, New Delhi, 2017.
9. https://nptel.ac.in/courses/105101087
10. https://www.smartzworld.com/notes/transportation-engineering-pdf-notes-te-pdf-notes/
11. https://jntukucen.ac.in/ebook_files/166.pdf

UNIT 5
TRACK GEOMETRICS, CONSTRUCTION, AND MAINTENANCE

UNIT SPECIFICS

This unit discusses the following aspects:

- Track Alignment - Factors governing alignment
- Track Cross sections - Single and Double line in cutting and embankment, in straight and at curves
- Railway track geometrics - Gradient, Curves, Super elevation, Cant deficiency, Negative cant
- Branching of tracks - Points and Crossings, Turn outs - types, components, functions, Track Junctions - types
- Stations - Purpose, requirements, types, factors affecting site selection
- Station Yards -Types, functions
- Track Maintenance - Necessity, Tools used, Organization of track maintenance, Duties of maintenance staff.

Multiple-choice questions along with answers, short and long answer type questions and practical work, relevant to the topics covered in the unit, are added. A list of references and suggested readings are also given at the end. It should be noted that dynamic QR codes are provided for additional reading in different sections, which can be scanned for relevant supportive information. A "KNOW MORE" section is also given, which has been carefully designed so that additional information relevant to this unit is provided for the users of the book. This section mainly contains some 'Activities' for the students to make them conversant with the topics he/she had studied, and some 'Interesting Facts' related with the contents of the unit.

RATIONALE

Trains need a path to run over it. The path which consists of formation, ballast, sleepers, rails and fasteners is called railway track. It is sometimes known as permanent way. In a railway track the rails are joined in series by welding and or with the help of fish plates and bolts. These rests on sleepers laid at right angles to them and fixed properly using fasteners. The sleepers spaced uniformly rest on ballast which is spread on sub grade formation. After understanding about these components of the track, the next phases of railway engineering include fixing up the alignment of the track, designing its geometrics, construction and maintenance of the track and traffic control. Once the track is aligned and constructed, it is very difficult and expensive to change the alignment at a later stage. Hence, utmost care should be taken in every step of the project. This unit discusses briefly the alignment, geometric design, construction and maintenance methods adopted for a railway track.

UNIT OUTCOMES

After completing this unit, student will be able

U5-O1: To describe the factors controlling the alignment of railway track, and their cross sections when cutting and filling areas come across.

U5-O2: To design the various geometric elements of railway track such as gradient, curves and super elevation

U5-O3: To identify the features of branching of railway tracks including that of different types of turn-outs and track junctions.

U5-O4: To identify the functions, requirements, and limitations of different types of railway stations and yards.

U5-O5: To identify the necessity and classification of track maintenance methods and tools, and organizational set-up of track maintenance.

Unit-5 Outcomes	**EXPECTED MAPPING WITH COURSE OUTCOMES** (1- Weak Correlation, 2-Medium Correlation, 3- Strong Correlation)				
	CO-1	CO-2	CO-3	CO-4	CO-5
U5-O1	-	-	-	3	3
U5-O2	-	-	-	3	3
U5-O3	-	-	-	3	3
U5-O4	-	-	-	2	2
U5-O5	-	-	-	1	3

5.1 TRACK ALIGNMENT

The fixing up of the centre line or route along which the railway track is constructed and upon which the train runs is defined as the alignment. As the routes are selected to connect different places, it may not be possible to have the alignment truly on level ground nor along a straight line. As such, there can be horizontal and vertical components for alignment. The horizontal components include straight path, its width, curves and vertical components include vertical curves, gradient, etc.

As it is rather difficult to change the alignment of a track already constructed, at a later stage, sufficient care should be taken during the alignment phase itself. Improper alignment would invariably result in huge loss in capital cost, maintenance cost and vehicle operating cost.

An ideal alignment must have the shortest possible route. It also must have minimum operational, construction and maintenance expenses. There must be safety, convenience and riding comfort. Besides, there must be aesthetically pleasing appearance.

5.1.1 Factors governing rail alignment

The alignment which has direct shortest route is the most economical but is rarely possible due to various practical difficulties such as intermediate obstructions, steep gradients, topography etc. Again, in many cases it may be necessary to deviate from the shortest route to connect obligatory points. (i.e. traffic generating points or places of importance).

An alignment, which is economical in the initial cost, may not be economical in long run due to maintenance cost or vehicle operation cost or both. It is also possible that shortest route may be costlier than other routes, when different alternatives are tried from the point of construction cost.

The various factors which control the alignment of a railway track are:

i) Obligatory points

ii) Traffic

iii) Geometric design standards

iv) Topography

v) Economics

vi) Other considerations

i. Obligatory points: These are points which control the alignment of railway track. These can be classified into two categories:

i) Points through which a track must pass

a) Important towns and cities: It is desirable that track alignment passes through places of social, commercial, political and defense importance.

b) Major bridges or river crossings: The construction of additional bridges over large rivers is a costly affair.

c) Hill passes or saddles: To avoid unnecessary requirements of deep cuttings or high banks or tunnels or viaducts, the existing passes or saddles should be connected, whenever crossing the hills.

d) Site for tunnels: Though passing of a track through tunnel should be avoided as far as possible. However, in case of high and thin ridges, a tunnel may be an economical option to avoid deep cuttings,

ii) Points through which a track should not pass:

a. Costly and fertile land

b. Religious places like temple, church, mosque or tomb

c. Areas liable to flooding (water logged areas), marshy land etc.

ii) Traffic: Growth of traffic, its location, nature and intensity have to be considered. The location of traffic affects control points, the nature of traffic (passenger or goods) and its intensity govern type of construction.

General considerations are:

a) Traffic varies with square of population. Hence, route with the highest population is the best.

b) Freight earnings are much more than passenger earnings.

c) Influence area of railway line increases from 15 km to 25 km over a few years.

iii) Geometric standards: Some points to be considered are:

a. Gauge of the track

b. Ruling gradient and minimum radius.

c. Provision long straight stretches in between two reverse curves.

d. Avoiding of curves at bridges, stations, etc.

iv) Topography: If topography of country is such that use of steep gradients is unavoidable, then in such cases the alignment of the track is made by special ways to reduce the rate and cost of high gradients. For alignment, topography may be classified as:

a) Valley alignment

b) Cross country alignment

c) Mountain alignment

v) Economy: Different alignments are analysed from cost point of view and best alignment which gives maximum annual return is selected.

$$Annual\ Return = \frac{Gross\ revenue - Annual\ running\ expenses}{Investment} \quad \text{Eq. 5.1}$$

vi) Other considerations:

a) Presence of geological formation such as faults, slips, slides, etc.

b) Effect of flood and climate.

c) Track should cross road at right angles.

d) Station sites should be on level ground.

e) Availability of construction materials.

f) Political interventions and social acceptability.

5.2 TRACK CROSS SECTIONS

The cross sectional elements of a railway track are:

i) Right of way or Permanent land

ii) Formation width

iii) Side slopes

iv) Side drains

i. *Right of Way or permanent land*

The area of land acquired by railways and used for construction of railway track along the proposed alignment is called right of way or permanent land. The width of the right of way is called permanent land width.

ii. *Formation width*

The prepared and finished surface of earthwork in cutting or embankment over which the railway track is laid is called the formation. The top width of a railway embankment or bottom width of formation of cutting, excluding the side drain is called formation width. The formation width of a railway track depends upon the gauge adopted, number of rail lines, etc.

The minimum formation width recommended by Indian Railway Board in embankment is 6.1m and 10.7m for single line and double line respectively. In cutting it is 5.5m and 10.1m respectively.

iii. *Side Slopes*

The slopes given to the sides of the earthwork of a track in cutting or embankment from slope stability consideration are called side slopes. It depends upon type of soil, climatic conditions, method of drainage, and slope protection measures adopted etc. Generally, the side slopes recommended are 2:1 for embankment and 1:1 for cutting.

iv. *Side Drains*

The drains provided on either side of railway tracks are known as side drains. Side drains are generally of trapezoidal shape with a minimum top width of 1.8m in embankment and 1.22m in cutting, and a bottom width of 0.9m.

Standard cross section of single line broad gauge track in embankment on a straight track is shown in Fig. 5.1 and a single line broad gauge track in cutting on a curved track is shown in Fig. 5.2. Similarly, standard cross sections of double line broad gauge track in cutting on a straight and a curved track are shown in Fig. 5.3 and Fig. 5.4 respectively.

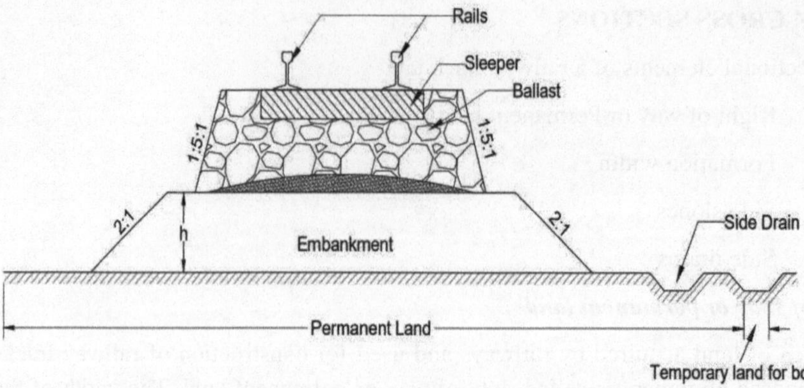

Fig. 5.1 Typical cross section of single line broad gauge track in embankment (on straight track)

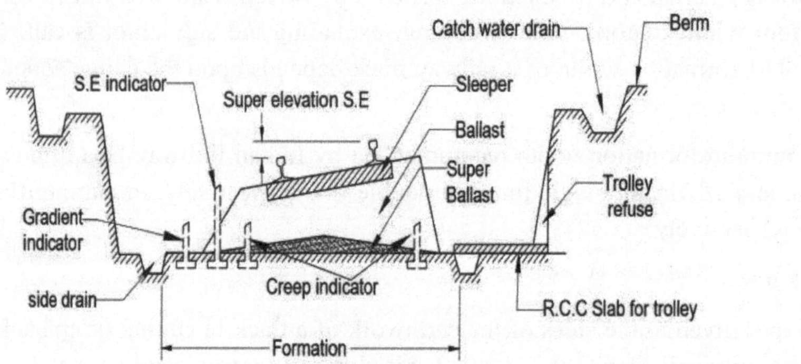

Fig. 5.2 Typical cross section of single line broad gauge track in cutting (on curved track)

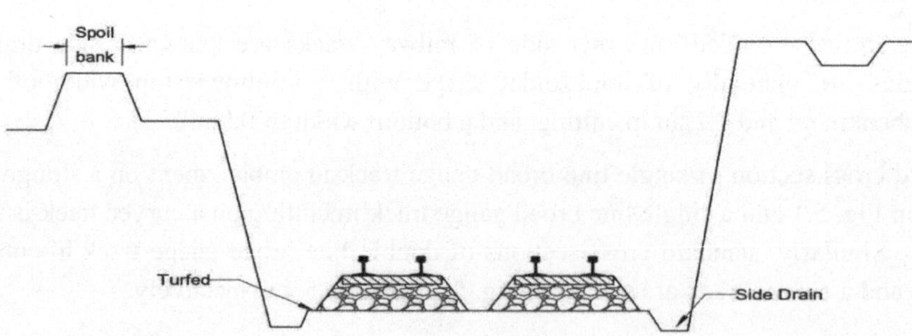

Fig. 5.3 Typical cross section of a double line broad gauge track in cutting (on straight track)

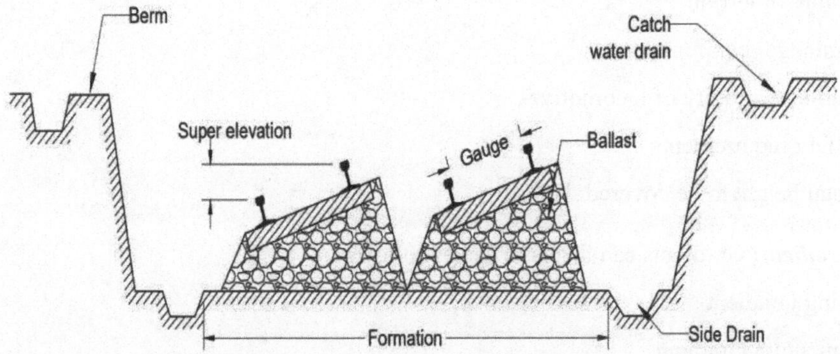

Fig. 5.4 Typical cross section of a double line broad gauge track in cutting (on curved track)

5.3 RAILWAY TRACK GEOMETRICS

The geometrics of any structure refer to its size and shape. The geometric elements to be designed for a railway track include:

i. Cross sectional elements (see section 5.2)
ii. Gradients
iii. Horizontal and vertical curves
iv. Super elevation
v. Speed of train.

The track should be designed in such a way that trains with heavy loads can run over it with maximum safety at maximum possible speed.

5.3.1 Gradient

It is the rate of rise or fall of the track. It is expressed as vertical to horizontal distance or as percentage. i.e., if there is a rise of 1m for a horizontal distance of 100m, the gradient is expressed as 1 in 100 or 1%.

Gradient is determined considering the satisfactory track drainage requirements. It economizes the earthwork. It also helps in reaching the stations situated at different elevations by providing uniform rate of rise or fall as far as practicable.

Factors affecting selection of gradient: The selection of a particular gradient depends upon:

a. Nature of terrain

b. Drainage requirements

c. Hauling capacity of locomotives

d. Safety requirements

e. Total height to be covered.

Types of Gradient: Gradients can be classified as follows:

a. Ruling Gradient

b. Momentum Gradient

c. Pusher Gradient

d. Gradient at station yards

e. Compensated Gradient

i. ***Ruling Gradient:*** It is the maximum gradient allowed on a certain section of railway track. It governs the maximum weight a locomotive can pull along that section. It depends on the type of terrain too.

In plains	1 in 150 to 1 in 200
In hilly regions	1 in 100 to 1 in 150.

ii. ***Momentum Gradient:*** Gradient steeper than ruling gradient, which is provided by utilizing the momentum attained by the train while traversing along the descending gradient of a valley curve to climb the up gradient. This up gradient is called momentum gradient. It should be noted that stop signals should not be provided on such stretches of valley curve.

iii. ***Pusher Gradient:*** This is also a steeper gradient than ruling one which requires one or more additional locomotives for pushing the train load up the track. They are provided at mountainous places to avoid deep cutting or to reduce the length of track. For e.g., a pusher gradient of 1 in 37 is provided at Bhorghat between Pune and Mumbai on Western Ghats, in Darjeeling Railway with NG track, pusher gradient of 1 in 25 has been provided at some places. It has been found that pusher gradient of 1 in 75 to 1 in 103 with additional one locomotive is generally sufficient.

iv. ***Gradient at station yards:*** Gradient provided at station yards are sufficiently low because standing bogies on steeper gradients are liable to move under heavy winds and cause accidents. Besides, it also prevents additional resistance due to grade or in other words it prevents extra force required by the locomotives to pull the train up a gradient while starting the train. Hence, the maximum gradient permitted in a station yard is kept as 1 in 400 and the minimum gradient to be provided is 1 in 1000 for easy drainage of rain water.

v. ***Compensated Gradient:*** At curves, in order to relieve from the additional resistance to traction, the ruling gradients should be eased by a certain percentage called 'grade compensation'. The grade compensation adopted in Indian Railways is as follows:

On BG curves - 0.04 percent per degree of curve

On MG curves - 0.03 percent per degree of curve

On NG curves - 0.02 percent per degree of curve

5.3.2 Curves

Often, track alignments are not straight nor level. Deviations with respect to horizontal or vertical plane will be necessitated. Any such deviations shall be designed properly by means of suitable curves such that safety, speed and comfort of travel are ensured. Curves are geometrical arcs provided at the change in alignment of a track. A curve is represented by the length of its radius or by the degree of curvature suspended by a chord of length 30.48m or 100 ft. The degree of curvature 'D' of a curve of radius 'R' is calculated as follows:

$$R = \frac{1750}{D} m \qquad \text{Eq. 5.2}$$

From the above equation, a 3° curve has a radius of 583.3m.

Necessity of Curves: Curves are necessary under the following situations:

a. To provide easier gradient.

b. To by pass obstacles.

c. To avoid excessive earthwork.

d. To adopt the alignment along the site suiting to bridge or tunnel, if required.

e. To avoid costly /fertile land, water logged areas, etc. coming in the straight route.

Types of Curves: Curves used on railways can be classified as:

a) Horizontal curves

b) Vertical curves

c) Transition curves

a) Horizontal curves: These are provided in horizontal plane to achieve gradual change of direction of alignment. They are of following types:

i. Simple curves - consists of a single arc of uniform radius

ii. Compound curves - consists of two or more simple curves of different radii turning in the same direction

iii. Reverse curves - consists of two simple curves of same or different radii which turn in the opposite directions

b) Vertical Curves: They are used to connect stretches with different gradients smoothly. They are usually designed as parabolic curves. They are of two types:

i. Summit curves or Crest curves with convexity upwards

ii. Valley curves or Sag curves with concavity upwards

c) Transition curves: They are provided to connect a straight stretch with a circular curve, whose radius varies point to point (infinity at the end meeting the straight stretch and radius of circular curve at the end meeting circular curve).

Functions of Transition curves: Transition curves are provided:

i. To introduce gradually the change in the radius of curvature from infinity at the end of straight to that of circular curve of selected radius.

ii. To introduce smoothly the rate of change of centrifugal acceleration so that riding comfort is ensured

iii. To introduce gradually the designed super elevation.

iv. To minimize wear of rails at curves.

v. To reduce the chances of derailment.

In Indian Railways, cubic parabola is adopted for designing transition curve.

The length of transition curve is determined from the following formulae:

i. As per Railway code:

$$L = 4.4\sqrt{R} \qquad \text{Eq. 5.3}$$

Where R = Radius of circular curve in m

L = Length of transition curve in m.

ii. Based on rate of change radial acceleration:

$$L = \frac{3.2\ V^3}{R} \qquad \text{Eq. 5.4}$$

where V = Speed of train in m

L and R in m.

iii. At the rate of change of super elevation of 1 in 360.

5.3.3 Superelevation

When a vehicle traverses a circular path, it will be subjected to a centrifugal force acting radially outward through its centre of gravity. The centrifugal force exerts a horizontal thrust on the outer rail and the weight on the outer rail increases. This horizontal thrust and uneven load distribution will cause derailment. This centrifugal force can be counteracted by introducing the centripetal force by raising the outer rail with respect to inner rail. This raising of outer rail with respect to inner rail is called 'superelevation' or 'canting'.

Objects of providing superelevation: The following are the objects of providing superelevation:

i. To counteract the centrifugal force acting on the vehicle and thereby to avoid derailment and to reduce side wear of rails.

ii. To distribute the train load equally on the two rails, reducing the top wear of rails and the maintenance cost.

iii. To ensure safe and comfortable travel for train.

Relation of Superelevation with Speed, Radius of the curve and Gauge: When a train moves over a circular track, it will be subjected to the following forces: (See Fig. 5.5).

i. The weight of the train (W) acting vertically downward through its C. G.

ii. The centrifugal force (F) acting horizontally outward through C. G.

iii. Reaction R_1 acting upward normal to the track.

Let R = radius of the circular path in m

G = gauge of the track in m

V = speed of the vehicle in kmph

v = speed of the vehicle in m/s

α = inclination of rail surface to horizontal

g = acceleration due to gravity in m/s^2

S = length of inclined surface in m

e = superelevation provided in m

Now, centrifugal force, $F = \frac{Wv^2}{gR}$ (i)

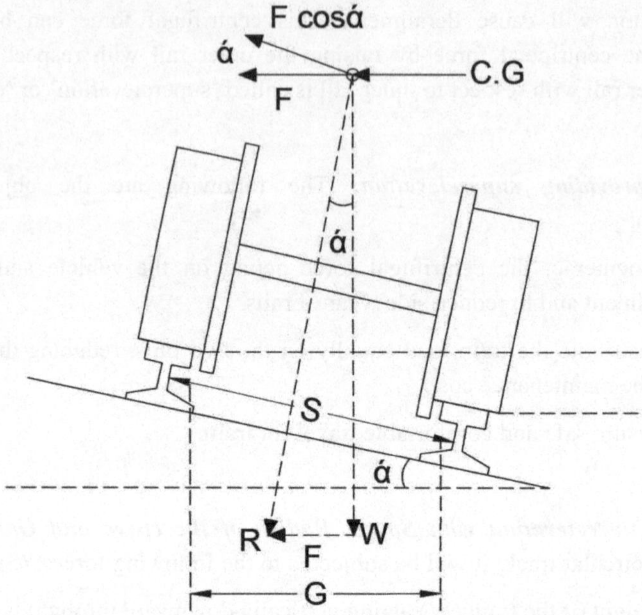

Fig. 5.5 Analysis of Superelevation

Resolving the forces along the inclined surface,

$$F \cos\alpha = W \sin\alpha \quad \text{(ii)}$$

Where, $\sin\alpha = \frac{e}{s}$ and $\cos\alpha = \frac{G}{s}$

$$\frac{Wv^2}{gR} \times \frac{G}{S} = W \times \frac{e}{S}$$

$$\therefore e = \frac{Gv^2}{gR}$$

$$e = \frac{G \times (0.278v)^2}{9.81R}$$

i.e.

$$e = \frac{GV^2}{127R} m \quad \text{Eq. 5.5}$$

where $v_{m/s} = 0.278V_{kmph}$

For BG, $e = \frac{1.676V^2}{127R} m$

For MG, $e = \frac{1.0V^2}{127R} m$

For NG, $e = \frac{0.762V^2}{127R} m$

In India, where the maximum allowable speed of trains on BG and MG is > 50 kmph, then average speed is assumed to be 75% of maximum speed or safe speed of the curve whichever is less.

At locations when the maximum allowable speed of trains on BG and MG is ≤ 50 kmph, then the average speed is taken as the maximum allowable speed or safe speed of the curve whichever is less.

Equilibrium speed of the trains is determined by estimation of weighted average calculated as under:

$$Veq = \frac{n_1V_1 + n_2V_2 + ...}{(n_1 + n_2 + ...)} = \sum \frac{n_iV_i}{N} \quad \text{Eq. 5.6}$$

Where, n_1, n_2, …. are the number of trains having speeds V_1, V_2, …… respectively.

$N = n_1 + n_2 + ...$ i.e. total no. of trains.

Limit of Superelevation: The superelevation provided in curved track should be such that safe movement of trains at different speeds is ensured. Generally, the maximum value of superelevation is 1/10th of gauge. Thus in India, the maximum values adopted for different gauges are:

For BG track - 167.6 mm

MG track - 100 mm

NG track - 76.2 mm

Recently, Indian Railways Board has recommended the following values of maximum superelevation for different gauges as shown in Table 5.1.

Table 5.1. Limits of superelevation for different gauges as recommended by I.R.B.

<table>
<tr><th rowspan="2">Sl. No.</th><th rowspan="2">Gauge</th><th colspan="2">Maximum Superelevation when V<100kmph</th><th colspan="3">Maximum Superelevation for high speeds</th></tr>
<tr><th>Under ordinary condition</th><th>Under special permission</th><th>120 kmph</th><th>160 kmph</th><th>200 kmph</th></tr>
<tr><td>1</td><td>BG</td><td>140 mm</td><td>165 mm</td><td>165 mm</td><td>185 mm</td><td>185 mm</td></tr>
<tr><td>2</td><td>MG</td><td>90 mm</td><td>100 mm</td><td>Not specified</td><td>Not specified</td><td>Not specified</td></tr>
<tr><td>3</td><td>NG</td><td>65 mm</td><td>76 mm</td><td>Not specified</td><td>Not specified</td><td>Not specified</td></tr>
</table>

Method of providing superelevation: The superelevation is provided gradually and smoothly along the transition curve which connects the straight stretch with the circular curve. Superelevation varies from zero at the beginning of transition curve (end of straight) to full design value at the start of circular curve (end of transition curve) at a uniform rate of change, so that no wear and tear occurs for rails and fixtures. The design value of superelevation has to be maintained throughout the length of circular curve.

5.3.4 Cant Deficiency

It is the numerical difference between the actual cant provided and the equilibrium cant that is required for the maximum permissible speed of the curve. Cant deficiency should be as minimum as possible because of the following reasons:

Higher cant deficiency leads to:

a. Extra pressure and lateral thrust on outer rails, which requires high strength track and more fastenings for stability.

b. Higher discomfort and inconvenience to passengers.

c. More side wears and creep of outer rails of the track.

Indian Railways prescribes the following values given in Table 5.2 as limits of cant deficiency for different gauges with respect to design speed.

Table 5.2 Limits of cant deficiency for different gauges on Indian Railways

<table>
<tr><th rowspan="2">Sl. No.</th><th rowspan="2">Gauge</th><th colspan="2">Cant Deficiency, mm</th></tr>
<tr><th>For speeds up to 100 kmph</th><th>For speeds more than 100 kmph</th></tr>
<tr><td>1</td><td>BG</td><td>76</td><td>100</td></tr>
<tr><td>2</td><td>MG</td><td>51</td><td>Not specified</td></tr>
<tr><td>3</td><td>NG</td><td>38</td><td>Not specified</td></tr>
</table>

5.3.5 Negative Cant

When a branch line takes off from a main line on a curve, then the superelevation necessary for average speed of trains running over the main line cannot be provided. See Fig. 5.6. Here, PT and QS are the inner and outer rails respectively of main line, and QV and PU are the inner and outer rails respectively of branch line. The point Q on the main line should be higher than point P by the amount e_1. When we consider the branch line, the point P should be higher than the point Q by an amount e_2. Obviously, it is not possible to satisfy both conditions simultaneously. In such cases, an amount of cant deficiency is allowed and the outer rail of the branch line will be lower than inner rail, thereby the superelevation obtained for branch line is negative. Such type of superelevation is known as 'negative superelevation' or 'negative cant'.

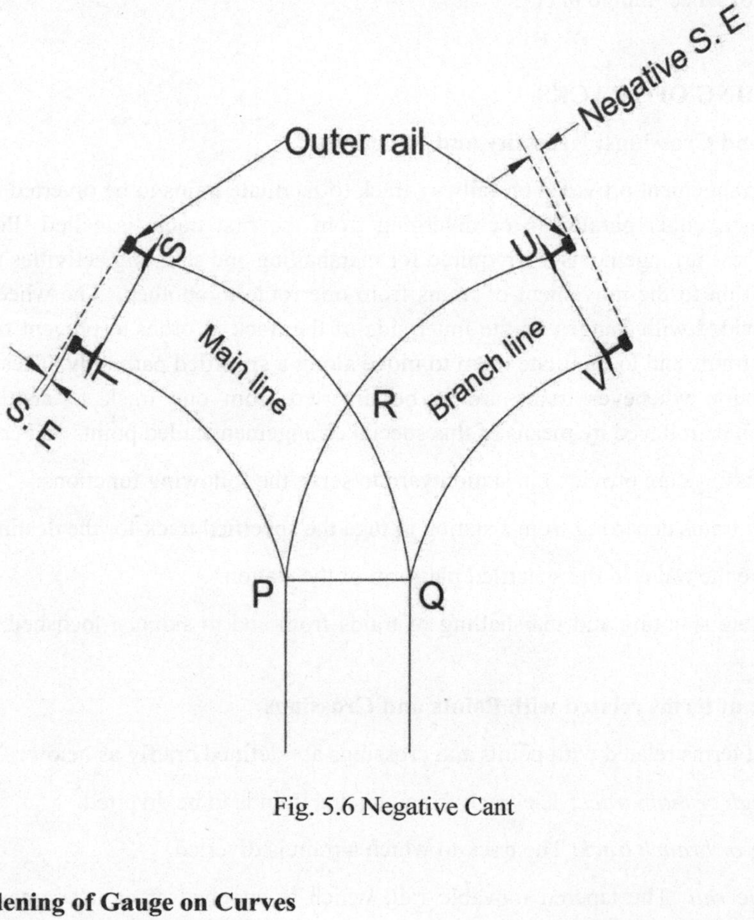

Fig. 5.6 Negative Cant

5.3.6 Widening of Gauge on Curves

It is the extra width of gauge provided on curved portion of a track to avoid tilting of trains. Due to rigidity of the wheel base of rolling stock, when the front axle strikes the outer rail, the inner axle wheel bears a gap with the outer rail. This gap should be allowed by widening the gauge in order to prevent derailment. The widening should be just adequate; otherwise it may result in derailment due to the lateral play of train. Extra width of gauge (W_e) in mm is given by the equation:

$$We = \frac{130(B+L)^2}{R} \qquad \text{Eq. 5.7}$$

Where B = rigid wheel base in m which is 6m for BG and 4.88m for MG tracks

R =radius of the curve in m

L = lap of flange in m $= 0.02\sqrt{h^2 + D \times h}$

h = depth of wheel flange below rails in cm

D = diameter of wheel flange in cm.

5.4 BRANCHING OF TRACKS

5.4.1 Points and Crossings: Necessity and Functions

The special arrangement provided on railway track to facilitate trains to be diverted from one track to another, either parallel to or diverging from the first track, is called 'Points and Crossings'. These arrangements are required for marshalling and shunting activities in station yards, in addition to the movement of trains from one route to another. The wheels of the trains are provided with flanges on the inner side of the track in order to prevent the lateral movement of trains and to facilitate them to move along a specified path only. These flanges cause obstruction whenever trains are to be diverted from one track to another. This obstruction can be relieved by means of this special arrangement called points and crossings.

Points and crossings are provided in station yard to serve the following functions:

a. To enable trains departing from a station to take the specified track for the destination

b. To receive the trains in the specified platform of the station.

c. To facilitate shunting and marshalling of trains from and to sidings, locoshed, washing lines, etc.

5.4.2 Important terms related with Points and Crossings

The important terms related with points and crossings are defined briefly as below:

i. *Through or main track*: The track from which a train is to be diverted.

ii. *Siding or branch track*: The track to which a train is diverted.

iii. *Tongue rail*: The tapered movable rail, which is attached at or near one end to a running rail.

iv. *Stock rail*: The running rail to which a tongue rail is attached.

v. *Switch :* A pair of tongue rails with necessary connections

vi. *Points:* A pair of tongue rails and stock rails with necessary connections

vii. *Heel of switch*: It is the untapered end of a switch rail which is fixed to the lead rail.

viii. *Toe of switch:* The thin tapering end of tongue rail.

ix. *Throw of switch:* The distance through which the toe of a tongue rail moves sideways when operated.

x. *Heel divergence:* The distance between the running face of stock rail and that of tongue rail measured at heel of the switch.

xi. *Heel block:* The cast iron block on which a tongue rail and lead rail are bolted to stock rail to keep heel of the tongue at the designed distance from the stock rail.

xii. *Lead rail:* The rail which lead the track from heel of the tongue rail to the toe of crossing.

xiii. *Point rail:* The rail of main track forming the nose of crossing.

xiv. *Splice rail:* The rail of branch track which meet the point rail at the nose of crossing.

xv. *Wing rail:* The bent portion of rail used in front of nose of crossing which guides the train wheels in their proper route.

xvi. *Check rail:* The rail length provided on the opposite side of crossing to check the tendency of wheel to climb over the crossing.

xvii. *Splice rail:* The rail of branch track meeting at the nose of crossing.

xviii. *Point rail:* The rail of main track forming the nose of crossing.

xix. *Theoretical nose of crossing (TNC)*: The point of intersection of the gauge lines of a crossing which is used as a reference point for the design of turn out.

xx. *Actual nose of crossing (ANC):* Since it is not practical to maintain the sharp end of the crossing, a short length of it is cut off to give a certain width to nose. This point is called Actual nose of crossing (ANC)

xxi. *Throat of crossing:* The location where the converging wing rails are the nearest.

xxii. *Angle of crossing:* The angle between the running faces of point rail and splice rail at a crossing.

xxiii. *Flange way clearance:* The distance between the adjacent faces of the stock rail which allows free movement of wheel flanges.

xxiv. *Flare:* The gradual widening of the flange way formed by bending the end of a check rail or a wing rail away from the gauge line.

xxv. *Toe of crossing:* The end point of a wing rail with lead rail.

xxvi. *Heel of crossing:* The end of the point or splice rail at a crossing.

xxvii. *Overall length of turn out*: The horizontal distance between the end of stock rail to end of the point rail of a turn out.

xxviii. *Stretcher bar*: The bar which connects the two tongue rails each other so that each tongue rail moves through the same distance while changing the point.

xxix. *Slide chairs:* The plates which support the tongue rails throughout their length and enable them to slide laterally while changing the points.

5.4.3 Turnout

Turnout is the simplest combination of points and crossings which permits movement of train from a main track to a siding or branch track. In Indian Railways, the speed of trains on turnout is limited to 15kmph. The running of train at these locations will not be as smooth as on normal track. A turnout is said to be 'right handed' or 'left handed' according as the diversion of the train from main track is towards right or left side of its facing direction. See Fig. 5.7.

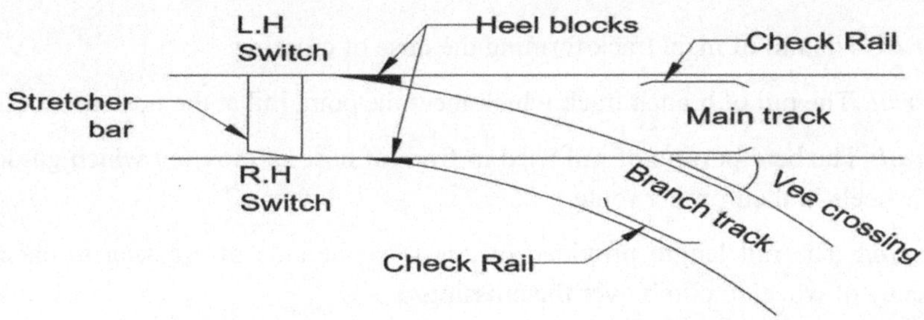

(a) Right hand Turnout

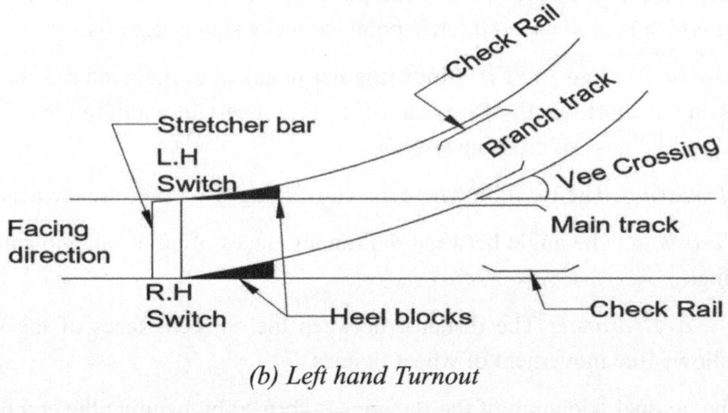

(b) Left hand Turnout

Fig. 5.7 Right hand and Left hand Turnouts

Component parts of a turnout and their functions: The component parts of a turnout and their functions are briefly described below: (See Fig. 5.8).

a. A pair of tongue rails: The tongue rails along with the stock rails in a turnout form a pair of points or switches. The tongue rails facilitate the diversion of trains from main track to a branch track.

b. A pair of stock rails: They are the main rails to which the tongue rails fit closely and they help in smooth working of tongue rails.

c. Two check rails: They are provided adjacent to the lead rails, one each in main tack and branch track to check or prevent the tendency of wheels to climb over the crossing.

d. Four lead rails: They are the outer straight lead rail, outer curve lead rail, inner straight lead rail and inner curve lead rail, provided to lead the track from heel of switches to the toe of crossing.

e. A Vee Crossing: It is formed by two wing rails, a point rail, and a splice rail. Its function is to provide sufficient gap between the rails for the easy passage of wheel flanges through them.

f. Slide chairs: They are provided to support the tongue rails throughout their length and to allow lateral movement for changing of points.

g. Stretcher bar: It connects toes of both the tongue rails so that each tongue rail moves through the same distance while changing the points.

h. A pair of heel blocks: These keep the heel ends of both the tongue rails at fixed distance from their respective stock rails.

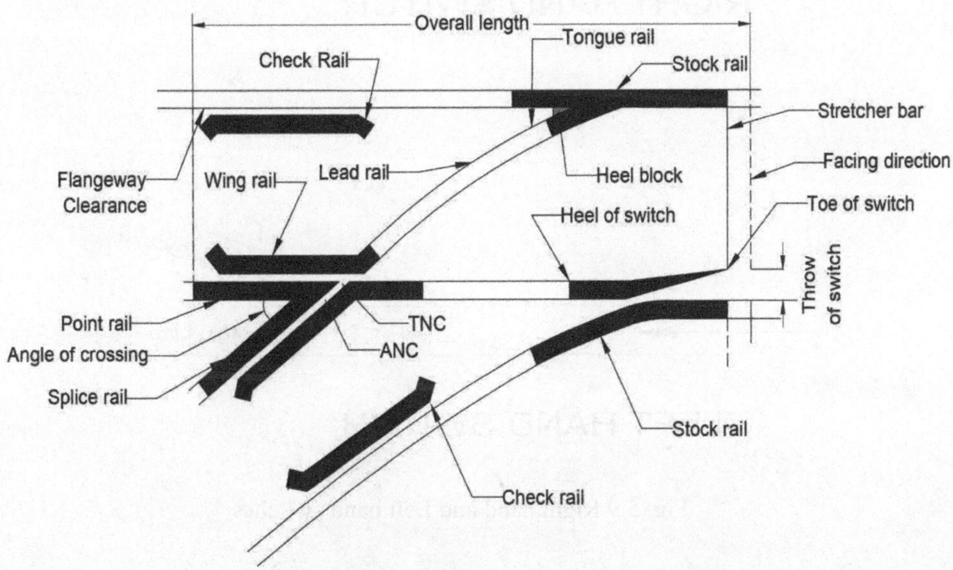

Fig. 5.8 Left hand turnout showing all the components

i. Switch tie plate or gauge tie bar: It is provided below the slide chairs and it holds the track rigidly to the definite gauge at the toe of switches.

j. Stops: These are the bent up plates fitted to the web of stock rails to prevent lateral bending of the tongue rail.

k. Rods, Cranks, levers, etc.: These are the devices for operating the points or switches.

l. Locking box, lock bar, plunger bar, etc.: These are the devices which form the parts of a locking system.

5.4.4 Switch or Point

The switch or point consists of two stock rails and a pair of tongue rails. Stretcher bars are used to join the two tongue rails together so that they can operate simultaneously. Point provides facility to divert the wheel passing over it in facing direction from one track to the other track. The point assembly is known as a right hand switch or left hand switch depending on which side a train running in the facing direction of switch is directed. See Fig. 5.9.

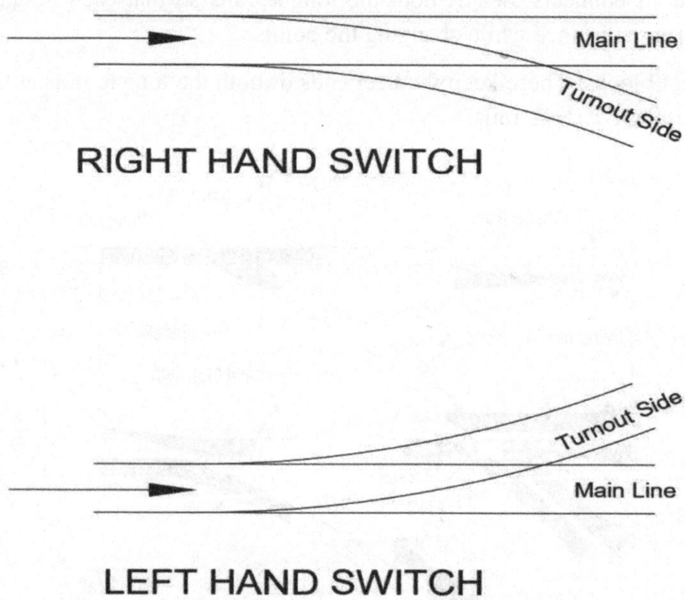

Fig. 5.9 Right hand and Left hand switches

The following are the component parts of switches:

a. A pair of tongue rails
b. A pair of stock rails
c. Switch tie plate
d. Heel blocks
e. Stretcher bar

f. Stops or studs

g. Slide chairs

h. Switch anchors

Various terms in connection with switch are described below.

Straight switch and curved switch: Straight switches have straight tongue rails. On such turnouts, vehicle will move on one straight track followed by another straight track whereas in the case of curved switch, tongue rail is made curved, but is not tangential to main line and there is no transition between straight and circular curve (Fig.5.10).

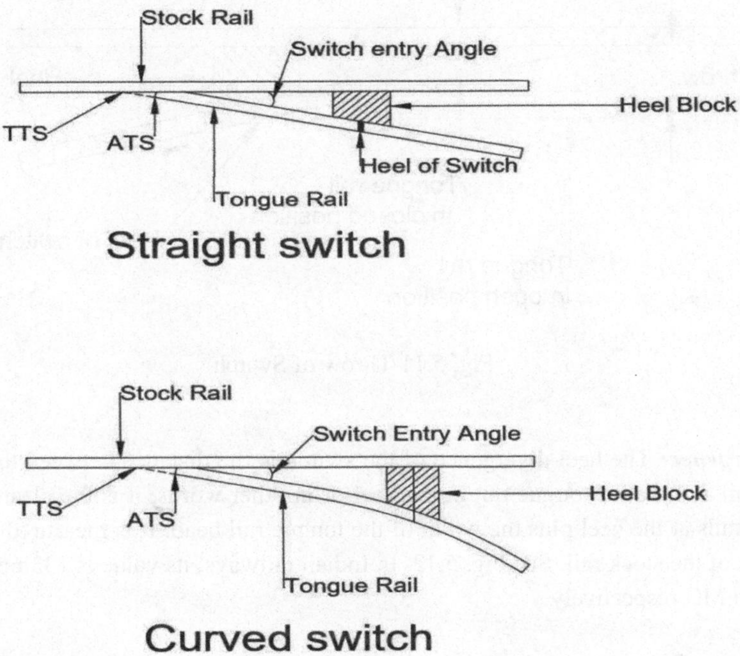

Fig. 5.10 Straight switch and Curved switch

Actual Toe of Switch (ATS): It is a point at which the tongue rail starts at the front end. It is the first tip of tongue rail visible to the eyes.

Switch angle: It is the angle between gauge lines of the tongue rail and its stock rail in the closed position, in case of straight switches. In case of curved switches, it is the angle between imaginary tangent drawn to the gauge line of tongue rail at Actual Toe of Switch (ATS) and the gauge line of the stock rail. It is also called Switch Entry Angle (SEA) or angle of switch divergence. (See Fig. 5.10)

Throw of switch: Throw of switch is the distance or gap through which a tongue rail moves at its toe from its closed position to open position. This distance is measured from the gauge line of the stock rail to inside of the open tongue rail. It is measured at actual toe of switch. In Indian Railways its value for BG track is 95mm and in MG track is 89mm.It is shown in Fig. 5.11.

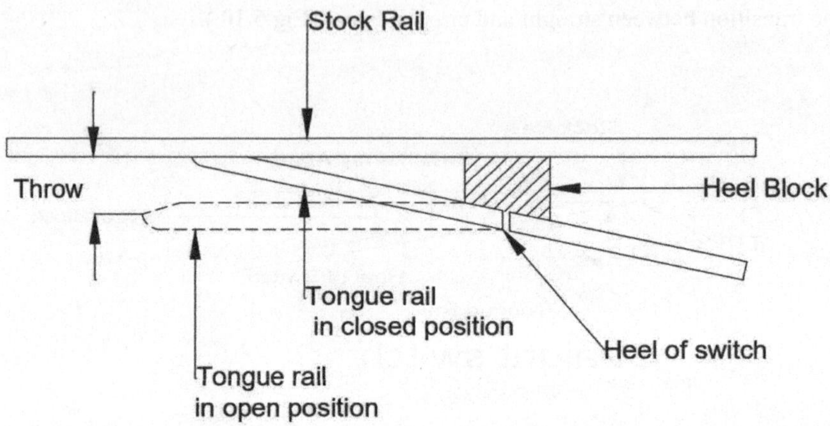

Fig. 5.11 Throw of Switch

Heel Divergence: The heel divergence of the switch is the distance between the gauge lines of stock rail and that of tongue rail at the heel or in other words, it is the clearance between these two rails at the heel plus the width of the tongue rail head. It is measured right angle to gauge face of the stock rail. See Fig. 5.12. In Indian railways, its value is 133mm and 117mm for BG and MG respectively.

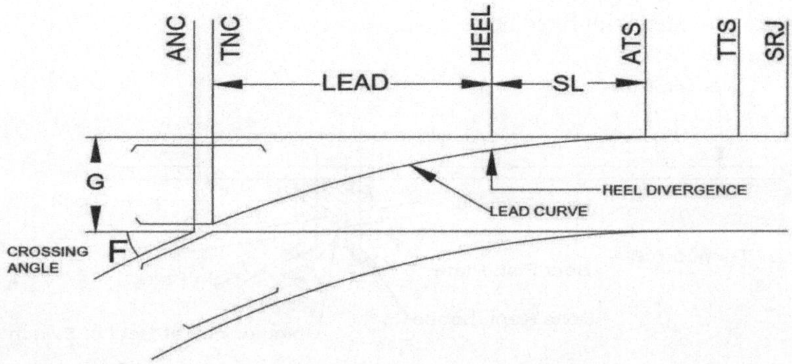

Fig. 5.12. Heel Divergence

Types of switches: In India, the following types of switches are generally used:

i. Stub switch

ii. Split switch

i. Stub Switch: Here, no separate tongue rail is provided and some portion of the track is placed on sliding chairs to move from side to side. See Fig. 5.13. It is an old type of switch and is structurally weak compared to split switch. Hence, they are being used only for temporary needs to divert the trains during maintenance and construction of new tracks.

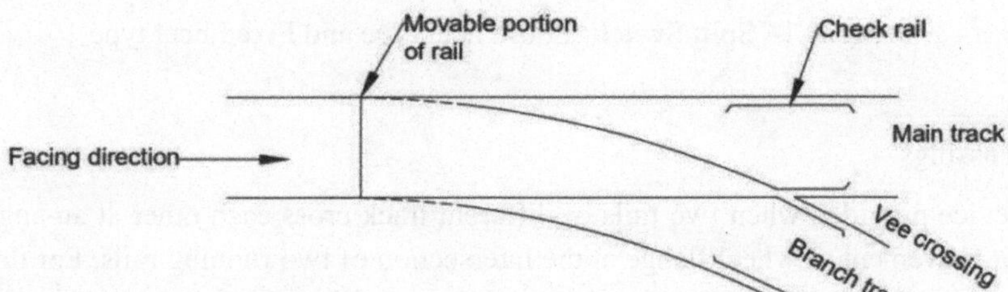

Fig. 5.13 Stub Switch

ii. Split Switch: They are of two types: (a) loose-heel type and (b) fixed heel type.

Loose Heel Type: In loose heel type of switch, fish plates join lead rails to tongue rail of the switch. The two front bolts are kept loose to allow for the throw of the switch. Hence the heel joint becomes weak. See Fig. 5.14(a).

Fixed heel Type: In this type, a tongue rail is combined with the stock rail as shown in Fig. 5.14(b) and they can move laterally about the heel points. The tongue rails are tapered at their toes in such a manner that they fit to the stock rails properly. Indian railways use this type of switch predominantly. For high speed tracks, fixed heel type switch is the best suited one because of its higher lateral rigidity. All the modern turnouts are provided with fixed heel.

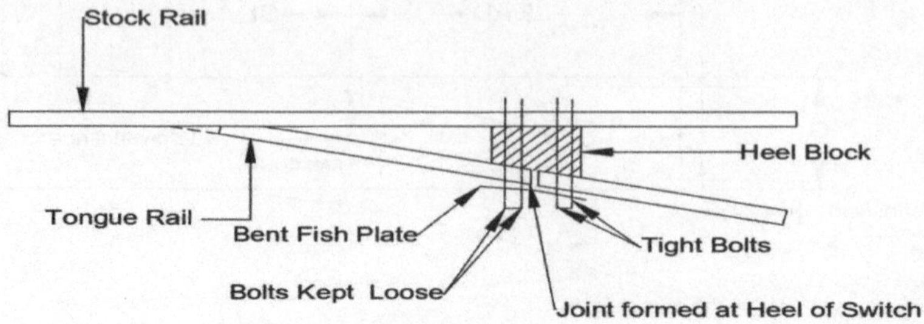

(a) Loose Heel Type Split Switch

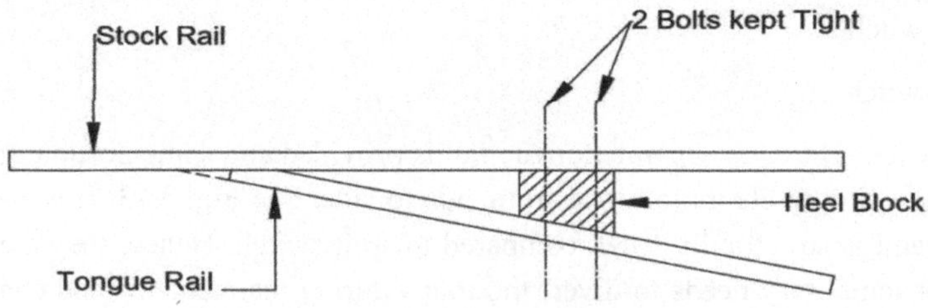

(b) Fixed Heel Type Split Switch

Fig. 5.14 Split Switch: Loose heel type and Fixed heel type

5.4.5 Crossings

It is a device provided when two rails of different track cross each other at an angle in order to permit movement of wheel flange at the intersection of two running rails. For this purpose, it is necessary to provide gap for movement of flange of the wheels to travel across a running rail. The flanged wheels jump over the gap from throat to nose of crossing. Even after the wheel passes for some distance after throat of crossing, wheel load is still born by wing rail. In order to check the wheel flanges from striking the nose, the opposite wheel flanges are guided by use of check rail inside the running rails.

Requirements of an ideal crossing: The following are the requirements of an ideal crossing:

i. Crossing assembly should be rigid enough to withstand severe vibrations.

ii. Wing rails and nose of crossing shall be made of special alloy steel, so that they should be able to resist heavy wear due to movement of trains.

iii. The nose of crossing should have adequate thickness to take all stresses acting on the crossing.

Component parts of a crossing: the different component parts of a crossing are listed below: (See Fig. 5.15).

i. A Vee piece
ii. A point rail
iii. A splice rail
iv. Two check rails
v. Two wing rails
vi. Heel blocks at throat, nose and heel of crossing
vii. Chairs at crossing, at toe and at heel.

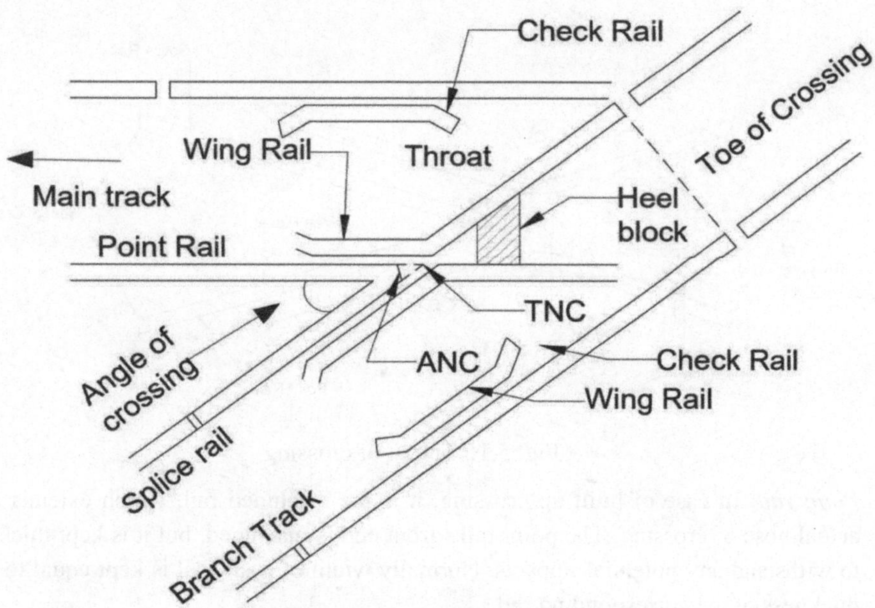

Fig 5.15 Component parts of a crossing

a. *Theoretical Nose of Crossing (TNC) &Actual Nose of Crossing (ANC)*: Theoretical nose of crossing is the theoretical point of intersection of the gauge lines of a crossing, which is used as a reference point for all layout calculations specially for the turnouts laid on curve (Fig. 5.15). The actual nose of crossing is the point at which the spread between the gauge lines of a crossing is sufficient to allow for adequate thickness, from consideration of manufacture and strength. Normally, ANC is provided with a width equal to thickness of web for the corresponding rail section.

b. *Crossing angle:* It is the angle contained between the gauge lines of the crossing measured at the theoretical nose of crossing (TNC).

c. *Number of crossing:* The number of crossing is the cotangent of angle of crossing. If the angle between legs of crossing is "F", the number of crossing "N" will be equal to "cotF". By measuring the spread between two gauge lines of crossing at a distance of about 1m from the ANC on both sides, the number of crossing can be determined in the field. If the spread is approximately 8.5cm, crossing is 1 in 12, if it is approximately 12cm; it is 1 in 8.5 crossing.

d. *Wing rails*: These are the two rails which start from toe of crossing. Wheel moves on wing rails up to actual nose of crossing (ANC) and further for some distance after ANC. Thereafter, wheel load is progressively transferred to nose of crossing.

e. *Throat of crossing*: It is the point at which the converging wing rails of a crossing are closest to each other. See Fig. 5.16.

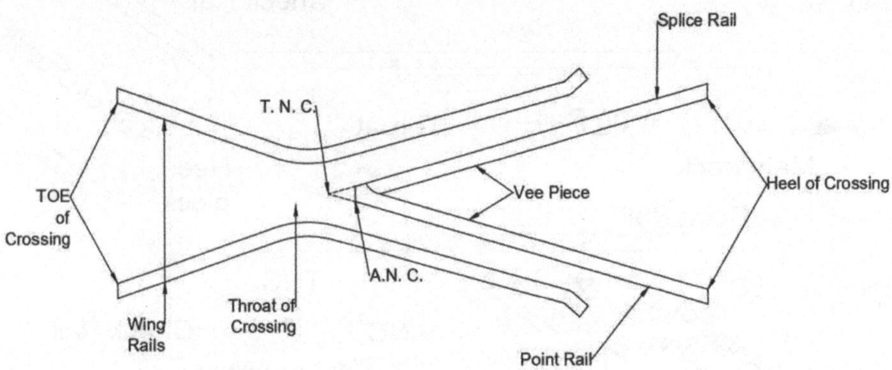

Fig. 5.16 Throat of crossing

f. *Point rail*: In case of built up crossing, it is the machined rail, which extends upto the actual nose of crossing. The point rail's front end is machined, but it is kept thick enough to withstand any potential impacts. Normally width of point rail is kept equal to the web thickness of the corresponding rail.

g. *Splice rail:* It is the rail which forms a part of nose of crossing but does not extend up to ANC. It is connected to the point rail with the help of bolts. Point rail and splice rail together form "V" of crossing.

h. *Toe of crossing:* It is the joint where wing rail of crossing meets the lead rail. Fish plated joint is provided at this location. The joint should be machined joint to reduce excessive hammering.

i. *Heel of crossing*: It is the last fish plated joint (6 bolts) at the end of crossing. This joint should also be machined joint to reduce the hammering effect of the wheel. (In case of turnout on concrete sleepers, the track going towards the turnout side is required to be made straight up to the centre of last long sleeper).

j. *Lead of turnout:* It is the track portion between heel of switch to the beginning of crossing assembly. Lead of turnout is measured from the theoretical nose of the crossing to the heel of the switch measured along the straight track. (See Fig. 5.12).

Types of crossings: Based on the shape of crossing, they are classified into three types as follows:

a. Acute angle crossing

b. Obtuse angle crossing

c. Square crossing

Acute angle crossing: When the left hand rail of one track meets the right hand rail of another track at an acute angle, or vice versa, this sort of crossing is formed. This type is widely used in Indian Railways. It consists of a pair of wing rails, a pair of check rails, a point rail and a splice rail. See Fig 5.15. It is also called V-crossing or Frog.

Obtuse angle crossing: It is formed when left hand rail of one track crosses right hand rail of another track at an obtuse angle or vice versa. The layout of this type of crossing resembles with diamond shape and hence it is called diamond crossing. Layout of a diamond crossing consists of two acute angle crossings and two obtuse angle crossings. See Fig. 5.17.

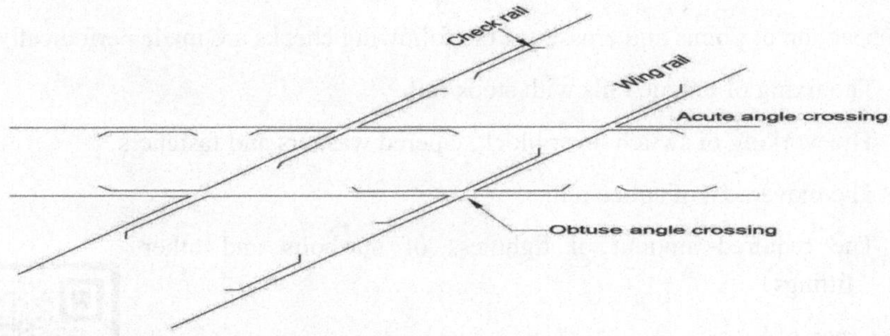

Fig. 5.17 Obtuse angle crossing

Square crossing: It is formed when two straight tracks of same or different gauge cross each other. See Fig. 5.18. This type of crossing shall be avoided on main lines as it causes heavy wear of rails due to impact of moving loads.

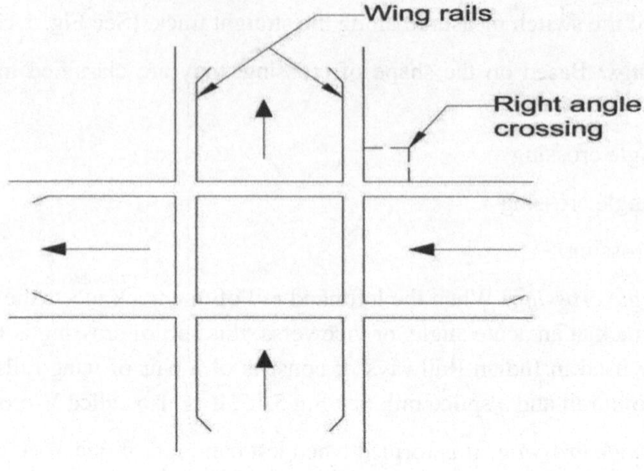

Fig. 5.18 Square Crossing

5.4.6 Inspection of Points and Crossings

For inspection of points and crossings, the following checks are made periodically:

- The fixing of tongue rails with stock rail.
- The working of switch lever block, tapered washers and fasteners.
- The movement of splice rail.
- The required amount of tightness of nut-bolts and other fittings.
- Creep of Stock.
- Wearing of rails.
- The packing of sleepers and ballast.
- Special care for drainage.
- Alignment of track.
- Interlocking connections.

SCAN ME
for
Points and Crossings
Railway

5.4.7 Track Junctions

Track junctions are formed by combining points and crossings with curved and straight lengths of tracks to transfer the trains from one track to another or to enable trains to cross the other crossing track. Depending upon the requirements of traffic, there can be several types of track junctions. The most commonly used layouts in Indian Railways are listed below:

a. Turnout

b. Acute angle crossing

c. Obtuse angle (diamond) crossing

d. Square crossing

e. Cross-over

f. Slips

g. Scissors cross over

h. Gauntlet track

i. Triangle track

j. Gathering lines or ladder track.

Different types of turnouts and crossings are briefly discussed already in sections 5.4.3 and 5.4.5. The other types of track junctions listed above are briefly explained below:

Crossovers: A crossover is a pair of switches that connects two parallel rail tracks, allowing a train on one track to cross over to the other. Fig. 5.19 shows a simple cross over between two parallel tracks having reverse curves on both sides.

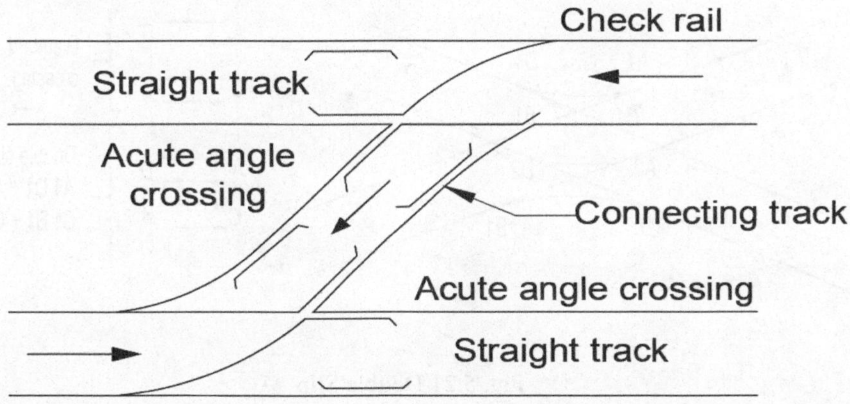

Fig. 5.19 Cross-over

Single Slip and Double Slip: In a diamond crossing, the tracks cross each other, but the trains from either track cannot change track. Slips are provided to enable vehicles to pass from one track to the other. The slip arrangement can be either single slip or double slip. The single slip arrangement is provided in a diamond crossing to enable the trains to change the track when approaching from one direction only. The different component parts of a single slip are two acute angle crossings, special curved lead rails, four check rails and two pairs of switches. See Fig. 5.20. In single slip, there are two sets of points, the vehicle from only one direction can change tracks.

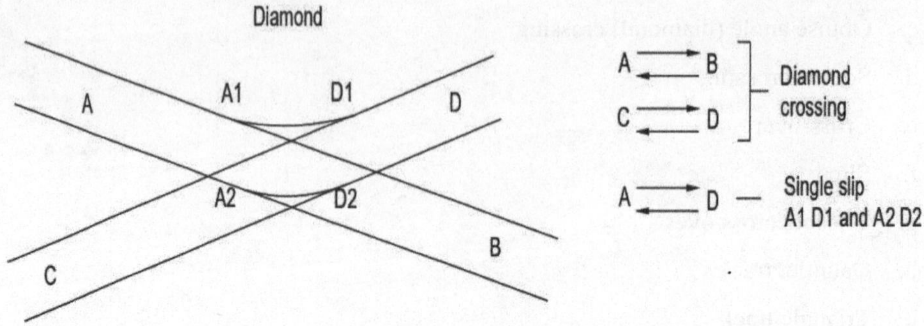

Fig. 5.20 Single Slip

In the case of double slip arrangement provided in diamond crossing, it is possible for the train to change the track when approaching from either direction. It consists of two acute angle crossings, two obtuse angle crossings, special curved lead rails, four check rails and four pairs of switches, there are four sets of points, and trains from both directions can change tracks. See Fig. 5.21.

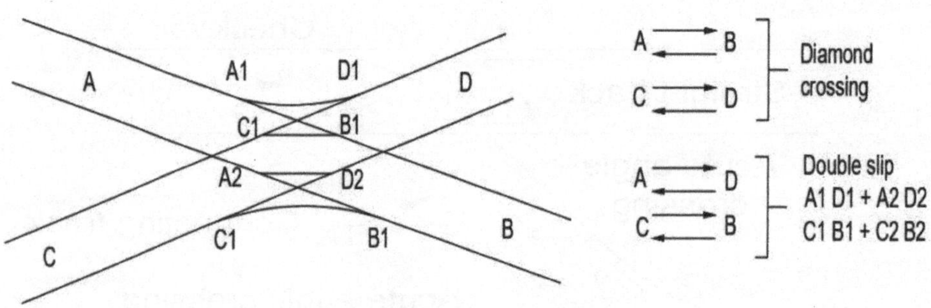

Fig. 5.21 Double Slip

Scissors Crossover: It consists of two crossovers provided between two adjacent parallel or slightly diverging tracks to enable the trains to change the track when approaching from either direction. The component parts of scissor cross over are: four pairs of switches, six acute angle crossings, two obtuse angle crossings, check rails, etc. See Fig. 5.22. This type of cross over is useful where space is limited and where much shunting has to be done. This arrangement has higher initial cost and requires careful maintenance.

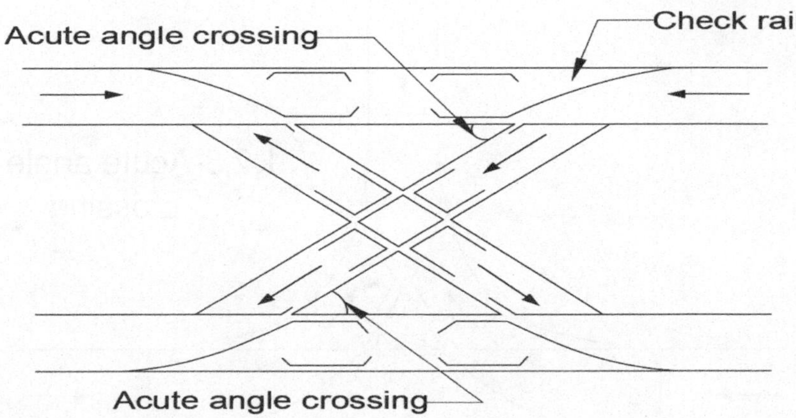

Fig. 5.22 Scissors Cross-over

Gauntlet track: This type of track arrangement is used when a double line track is to be narrowed down for a short distance. This is provided when one of the two tracks is under repair or on bridges. The components of this track include: two sets of crossings and a fixed point system. See Fig. 5.23.

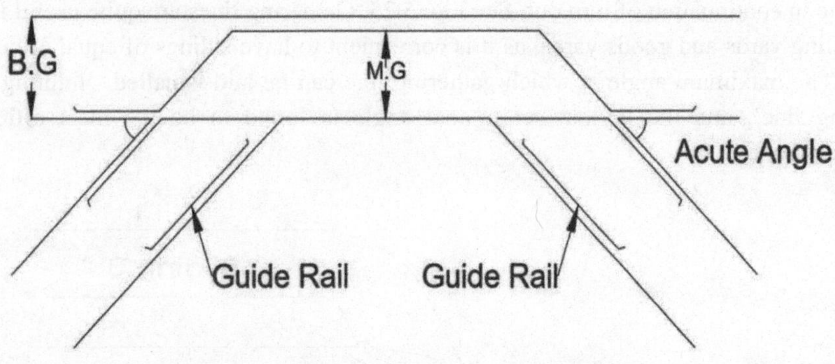

Fig. 5.23 Gauntlet Track

Triangle: A triangle (Fig. 5.24) is mostly provided in terminal yards for changing the direction of an engine. Through turntables are also used for the same purpose, but they are costlier. A triangle is provided where sufficient land is available and stations are not very important. It consists of one symmetrical split and two turnouts with lead rails, check rails, etc.

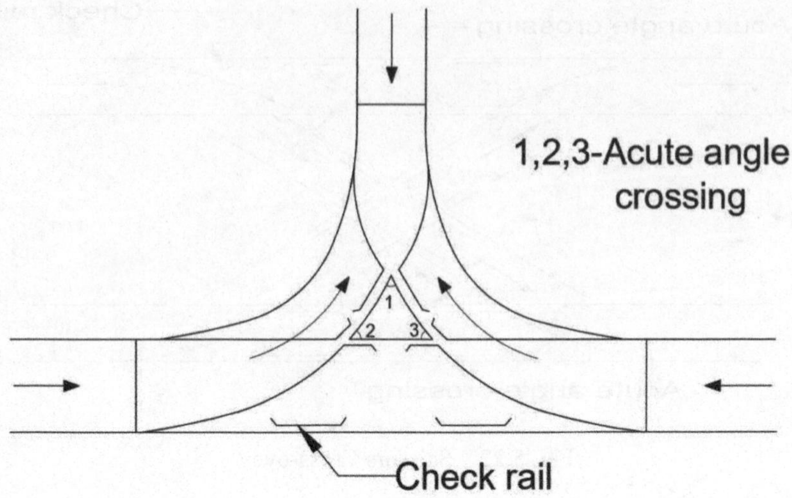

Fig 5.24 Triangle Track

Gathering Lines or Ladder track: These are inclined turn out tracks taken from a main track of turn out. This arrangement is adopted when a number of lines are branched off from a main line in continuation of turn out. See Fig. 5.25. Gathering lines are quite useful in case of marshalling yards and goods yards, as it is convenient to have sidings of equal or convenient length. The maximum angle at which gathering line can be laid is called 'limiting angle of gathering line', and the lay-out set in that angle is found to be the most efficient and economical one.

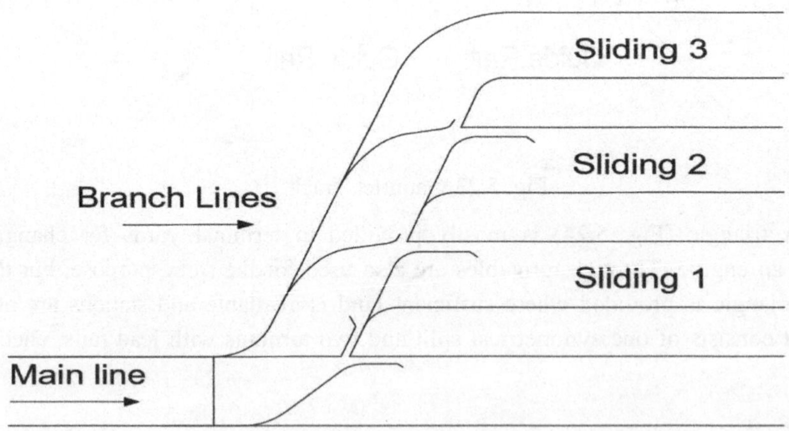

Fig. 5.25 Gathering Lines or Ladder Track

5.5 STATIONS

A railway station is a place on a railway line where (i) passengers and goods are booked and dealt with, (ii) watering and cooling of engines is done, (iii) changing of running staff, sorting of wagons, and control of train movements are carried out and (iv) where an authority to proceed is given to the trains. In some stations, only one of the above functions is carried out. For example, flag stations deal with traffic only, and block stations control the movement of trains only.

5.5.1 Purpose of Railway Station

A railway station is provided for one or more of the following purposes:

a. Boarding and alighting of passengers.

b. Loading and unloading of the goods or parcels.

c. Control the movement of trains.

d. Enable the trains to cross each other in case of single line section.

e. Enable the faster trains (Super fast, Rajadhani etc.) to overtake the slower trains.

f. Enable the locomotives to fill fuel, water or coal.

g. Attaching or detaching of coaches and wagons to trains.

h. Provide facilities for changing of engines and crew/staff.

i. To provide facilities and hold the passengers in case of emergencies like floods and accidents etc., when traffic is disrupted.

Many of the operational and non-operational activities of railways listed below are being carried out at stations:

Operational Activities:

i. Train operation: This includes train reception and despatch, shunting operation including loco movement, traction changing, crew management and operations during emergency.

ii. Infrastructure Operation and Maintenance: This includes Over Head Equipment (OHE) operation and maintenance, signal operation and maintenance, track maintenance and electricity supply for traction, signal, coach and locomotive maintenance depot area.

iii. Coach maintenance: This includes washing line operation, cleaning of coaches, watering of coaches, train cleaning including toilet discharge collection facilities.

iv. Locomotive Operation: This includes fuelling of locomotives, locomotive operation and maintenance and attaching/detaching locomotive.

v. Information System: This includes coaching operation information system, coach cabinet office working, announcements on Passenger Address (PA) system, train announcement and train enquiry.

vi. Ticketing/booking: This includes parcel booking, unreserved/reserved ticketing, feeding of quota/charting, luggage booking and ticket checking.

vii. Tourism and catering services: This includes on-board catering, bed-roll storage and services to AC coaches in trains, specified catering stalls, book stalls and miscellaneous passenger related stalls in the platforms, tourist reception centre management, Yatri Nivas and budget hotels built by railways, supply and distribution of bottled drinking water and food courts.

viii. Parcel Activities: This includes parcel handling and related operations.

ix. Security: This includes security of railway installations by RPF/GRP and crime prevention/control by RPF/GRP.

Non Operational Activities

i. Utilities: This include electricity supply and drainage management.

ii. Passenger Utilities: This include communication systems operation and maintenance, cloak room management, operation and maintenance of pay & use toilets, provision of Cyber Cafes/ATMs, Book stalls and miscellaneous stalls in commercial areas, food Courts/ Catering stalls, Waiting rooms, Escalator/lift upkeep and operation, Supply and distribution of potable and non potable water and Emergency medical care facilities.

iii. Cleaning : This includes station cleaning, staff offices and other building cleaning, and garbage collection and disposal

iv. Inter-modal Connectivity: This includes parking management, pre-paid taxi/auto rickshaw and maintenance of circulating area and approach roads including parking area.

v. Building Services: This include maintenance of station lighting/ ventilation/ air conditioning/power supply substation, station building maintenance, renovation and upgradation of infrastructure, development and maintenance of drainage system and sewerage system for yard and landscaping of the station complex.

vi. Railway Staff services : This include maintenance and cleaning of railway staff office, crew running room management including housekeeping, maintenance and catering.

5.5.2 Requirements of Railway Station

i) Passenger requirements:

- Enquiry office and reservation office
- Platforms for passengers and goods
- Waiting halls and retiring rooms
- Refreshment rooms, tea stalls, book stalls, etc.
- Bathrooms and toilets

- Drinking water supply arrangements
- Lighting and ventilation
- Display boards for schedule of trains
- Announcement system for train arrivals and departures
- Guides to help illiterate/ differently abled passengers

ii) Traffic requirements:

- Arrangement for controlling the movement of trains by signal.
- Sufficient space available for receiving, sorting and dispatching the trains.
- Sufficient number of platform for passengers and apparatus for issuing tickets.
- Goods Sheds and goods platforms
- Arrangement for inspection and maintenance of tracks

iii) Loco, Carriage and Wagon requirements:

- Loco shed and turn table
- Watering and fuelling facilities
- Inspection pits, water columns etc.

iv) Staff requirements:

- Accommodation for the staff of loco department
- Quarters for office staff
- Running rooms for train pilots and managers
- Canteen for staff, etc.

5.5.3 Types of Railway Stations

The layout of railway stations vary in size and importance according to the type and volume of traffic handled and as per their location. Stations are classified according to their operational and functional characteristics.

Classification of stations as per operational characteristics: According to operational characteristics, stations are classified as follows:

i. Block Stations

ii. Non-block stations

iii. Special class stations

Block Stations: They are places along the railway line where permission to approach and authority to proceed are granted. The railway track is divided into different 'block sections' to provide a proper space between the trains moving in one direction. Block stations are provided at the end of block sections and are equipped with proper signals to indicate the limits of block sections. Block stations are further classified into three types are as follows:

a. Class 'A' stations

b. Class "B' stations

c. Class 'C' stations

Class 'A' stations: In Class 'A' Stations, the permission to approach is given to trains only after clearing the line upto a distance of 400m beyond the home signal of the station. The minimum requirements of signals at Class A station are:

i. Home signal

ii. Warner signal

iii. Starter signal

Fig. 5.26 shows the lay-out of a Class A station.

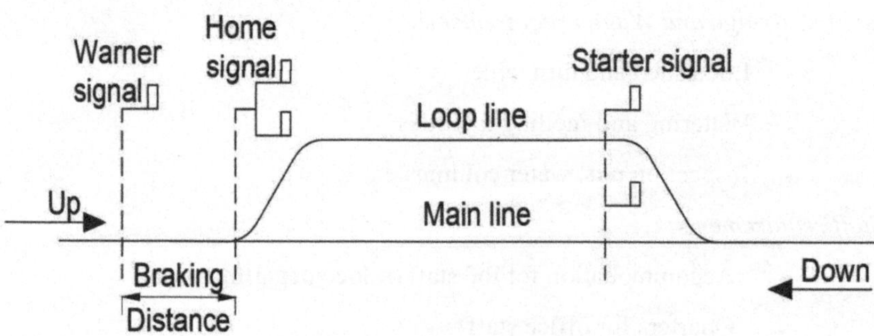

Fig. 5.26 Lay-out of a Class A station

Class 'B' stations: In Class 'B' Stations, the permission to approach is given to trains only after clearing the line up to an adequate distance beyond the outer signal of the station. The minimum requirements of signals at Class B station are:

i. Outer signal

ii. Home signal

iii. Starter signal

Fig. 5.27 shows the lay-out of a Class B station.

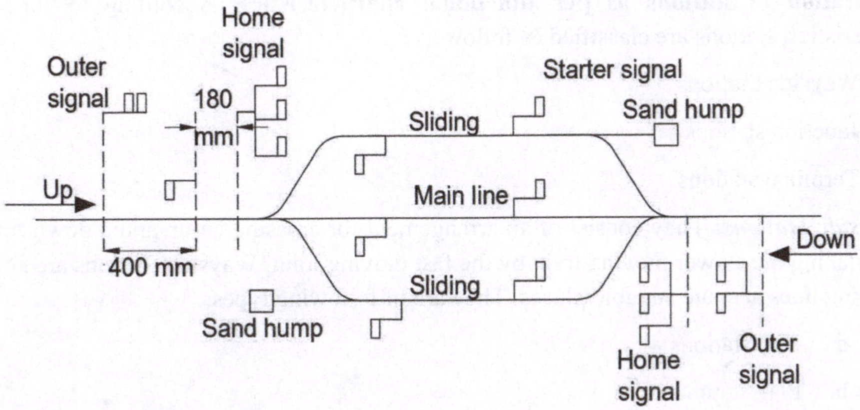

Fig. 5.27 Lay-out of a Class B station

Class 'C' Stations: They act as block huts where no trains are liable to stop. Class C stations are used to split a long block station such that the distance between successive trains is reduced. The minimum requirements of signals at Class C station are:

i. Home signal

ii. Warner signal(See Fig. 5.28)

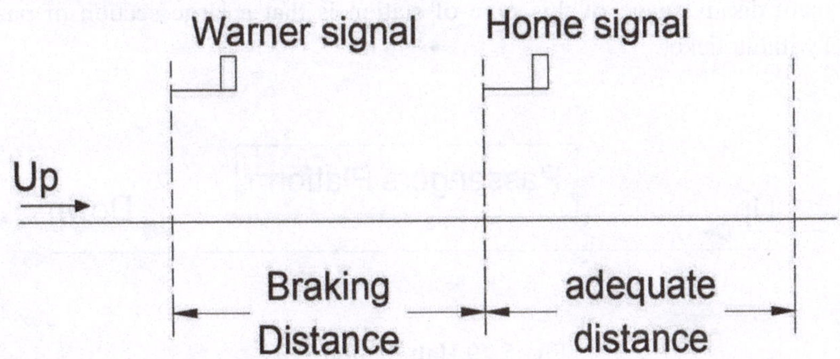

Fig. 5.28 Lay-out of a Class C station

Non-Block Stations: They are the stations located between two consecutive block stations which are also called Class 'D' or 'flag' stations. Non-block stations are neither telegraphically connected with any adjacent block stations nor have any signal or staff to control the movement of trains.

Special Class Stations: They are stations which are not covered under Class A, B, C and D.

Classification of stations as per functional characteristics: According to functional characteristics, stations are classified as follows:

i. Wayside Stations

ii. Junction stations

iii. Terminal stations

(i) Wayside Stations: They consist of an arrangement for crossing an up and a down train or for overtaking the slower moving train by the fast moving train. Wayside Stations are situated on running lines at some suitable places. They are of following types:

a. Halt stations

b. Flag stations

c. Crossing stations

Halt stations: A halt station (see Fig.5.29) is a stopping place of the simplest kind on a railway line. It is usually a rail level platform only with a name board at either end of it. There is neither yard nor station building/staff. Some selected local trains stop at halts to entrain and detrain passengers. The tickets to the passengers of these trains are issued by T.T.E. Separate compartment is provided for the issue of tickets in such trains. These types of stations are provided on light traffic and long block sections. The main disadvantage of this type of station is that a large section of passengers travel without ticket.

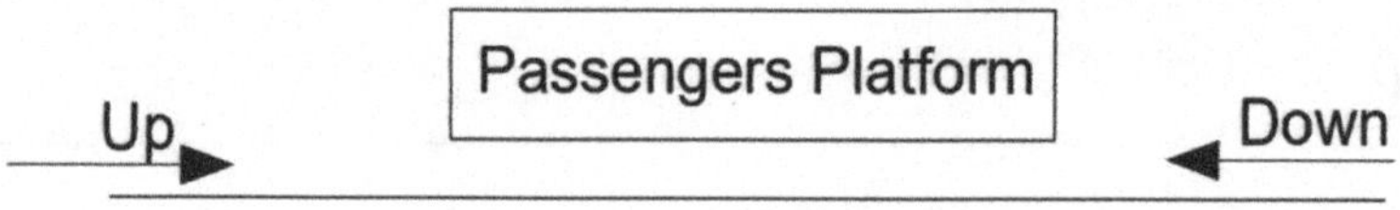

Fig. 5.29 Halt Station

Flag stations: These stations are similar to halt, but have buildings and staff. There are no arrangements for controlling movement of trains and crossing facilities. On controlled sections, a flag station has got communication with stations on either side. A flag station is usually provided with a small waiting hall and booking office, platforms with benches and with drinking water arrangements. Some of the flag stations have sidings in the form of loops. These stations are called flag stations, because the movement of trains are controlled by showing flags.Typical layout of a flag station is shown in Fig. 5.30.

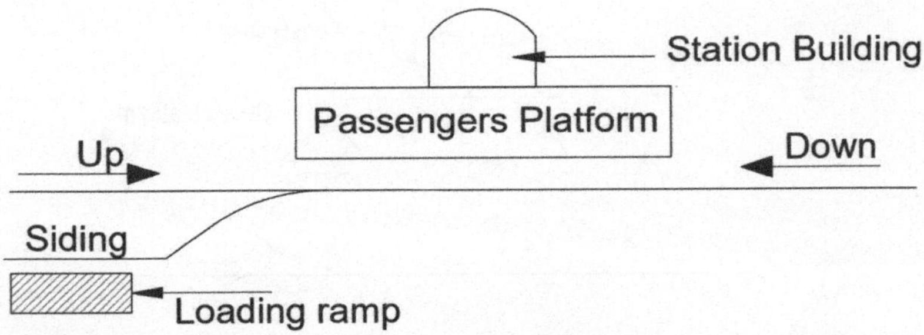

Fig. 5.30 Flag Station

Crossing Stations: These stations have facilities for crossing of an up and down train. Crossing stations are provided with one loop line so that when one train is standing on the loop, the other train can cross it. The loop line may or may not have dead end sidings. See Fig. 5.31.

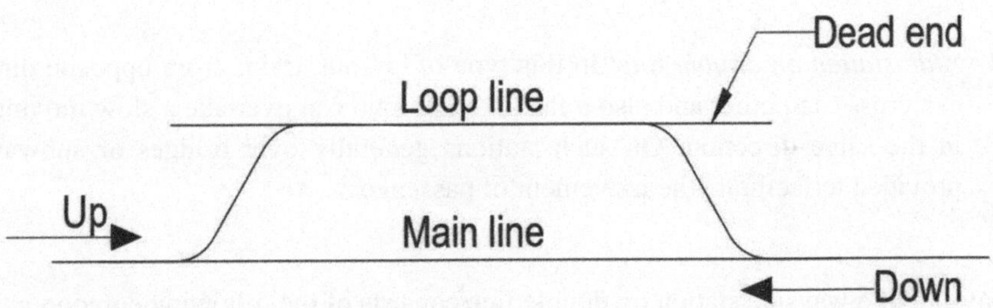

Fig. 5.31 Crossing Station

By providing different types of arrangements for crossing and overtaking trains, wayside station (crossing station) lay-outs are provided in the following ways:

i. *Wayside station on single line:* This is the simplest lay-out of a wayside station which consists of the following components:

   a. A through or main line

   b. A loop line

   c. A passenger platform and station building

   d. A goods loop

   e. A goods platform and shed

The lay-out is shown in Fig. 5.32.

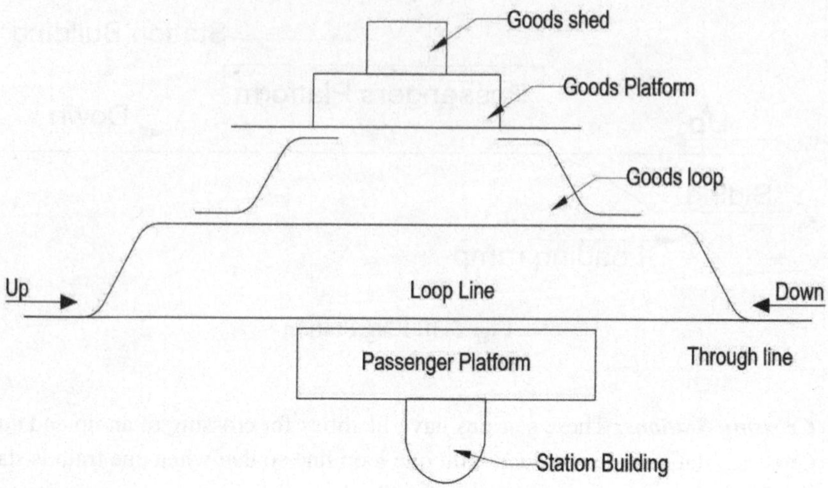

Fig. 5.32 Lay-out of a wayside station on single line track

iii) *Wayside station on double line*: In this type of lay-out, trains from opposite direction can cross each other and also a fast moving train can overtake a slow moving train in the same direction. On such stations generally over bridges or subways are provided to facilitate the movement of passengers.

The lay-out of a wayside station on double line consists of the following components:

a. Two main lines

b. A passenger platform and station building and an island platform

c. An over bridge

d. A goods loop

e. A cross over

f. A refuge line

The lay-out is shown in Fig. 5.33.

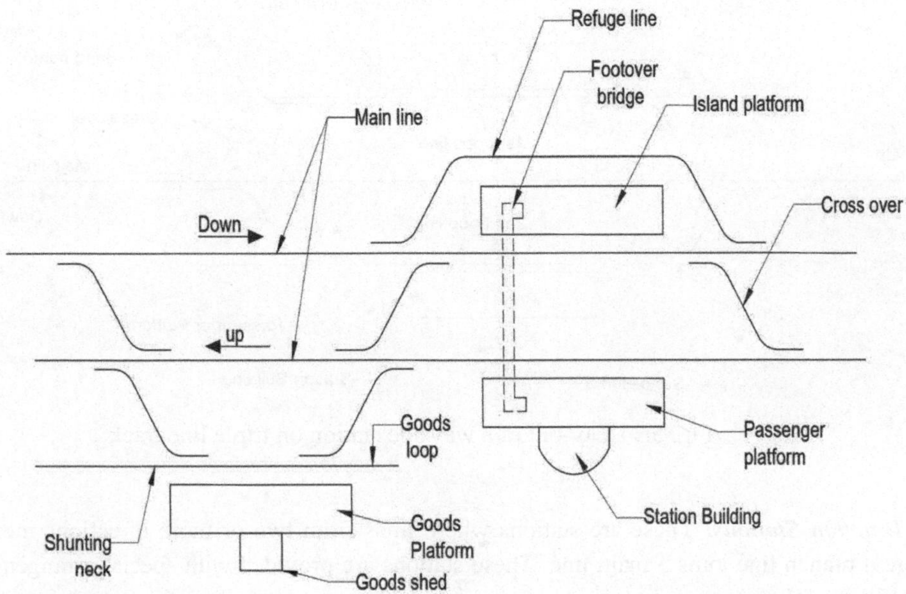

Fig. 5.33 Lay-out of a wayside station on double line track

ii. *Wayside station on triple line:* In this type of lay-out, a main line has two loop lines on either side. This arrangement facilitates simultaneous reception of all up trains in one line and down trains in other line. The lay-out of a wayside station on triple line consists of the following components:

a. One main line

b. Two loop lines

c. One or more passenger platforms and a station building

d. Cross over

e. Sand hump

The lay-out is shown in Fig. 5.34.

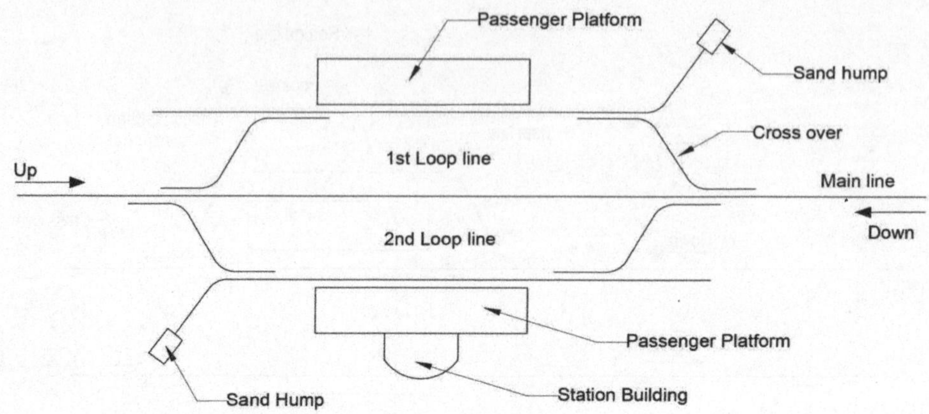

Fig. 5.34 Lay-out of a wayside station on triple line track

(ii) Junction Stations: These are stations where lines from two or more directions meet or where a branch line joins a main line. These stations are provided with special arrangements to fulfill the following requirements:

a. To facilitate the interchange of traffic between main and branch lines

b. To change the direction of engines

c. To repair and clean the train

The simplest lay-out of a junction station is shown in Fig. 5.35, where two trains, one from main line and one from branch line, can be received simultaneously.

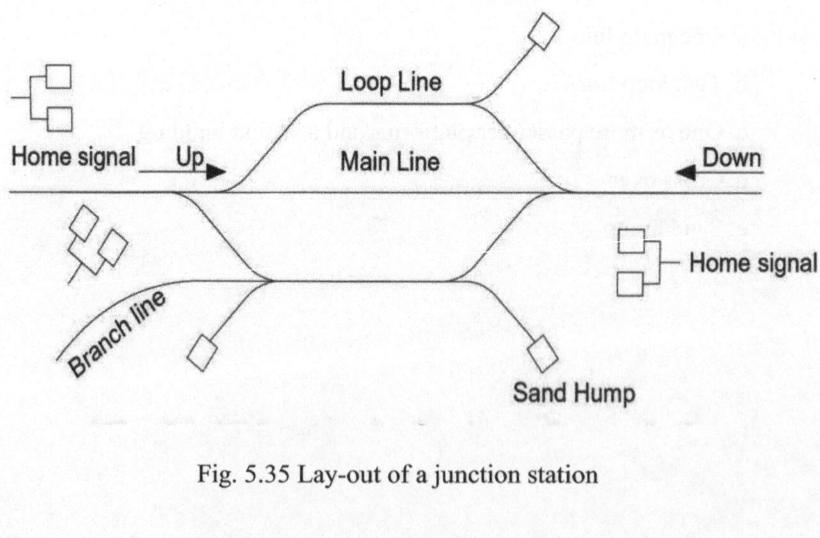

Fig. 5.35 Lay-out of a junction station

(ii) Terminal Stations: These are stations to which a railway line or one of its branches terminates or ends. The facilities provided at a terminal station are:

SCAN ME
for
Classification of
Railway Stations

a. Turn-table or triangle for changing the direction of the engine

b. Fuelling, watering and cleaning of engine

c. For dealing with goods traffic

All types of facilities are provided on main terminal stations, but only required facilities are provided at branch line terminal stations. At the ends to stop trains without much damage in case of brake failure, hydraulic buffers are provided. Ticket office, restaurants, etc. are also provided in the circulating area. Fig. 5.36 shows the layout of a terminal station with several platforms.

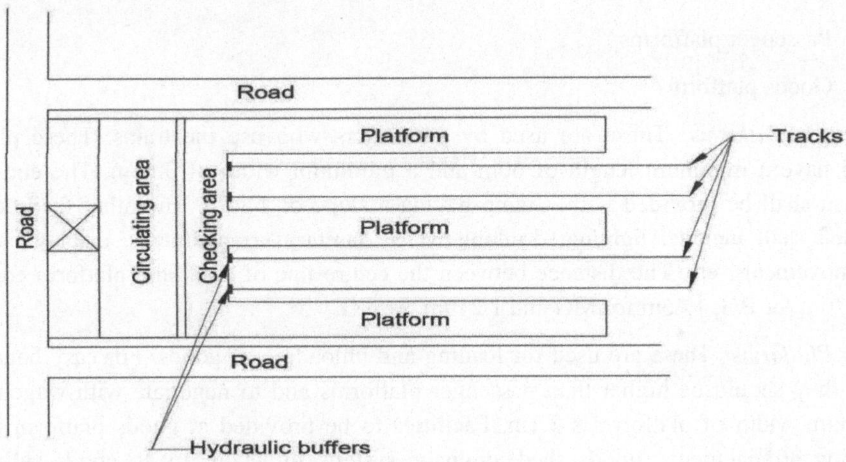

Fig. 5.36 Lay-out of a terminal station

5.5.4 Selection of Site for Railway Stations

The location of stations plays a vital role in the safe and efficient operation of train traffic. They should be located at suitable sites which are properly planned to provide maximum facilities and comfort to the passengers and railway staff. The following are the points to be considered in the selection of site for a railway station:

i. The site should be on a fairly level ground.

ii. It should have adequate drainage facility.

iii. It should have adequate land for the provision of single or double track, additional line, platforms, station building, staff quarters and for future development.

iv. It should have availability of unskilled and skilled labour for different trades required for construction.

v. It should have facilities of water supply, electricity, etc. for labour involved during construction.

vi. It should be situated on a straight portion of track, having no sharp curves in the approaches too.

vii. It should have proximity to town or village to be served.

viii. It should enable to construct the station building with minimum expenses and at the same time, satisfying the requirements of traffic, safety as well as aesthetics.

5.5.5 Platforms

A platform is the raised level surface from where passengers board and alight from trains or loading and unloading of goods is done. Thus, the platforms are divided into two categories based on the function they serve:

i. Passenger platforms

ii. Goods platforms

Passenger platforms: These are used by passengers who use the trains. These platforms should have a minimum length of 60m and a minimum width of 3.66m. The ends of the platform shall be provided with a ramp having a slope of 1 in 6. The other facilities to be provided shall include: lighting, drinking water, sanitary arrangements, display boards of train movements, etc. The distance between the centre line of track and platform edge shall be 1.676m for BG, 1.46m for MG and 1.219m for NG.

Goods Platforms: These are used for loading and unloading of goods. For easy handling of goods they should be higher than passenger platforms and to negotiate with wagon floors. Minimum width of platform is 3.1m. Facilities to be provided at goods platform include: weighing arrangements, goods shed, drainage system, direct access to goods sidings and marshalling yard, etc.

5.6 RAILWAY STATION YARDS

A station yard is defined as a system of tracks laid out within limits for various purposes like receiving, sorting, making up trains, etc., over which movement of trains is controlled by prescribed rules, regulations and signals.

5.6.1 Types of Yards

Station yards are normally classified into the following types:

a. Passenger yards

b. Goods yards

c. Marshalling yards

d. Locomotive yards

Passenger yards: The main function of passenger yard is to deal with the reception and dispatch of passenger trains. It shall provide all the facilities for the safe movement and convenience of passengers. These yards are significant at terminal and junction stations where extra passenger bogies are accommodated, and cleaning, washing or storing is done. The main requirements of passenger yards are listed below:

a. Ticket booking office, enquiry office, cloak room, and luggage booking room.

b. Sufficient parking area for vehicles outside the station.

c. Signals for receiving and departure of both up and down trains.

d. Facilities for passing a through train at full speed without any interference.

e. Sufficient number of platforms with sidings.

f. Sufficient number of stabling lines, washing lines and sick lines.

g. Sufficient number of shunting necks for withdrawals and placement of rakes without causing interference to other trains.

h. Facilities for charging of train batteries.

Goods yards: The receiving, stalling, loading, unloading, and dispatch of goods wagons are allowed in a goods yard. Most goods yards deal with a full train load of wagons. At goods yards, sorting, marshalling, or reforming are not done normally, except in the case of a few wagons which are booked for that particular station or a wagon is considered "sick." Separate goods sidings are provided with the platforms for the loading and unloading of the goods being handled at a particular station. Goods yards are provided in all stations except flag stations. The main requirements of goods yards are listed below:

a. Goods platforms for loading and unloading of goods.

b. Approach roads to each platform for movement of trucks.

c. Sufficient number of godowns for storage of goods.

d. Weighing machines, cranes and loading gauge for handling goods.

e. Booking office for goods.

f. Gathering lines with dead end sidings provided with buffer stops.

Marshalling Yards: Trains are received, sorted, and new trains are formed at a yard known as a marshalling yard, before being sent to various locations. In essence, these yards serve as distribution hubs. From several stations, this yard receives loaded and unloaded freight wagons and these are separated, sorted out, properly marshalled, and finally dispatched as full trains to various destinations. The marshalling of trains is done in such a way that the wagons can be conveniently detached without much shunting in transit at wayside stations. Marshalling yards are very expensive in construction and maintenance.

Functions of marshalling yards: Marshalling yards serve the following functions at the specified locations within the yard itself.

i) Receptions of trains - Trains are received in the reception yards with the help of various lines.

ii) Sorting of trains - Trains are normally sorted with the help of a hump with a shunting neck and sorting sidings.

iii) Departure of trains- Trains depart from departure yards where various lines are provided for this very purpose. Separate yards may be provided to deal with up and down traffic as well as through trains, which need not be sorted out.

Drawbacks of Marshalling yards: The following are the drawbacks of marshalling yards:

i. Traffic congestion at approaches to the yard due to continuous shunting work in the yard.

ii. Delay in transit of wagons

iii. Damage of wagons while shunting

A marshalling yard should be so designed that there is minimum detention of wagons in the yard and as such, sorting can be done as quickly as possible. Depending on the amount of traffic, these yards should have the essential amenities like a long shunting neck, properly designed hump, a braking system in the form of mechanical retarders, etc. The following points should be kept in mind while designing a marshalling yard.

a. Through traffic should be received and dispatched as expeditiously as possible, avoiding any idle time.

b. There should be a unidirectional movement of the wagons as far as possible and no conflicting movement of wagons and engines in the various parts of the yard.

c. The leads that permit the movement of wagons and train engines should be kept as short as possible.

d. There should be good lighting.

e. There should be adequate scope for the future expansion.

Types of Marshalling yards: Marshalling yards are of following three types:

i. Flat yard

ii. Gravity yard

iii. Hump yard

i) Flat yard: In this type of yard, all the tracks are laid almost level and the sorting of wagons is carried out with the help of shunting engines. This method is costly, as it involves frequent shunting, and the time required is also more as the engine has to traverse the same distance twice. This arrangement is adopted where space available is limited.

ii) Gravity yard: In this type of yards, the tracks are laid at suitable gradients so that wagons move under gravity. This is an ideal one, but very rarely constructed due to the unfavourable topography of the site. Manual wagon brakes are used to control the movement of wagons.

iii) Hump yard: In this type, a hump is constructed. Wagons are pushed up to the top of the hump with the help of engines from where they slide down and reach the sidings under the effect of gravity. Hump yards are more popular, because shunting operation is quicker than that of flat or gravity yards. The gradients commonly adopted are shown in the Fig. 5.37. The topography of the location of the yard also plays an important role in deciding the gradient. The speed of the wagons is to be regulated to ensure that they are kept in a stable condition while doing the sorting in order to avoid damages to wagons.

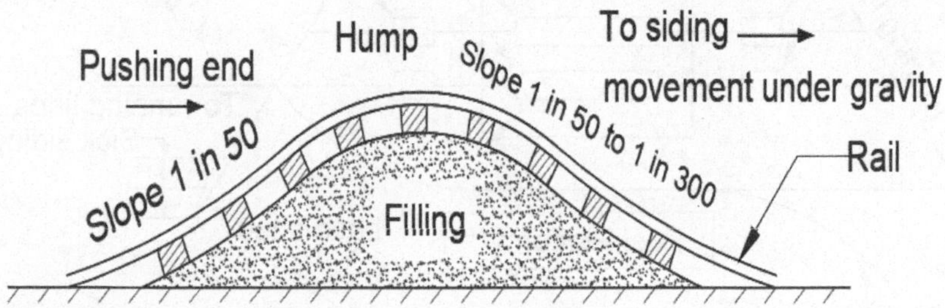

Fig. 5.37 Hump yard

SCAN ME
for
Types of Railway Yards

Lay-out of marshalling yards: The ideal lay-out of a marshalling yard consists of reception sidings, sorting sidings and departure sidings. Reception sidings are generally laid in the form of a grid and their lengths are kept equal. These are used to receive incoming trains where they wait for the shunting operations. Sorting sidings are used for shunting operations. The number of destinations for which the trains are to be assembled determines how many lines should be included in the sorting sidings. Each sorting line is kept around 15 to 20% longer than the length of a typical train so that there is some space behind the wagons. The layout of the sorting yard may be of the ladder or the balloon type. Departure sidings are similar to reception sidings. The number of lines to be included in a departure siding depends upon the number of trains proposed to be dispatched from the yard and on the frequency of their departure.

Whenever a wagon or coach becomes defective, it is marked 'sick' and taken to sick lines /sidings in the sick line yards for repair. Adequate facilities are provided in the sick line yards for the repair of coaches and wagons viz. examination pits, crane arrangements, train examiner's office and workshop, etc.

Locomotive yards: This is the yard where the locomotives are kept. In this yard, there are facilities for fueling, inspecting, repairing, and watering locomotives. The yard layout is designed depending upon the number of locomotives required to be housed in the locomotive shed. Sufficient number of tracks leading the engine to engine shed, ash pit, inspection pit, repair shed, turn table etc. are provided. Adequate water supply for washing the locomotives and servicing them is made available here. Typical layout of loco shed is shown in Fig. 5.38.

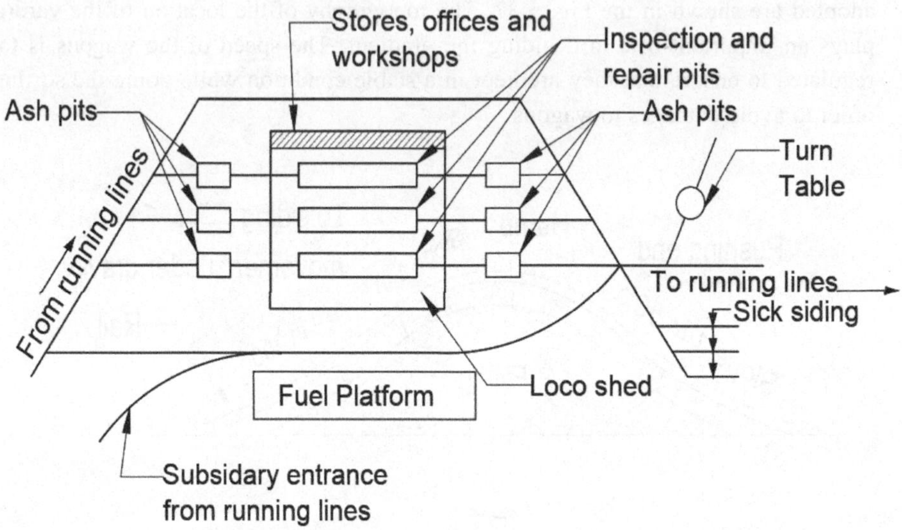

Fig. 5.38 Locomotive Yard

5.7 TRACK MAINTENANCE

Track maintenance is intended to keep the track structure in a serviceable condition as long as possible and as best as practicable. The track formation, side slopes, ballast, sleepers, rails, fixtures and fastenings, etc. get damaged due to the repeated movement of trains and under adverse climatic conditions. Poor or faulty maintenance results in in the drastic reduction not only in the useful life of the track structure, but also, in the safety to life of the public.

Even if the tracks are well designed and constructed, they may require periodic maintenance of its components. Railway track can be maintained by conventional manual labour or by modern methods using machines or by a combination of machines and manual labour. The extent of maintenance depends upon the importance of the track, intensity of traffic, topographical and geological conditions of the area in which the track is located.

5.7.1 Necessity of Track Maintenance

In order to run trains safely at the maximum permissible speed and to give passengers a reasonable level of riding comfort, the railway track must be properly maintained. The necessity of track maintenance arises due to following reasons:

(i) The packing under the sleepers becomes loose and the track geometry gets disturbed because of the constant movement of heavy and fast trains. The gauge, alignment, longitudinal and cross levels thus get affected adversely, which may result in derailment.

(ii) Fast moving trains cause vibrations and impacts that make track fittings to become loose leading to heavy wear and tear of the track and its components.

(iii) Because of the weathering effect of rain, water, sun and sand, the track and its components get deteriorated.

5.7.2 Classification of Track Maintenance

Maintenance operations of railway track can be divided into following categories:

i. Routine or periodic maintenance
ii. Special repairs

(i) ***Routine or periodic maintenance:*** This type of maintenance is carried out on railway tracks either daily or periodically.

Daily maintenance is done by the departmental labour throughout the year. The labour so engaged is known as 'maintenance gang'. The track is divided into suitable sections of length 5 to 8 km, and each gang is in charge of one section to carry out the following works:

a. Upkeep of the track section by daily inspection
b. Tightening of fish bolts, keys, gibs, cotters, etc.
c. Cleaning of flange way clearances at turnouts, level crossings, etc.
d. Oiling of slide chairs at points and crossings.

Periodic Maintenance work is carried out by departmental labour after an interval of 2 to 3 years. A study about the causes of defects in (i) gauge and alignment of the track, (ii) level of rail, (iii) points and crossings is carried out. On the basis of the findings of the study, the remedial measures are taken to make the track in perfect condition. The routine maintenance works to be carried out are listed below:

To rectify the defects of:

a. Track alignment

b. Gauge

c. Track components

d. Rail surface

e. Points and crossings

f. Level crossings

g. Bridges and approaches

h. Tunnels

i. Drainage system

Special Repairs or Maintenance: This type of maintenance work is carried out in case of special problems or major issues attributed to the track failures, whenever necessary, such as train accident, natural disasters, etc. The maintenance jobs in such cases become even more complex than planning and designing a new railway track. They include:

i. Replacement of defective rails

ii. Replacement of defective sleepers

5.7.3 Tools Required for Track Maintenance and their functions

The various hand tools and machine tools used in track maintenance operations and their respective functions are listed below.

Hand Tools:

a. *Hammers*: To drive keys, spikes, nails, bolts and wedges.

b. *Jim crow:* To bend rails.

c. *Rail Tongs*: To lift up the rails.

d. *Spanners:* For tightening the nuts.

e. *Ballast Rake:* For handling of ballast.

f. *Spade*: For surface dressing, clearing coarse weeds, dragging soil and sand, manual excavation and opening of ballast for track maintenance.

g. *Pick axe:* For breaking road surface on level crossing gates.

h. *Pick beater*: For digging, loosening and breaking up hard and semi hardearth in between the sleepers, digging below the sleepers, packing small ballast under the sleepers and for creating space in between the ballast.

i. *Rail gauge*: To check the gauge of track.

j. *Crow Bar*: To take out dog spike from wooden sleepers and to lift the track for surfacing. It is also used for packing ballast and to correct the alignment.

k. *Pan mortar:* For filling ballast, earth and muck etc.

l. *Shovel:* To take up, removing and placing of ballast on the sleepers. Also used to remove earth from the track.

m. *Straight Bar with ball and point ends:* For slewing, sleeper spacing, handling of material, packing of sleepers.

n. *Bar claw:* As a lever for lifting of track.

o. *Tommy bar: T*o clean the gaps in between running rails and check rails, to create gap to accommodate the liners in between rail foot and sleeper, for aligning the fish bolt hole to rail hole to insert bolt.

p. *Wire claw:* To open or close the track by pulling the ballast inside or outside the rail foot, to fill the ballast or earth in pan mortar.

q. *Ballast screen:* For screening ballasts manually.

r. *Sleeper tongs*: To lift up the sleepers.

s. *Adzes:* To do adzing of timber sleepers.

t. *Lifting jacks:* To lift the track.

u. *Cant board:* To check the cant on curves.

v. *Rail roller*: For longitudinal movement of rail panels.

Some of the above-mentioned tools are shown in Fig. 5.39.

Spiking Hammer

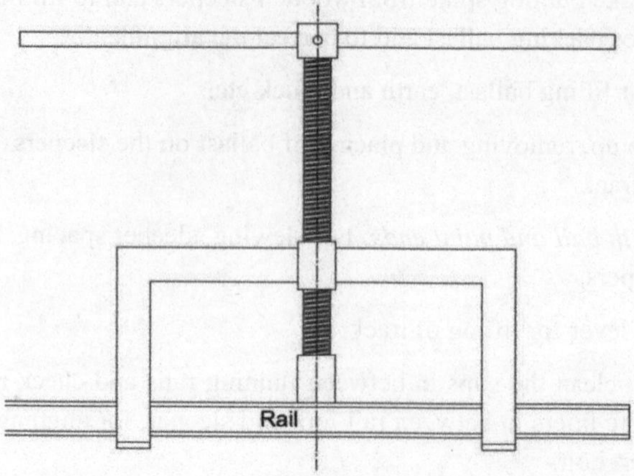

Jim crow

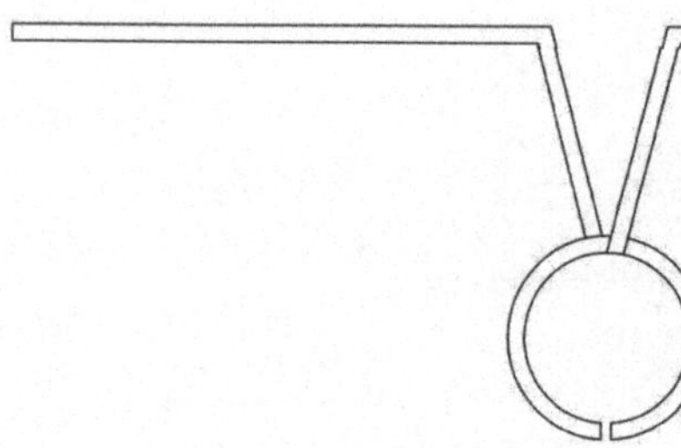

Rail Tongs

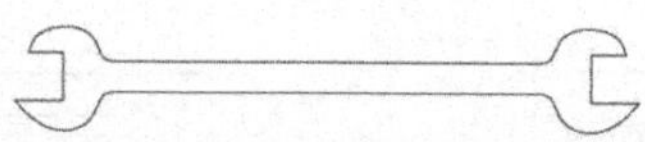

Double open ended spanner

Keyman/Patrolman's fish bolt spanners

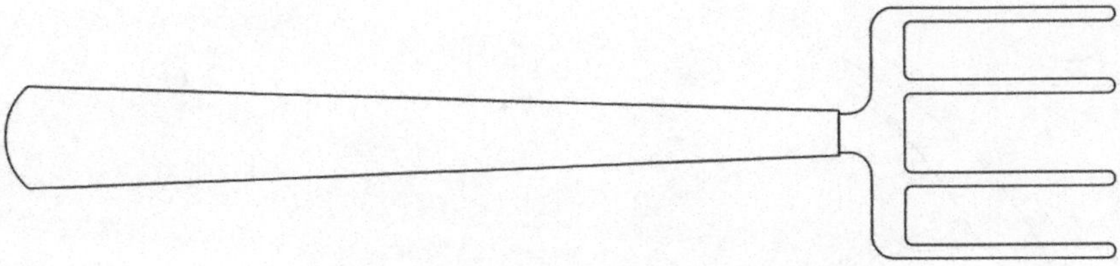

Ballast Rake

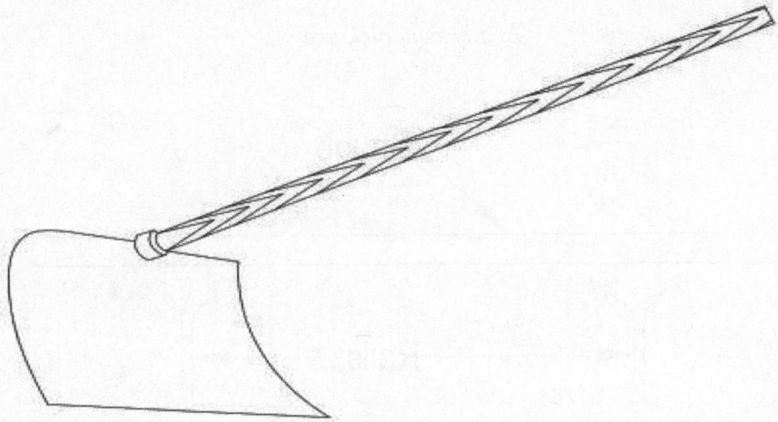

Spade

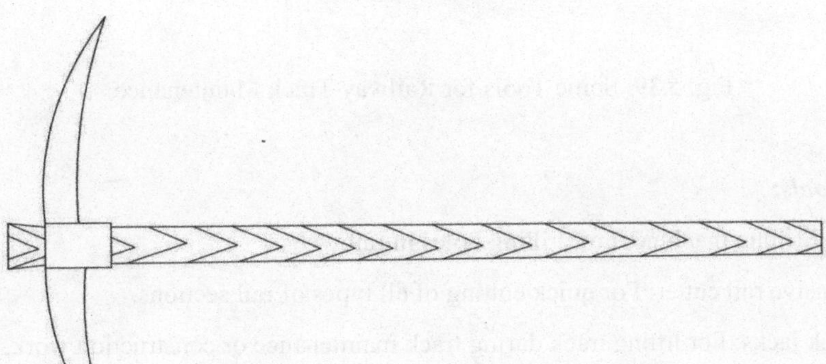

Pick Axe

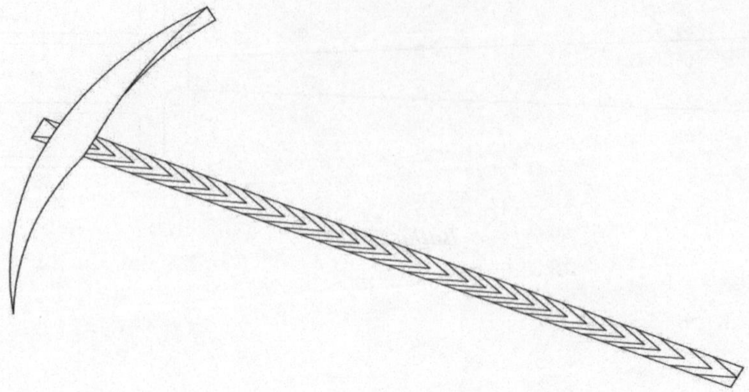

Beater cum pick axe

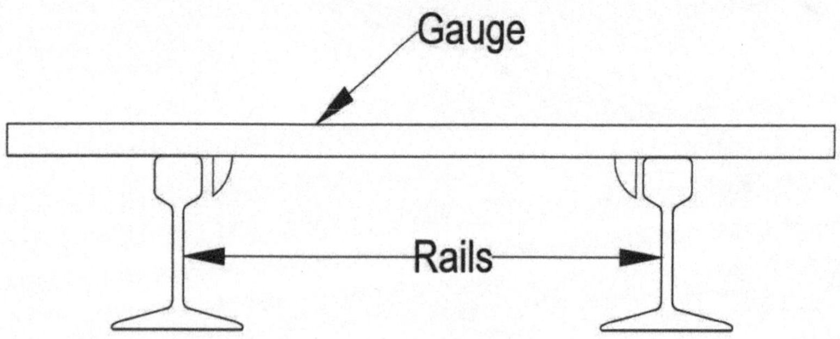

Rail Gauge

Fig. 5.39. Some Tools for Railway Track Maintenance

Machine Tools:

a. Rail drilling machine: For drilling holes in rail webs.
b. Abrasive rail cutter: For quick cutting of all types of rail sections.
c. Track jacks: For lifting track during track maintenance or construction work.
d. Hydraulic Rail Tensor: For rail de-stressing operations and for stress-free welding.
e. Rail Bender(Jim crow): For bending or de-kinking of flat-footed rails

f. Rail Joint Straightener: For straightening the dipped fish plated joint.

g. Rail creep adjuster: For creep adjustment of fish plated track.

h. Hydraulic sleeper spacer: For re-spacing of sleepers.

i. Concrete sleeper breaker

j. Concrete drilling machine: For drilling holes in concrete sleeper.

k. TRALIS- Portable Track Lifting and Slewing Device: For lifting and slewing of all types of tracks.

5.7.4 Organizational Set-up of Track Maintenance

The organizational set-up of the technical staff for track maintenance in Indian Railways is detailed as follows:

Organization at the Headquarters: In Indian Railways, the primary responsibility of track maintenance rest with its Civil engineering department headed by the Principal Chief Engineer, who is stationed at the head quarters of each zonal railway. He is assisted by a number of functional chief engineers such as, the Chief Track Engineer (CTE), the Chief Bridge Engineer (CBE), the Chief Engineer Planning and Design (CPDE), and the Chief Engineer General (CGE). A functional chief engineer is often in charge of one or more divisions and oversees their work on all civil engineering projects. Deputy Chief Engineers, Executive Engineers, etc., who support each Chief Engineer, are in charge of organizing, designing, and delivering the appropriate supplies as well as any other help the field engineers may need.

Organization at the Divisions: The division is in direct charge of maintaining the track and other civil engineering infrastructure. One or more Divisional Superintending Engineers (DSE) or Senior Divisional Engineers (Sr DEN) are there in each division, who are under the administrative control of the Divisional Railway Manager and technical control of the Chief Engineer. Details of the divisional structure for track maintenance are shown in Figure 5.40.

A division is under the complete control of a Divisional Superintending Engineers (DSE) or Senior Divisional Engineers (Sr DEN), who is supported by two to three Divisional Engineers (DENs), each of whom is in charge of around 1000 km of integrated track. Two to three Assistant Engineers (AENs), each in charge of around 400 km of track, support each DEN. Two to three Permanent Way Inspectors (PWI), who are directly in charge of track safety and upkeep, support an AEN in turn. One or more Inspectors of Works (IOW) who oversee all the works help each AEN as well. Numerous gangs work on maintaining the tracks; each gang is led by a mate who is assisted by 10 to 20 gangmen. A keyman from each gang daily inspects the track to ensure its safety.

The length of a railway track section under a gang depends upon:

i. Speed of the train

ii. Number of trains per day

iii. Type of sleepers in track

iv. Number of crossings and turnouts

v. Type of formation soil

vi. Length of sidings

vii. Age and condition of permanent way

The following sections provide a brief explanation of the responsibilities of AENs, PWIs, and other permanent way authorities.

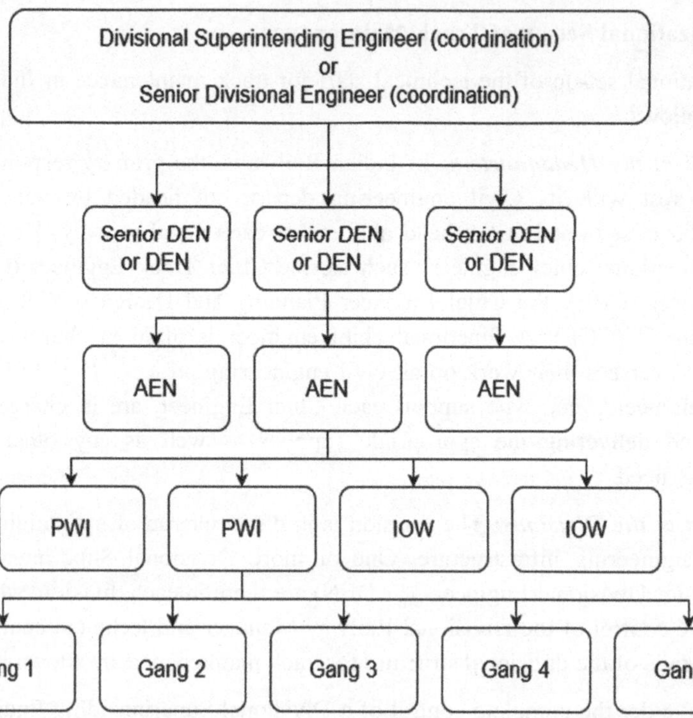

Figure 5.40 Divisional organization structure for track maintenance

5.7.5 Duties of Assistant Engineer (AEN)

Normally, the assistant engineer is in charge for the maintenance and safety of all works under his charge, for the precision, quality, and progress of any new work that may be undertaken and for the control of expenses with respect to the budget allotment.

The primary duties of an AEN are as follows:

a. Inspection and maintenance of track and related structures to ensure satisfactory and safe performance.

b. Preparation of plans and estimates, execution and assessment of work.

c. Verification of stores held by stockholders.

d. Submission of proposals for inclusion in the track renewal programme, estimates of revenue budget, and work programme.

5.7.6 Duties of Permanent Way Inspector (PWI)

Following are the main duties of Permanent Way Inspector:

a) Inspection and maintenance of track in a satisfactorily and safe condition.

b) Efficient execution of all works incidental to track maintenance, including track relaying work.

c) Accounting and periodical verification of the stores and tools in his charge.

d) Maintenance of land boundaries between stations as may be specified by the administration.

e) Ensuring safe movement of machine from siding to block section and back as per the provisions.

f) Execution and monitoring of track works.

g) Co-ordination with staff of other departments.

h) Training of permanent way officials.

i) Actions in case of emergencies such as accidents, breaches etc. and in extreme weather conditions.

j) Upkeep of station yards.

k) Observe track movement in yards especially at turnouts.

l) Inspection and preparation of inspection diagrams of tracks, points and crossings, curves, level crossings, bridges, tunnels, cuttings, etc.

m) Responsible for the safety of the track by way of being vigilant in locating faults promptly in the track and getting them repaired without delay.

5.7.7 Duties of Gang mate or Ganger

Gang mate is the head of the gang and he is responsible for the upkeep of the track. Following are the essential duties of the Gang mate:

The gang mate should:

i) See that the line is kept safe and in good running condition at all times.

ii) Ensure that every track maintainer is having the knowledge of safety rulesbefore deploying them on track.

iii) Ensure that safety equipment and signals are supplied to gangs and kept in good order.

iv) Ensure that all site equipment required are with trackmen at the work site.

v) Ensure custody and recording of muster and gang chart/diary.

vi) Observe sleeper packing during passage of train.

vii) Ensure safe custody of tools.

viii) Carryout patrolling during abnormal rainfall.

ix) Conduct weekly inspection of entire gang length.

x) Make relief arrangements in emergencies.

xi) Can stop or slow down a running train in case of emergency.

xii) Prevent all unauthorized construction in his section.

xiii) Ensure safety of his gang persons when on duty.

5.7.8 Duties of Key man

Key man is next to ganger in a gang. Following are the duties of Key man:

The key man should:

i) Inspect the entire beat once a day on foot, both the tracks and bridges.

ii) While walking, look for defects such as loose fish bolts on fish plates, fittings in switches and crossings, etc.

iii) Keep a special watch on rails and welds marked for observation.

iv) Attend one overhead equipment mast on one line thoroughly on everyday.

v) Carry out rail end examination and lubrication of fish plate joints with the assistance of track maintainers.

vi) Rectify and report serious defects noticed, if any, like broken rails, washed away ballast, etc. To higher authorities.

vii) Open out all joints once in a year and refit them.

viii) Upkeep and be in-charge of keyman book.

UNIT SUMMARY

Alignment

The fixing up of the centre line or route along which the railway track is constructed and upon which the train runs is defined as the alignment.

Factors governing rail alignment

a. Obligatory points
b. Traffic
c. Geometric design standards
d. Topography
e. Economics
f. Other considerations

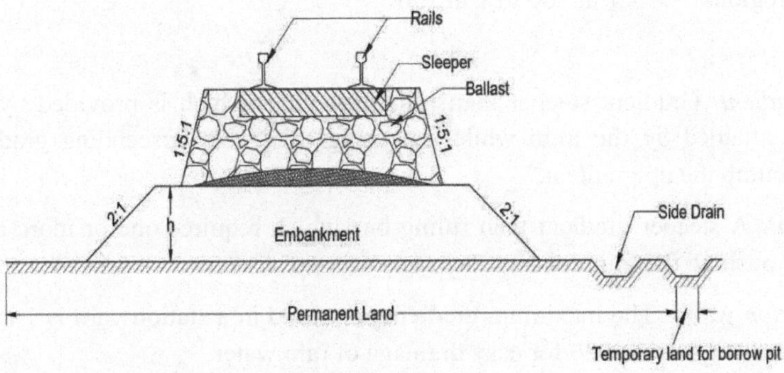

Typical cross section of permanent way showing its components

Railway Track Geometrics

a. Cross sectional elements (see section 5.2)
b. Gradients
c. Horizontal and vertical curves
d. Super elevation
e. Speed of train.

Gradient: The rate of rise or fall of the track. Expressed as vertical to horizontal distance or as percentage.

Factors affecting selection of gradient:

a. Nature of terrain
b. Drainage requirements

c. Hauling capacity of locomotives

d. Safety requirements

e. Total height to be covered.

Types of Gradient:

a. Ruling Gradient

b. Momentum Gradient

c. Pusher Gradient

d. Gradient at station yards

e. Compensated Gradient

Ruling Gradient: The maximum gradient allowed on a certain section of railway track.

In plains	1 in 150 to 1 in 200
In hilly regions	1 in 100 to 1 in 150.

Momentum Gradient: Gradient steeper than ruling gradient, which is provided by utilizing the momentum attained by the train while traversing along the descending gradient of a valley curve to climb the up gradient.

Pusher Gradient: A steeper gradient than ruling one which requires one or more additional locomotives for pushing the train load up the track.

Gradient at station yards: The maximum gradient permitted in a station yard is 1 in 400 and the minimum gradient is 1 in 1000 for easy drainage of rain water.

Compensated Gradient: At curves, in order to relieve from the additional resistance to traction, the ruling gradients should be eased by a certain percentage called 'grade compensation'. The grade compensation adopted in Indian Railways is 0.04/0.03/0.02 percent respectively for BG/MG/NG.

Types of Curves:

a. Horizontal curves - simple, compound, reverse

b. Vertical curves - summit and valley

c. Transition curves

Superelevation: The raising of outer rail with respect to inner rail.

Objects of providing superelevation:

a. To counteract the centrifugal force acting on the vehicle and thereby to avoid derailment and to reduce side wear of rails.

b. To distribute the train load equally on the two rails, reducing the top wear of rails and the maintenance cost.

c. To ensure safe and comfortable travel for train.

$$e = \frac{GV^2}{127R} m$$

$$e = \frac{1.676V^2}{127R} m \quad \text{For BG}$$

$$e = \frac{1.0V^2}{127R} m \quad \text{For MG}$$

$$e = \frac{0.762V^2}{127R} m \quad \text{For NG}$$

Limit of Superelevation: The maximum value of superelevation is 1/10th of gauge.

For BG track - 167.6 mm

MG track - 100 mm

NG track - 76.2 mm

Limits of superelevation for different gauges as recommended by I.R.B.

Sl. No.	Gauge	Maximum Superelevation when V<100kmph		Maximum Superelevation for high speeds		
		Under ordinary condition	Under special permission	120 kmph	160 kmph	200 kmph
1	BG	140 mm	165 mm	165 mm	185 mm	185 mm
2	MG	90 mm	100 mm	Not specified	Not specified	Not specified
3	NG	65 mm	76 mm	Not specified	Not specified	Not specified

Cant Deficiency: The numerical difference between the actual cant provided and equilibrium cant necessary for the maximum permissible speed on a curve.

Limits of cant deficiency for different gauges on Indian Railways

Sl. No.	Gauge	Cant Deficiency, mm	
		For speeds up	For speeds more than

		to 100 kmph	100 kmph
1	BG	76	100
2	MG	51	Not specified
3	NG	38	Not specified

Negative Cant: When a branch line takes off from a main line on a curve, an amount of cant deficiency is allowed and the outer rail of the branch line will be lower than inner rail, thereby the superelevation obtained for branch line is negative. Such type of superelevation is known as 'negative superelevation' or 'negative cant'.

Points and crossings: Functions:

a. To enable trains departing from a station to take the specified track for the destination

b. To receive the trains in the specified platform of the station.

c. To facilitate shunting and marshalling of trains from and to sidings, loco shed, washing lines, etc.

Turnout: The simplest combination of points and crossings which permits movement of train from a main track to a siding or branch track. It is 'right handed' or 'left handed' according as the diversion of the train from main track is towards right or left side of its facing direction.

Switch or point: Comprises of pair of tongue rails between two stock rails, connected to each other with the help of stretcher bars, so that they are operated simultaneously. It provides facility to divert the wheel passing over it in facing direction from one track to the other track.

Crossings: Device provided when two rails of different track cross each other at an angle in order to permit movement of wheel flange at the intersection of two running rails.

Types of crossings:

a. Acute angle crossing

b. Obtuse angle crossing

c. Square crossing

Inspection of Points and Crossings: The following checks are made periodically:

- The fixing of tongue rails with stock rail.
- The working of switch lever block, tapered washers and fasteners.
- The movement of splice rail.
- The required amount of tightness of nut-bolts and other fittings.
- Creep of Stock.
- Wearing of rails.
- The packing of sleepers and ballast.

- Special care for drainage.
- Alignment of track.
- Interlocking connections.

Track Junctions: Formed by combining points and crossings with curved and straight lengths of tracks to transfer the trains from one track to another or to enable trains to cross the other crossing track.

Types of Track Junctions:

a. Turnout

b. Acute angle crossing

c. Obtuse angle (diamond) crossing

d. Square crossing

e. Cross-over

f. Slips

g. Scissors cross over

h. Gauntlet track

i. Triangle track

j. Gathering lines or ladder track.

Stations: A place on a railway line where (i) passengers and goods are booked and dealt with, (ii) watering and cooling of engines is done, (iii) changing of running staff, sorting of wagons, and control of train movements are carried out and (iv) where an authority to proceed is given to the trains.

Purpose of Railway Station:

a. Boarding and alighting of passengers.

b. Loading and unloading of the goods or parcels.

c. Control the movement of trains.

d. Enable the trains to cross each other in case of single line section.

e. Enable the faster trains (Super fast, Rajadhani etc.) to overtake the slower trains.

f. Enable the locomotives to fill fuel, water or coal.

g. Attaching or detaching of coaches and wagons to trains.

h. Provide facilities for changing of engines and crew/staff.

i. To provide facilities and hold the passengers in case of emergencies like floods and accidents etc., when traffic is disrupted.

Requirements of Railway Station

Passenger requirements:

- Enquiry office and reservation office
- Platforms for passengers and goods
- Waiting halls and retiring rooms
- Refreshment rooms, tea stalls, book stalls, etc.
- Bathrooms and toilets
- Drinking water supply arrangements
- Lighting and ventilation
- Display boards for schedule of trains
- Announcement system for train arrivals and departures
- Guides to help illiterate/ differently abled passengers

Traffic requirements:

- Arrangement for controlling the movement of trains by signal.
- Sufficient space available for receiving, sorting and dispatching the trains.
- Sufficient number of platform for passengers and apparatus for issuing tickets.
- Goods Sheds and goods platforms
- Arrangement for inspection and maintenance of tracks

Loco, Carriage and Wagon requirements:

- Loco shed and turn table
- Watering and fuelling facilities
- Inspection pits, water columns etc.

Staff requirements:

- Accommodation for the staff of loco department
- Quarters for office staff
- Running rooms for train pilots and managers
- Canteen for staff, etc.

Types of Railway Stations:

As per operational characteristics:

a. Block Stations - Class A, B, C

b. Non-block stations - Class D

c. Special class stations

As per functional characteristics:

a. Wayside Stations: Halt stations, Flag stations, Crossing stations

b. Junction stations

c. Terminal stations

Selection of Site for Railway Stations: Factors to be considered

a. The site should be on a fairly level ground.

b. It should have adequate drainage facility.

c. It should have adequate land for the provision of single or double track, additional line, platforms, station building, staff quarters and for future development.

d. It should have availability of unskilled and skilled labour for different trades required for construction.

e. It should have facilities of water supply, electricity, etc. for labour involved during construction.

f. It should be situated on a straight portion of track, having no sharp curves in the approaches too.

g. It should have proximity to town or village to be served.

h. It should enable to construct the station building with minimum expenses and at the same time, satisfying the requirements of traffic, safety as well as aesthetics.

Platforms: Types

a. Passenger platforms

b. Goods platforms

Types of Station Yards:

a. Passenger yards

b. Goods yards

c. Marshalling yards

d. Locomotive yards

Functions of marshalling yards:

a. Reception of trains

b. Sorting of trains

c. Departure of trains

Drawbacks of Marshalling yards:

a. Traffic congestion at approaches to the yard due to continuous shunting work in the yard.

b. Delay in transit of wagons

c. Damage of wagons while shunting

Types of Marshalling yards:

a. Flat yard

b. Gravity yard

c. Hump yard

Necessity of Track Maintenance:

a. Due to constant movement of heavy and fast moving trains, the packing under the sleepers gets loose and track geometry gets disturbed. The gauge, alignment, longitudinal and cross levels thus get affected adversely and safety of the track is likely to be jeopardized.

b. Due to vibrations and impact of fast moving trains, fittings of track get loose and there is heavy wear and tear of track and its components.

c. The track and its components get worn out due to weathering effect of rain, water, sun and sand.

Classification of Track Maintenance

a. Routine or periodic maintenance

b. Special repairs

Tools Required for Track Maintenance and their functions:

Hand Tools:

a. *Hammers* : To drive keys, spikes, nails, bolts and wedges.

b. *Jim crow:* To bend rails.

c. *Rail Tongs*: To lift up the rails.

d. *Spanners:*For tightening the nuts.

e. *Ballast Rake:* For handling of ballast.

f. *Spade*: For surface dressing, clearing coarse weeds, dragging soil and sand, manual excavation and opening of ballast for track maintenance.

g. *Pick axe:* For breaking road surface on level crossing gates.

h. *Pick beater*: For digging, loosening and breaking up hard and semi hardearth in between the sleepers, digging below the sleepers, packing small ballast under the sleepers and for creating space in between the ballast.

i. *Rail gauge*: To check the gauge of track.

j. *Crow Bar*: To take out dog spike from wooden sleepers and to lift the track for surfacing. It is also used for packing ballast and to correct the alignment.

k. *Pan mortar:* For filling ballast, earth and muck etc.

l. *Shovel:* To take up, removing and placing of ballast on the sleepers. Also used to remove earth from the track.

m. *Straight Bar with ball and point ends:* For slewing, sleeper spacing, handling of material, packing of sleepers.

n. *Bar claw:* As a lever for lifting of track.

o. *Tommy bar:* To clean the gaps in between running rails and check rails, to create gap to accommodate the liners in between rail foot and sleeper, for aligning the fish bolt hole to rail hole to insert bolt.

p. *Wire claw:* To open or close the track by pulling the ballast inside or outside the rail foot, to fill the ballast or earth in pan mortar.

q. *Ballast screen:* For screening ballasts manually.

r. *Sleeper tongs*: To lift up the sleepers.

s. *Adzes:* To do adzing of timber sleepers.

t. *Lifting jacks:* To lift the track.

u. *Cant board:* To check the cant on curves.

v. *Rail roller*: For longitudinal movement of rail panels.

Machine Tools:

a. Rail drilling machine: For drilling holes in rail webs.

b. Abrasive rail cutter: For quick cutting of all types of rail sections.

c. Track jacks: For lifting track during track maintenance or construction work.

d. Hydraulic Rail Tensor: For rail de-stressing operations and for stress-free welding.

e. Rail Bender(Jim crow): For bending or de-kinking of flat-footed rails

f. Rail Joint Straightener: For straightening the dipped fish plated joint.

g. Rail creep adjuster: For creep adjustment of fish plated track.

h. Hydraulic sleeper spacer: For re-spacing of sleepers.

i. Concrete sleeper breaker

j. Concrete drilling machine: For drilling holes in concrete sleeper.

k. TRALIS- Portable Track Lifting and Slewing Device: For lifting and slewing of all types of tracks.

Organisational Set-up of Track Maintenance:

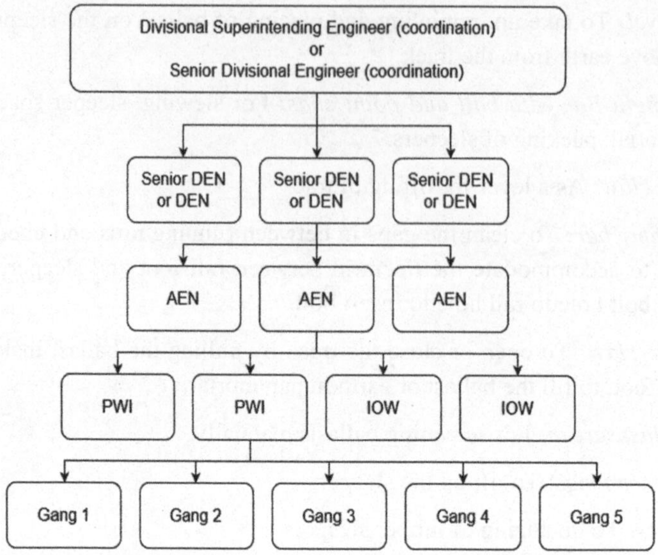

Duties of Assistant Engineer (AEN):

a. Inspection and maintenance of track and related structures to ensure satisfactory and safe performance.

b. Preparation of plans and estimates, execution and assessment of work.

c. Verification of stores held by stockholders.

d. Submission of proposals for inclusion in the track renewal programme, estimates of revenue budget, and work programme.

Duties of Permanent Way Inspector (PWI):

a) Inspection and maintenance of track in a satisfactorily and safe condition.

b) Efficient execution of all works incidental to track maintenance, including track relaying work.

c) Accounting and periodical verification of the stores and tools in his charge.

d) Maintenance of land boundaries between stations as may be specified by the administration.

e) Ensuring safe movement of machine from siding to block section and back as per the provisions.

f) Execution and monitoring of track works.

g) Co-ordination with staff of other departments.

h) Training of permanent way officials.

i) Actions in case of emergencies such as accidents, breaches etc. and in extreme weather conditions.

j) Upkeep of station yards.

k) Observe track movement in yards especially at turnouts.

l) Inspection and preparation of inspection diagrams of tracks, points and crossings, curves, level crossings, bridges, tunnels, cuttings, etc.

m) Responsible for the safety of the track by way of being vigilant in locating faults promptly in the track and getting them repaired without delay.

Duties of Gang mate or Ganger:

a. See that the line is kept safe and in good running condition at all times.

b. Ensure that every track maintainer is having the knowledge of safety rulesbefore deploying them on track.

c. Ensure that safety equipment and signals are supplied to gangs and kept ingood order.

d. Ensure that all site equipment required are with track men at the work site.

e. Ensure custody and recording of muster and gang chart/diary.

f. Observe sleeper packing during passage of train.

g. Ensure safe custody of tools.

h. Carryout patrolling during abnormal rainfall.

i. Conduct weekly inspection of entire gang length.

j. Make relief arrangements in emergencies.

k. Can stop or slow down a running train in case of emergency.

l. Prevent all unauthorized construction in his section.

m. Ensure safety of his gang persons when on duty.

Duties of Key man:

a. Inspect the entire beat once a day on foot, both the tracks and bridges.

b. While walking, look for defects such as loose fish bolts on fish plates, fittings in switches and crossings, etc.

c. Keep a special watch on rails and welds marked for observation.

d. Attend one overhead equipment mast on one line thoroughly on everyday.

e. Carry out rail end examination and lubrication of fish plate joints with the assistance of track maintainers.

f. Rectify and report serious defects noticed, if any, like broken rails, washed away ballast, etc. To higher authorities.

g. Open out all joints once in a year and refit them.

h. Upkeep and be in-charge of keyman book.

EXERCISES

Multiple Choice Questions

5.1. Track geometrics include

(a) Cross sectional elements (b) Gradient (c) curves (d) All of the above

5.2. The top width of track embankment is called

(a) Right-of-way (b) formation width (c) subgrade (d) none of these

5.3. Minimum formation width in embankment for single track as recommended by Indian Railways is

(a) 5.5 m (b) 6.1 m (c) 10.1 m (d) 10.7 m

5.4. The rate of rise or fall provided to the formation of a railway track is called

(a) gradient (b) superelevation (c) gauge (d) none of these

5.5. Recommended side slope for embankment of permanent way is

(a) 1: 1 (b) 1.5 : 1 (c) 2 : 1 (d) none of these

5.6. Grade compensation recommended for Broad Gauge on Indian Railways is

(a) 0.04 % (b) 0.03 % (c) 0.02 % (d) 0.01%

5.7. The gradient which requires more than one locomotive for pulling the train up a track is called

(a) Ruling gradient (b) Momentum gradient (c) Pusher gradient (d) Minimum gradient

5.8. Which type of the gradients given below is related with the valley curve having no stop signals?

(b) Ruling gradient (b) Momentum gradient (c) Pusher gradient (d) Minimum gradient

5.9. Maximum permissible value of superelevation for a Broad Gauge track on Indian Railways is

(a) 167.6 mm (b) 140 mm (c) 100 mm (d) 76.2 mm

5.10. Permissible value of cant deficiency for Broad Gauge for speed up to 100 kmph is

(a) 76 mm (b) 71 mm (c) 38 mm (d) 10 mm

5.11. Curves provided at the change of gradients are called

(a) Horizontal curve (b) Vertical curve (c) Compound curve (d) Transition curve

5.12. The raised elevation of outer rail above the inner rail at a horizontal curve is called

(a) Gradient (b) grade compensation (c) cant (d) cant deficiency

5.13. The difference between equilibrium cant required and actual cant is called

(a) Cant deficiency (b) negative cant (c) cant excess (d) none of these

5.14. Superelevation is

(a) $GV^2/(1.25R)$ (b) $GV^2/(1750R)$ (c) $GV^2/(127R)$ (d) $GV^2/(1.27R)$

5.15. Negative cant arises in case of

(a) Main and loop lines (b) Transition curves (c) similar flexure (d) contrary flexure

5.16. Maximum ruling gradient permitted in plain terrain in Indian Railways is

(a) 1 in 50 (b) 1 in 100 (c) 1 in 150 (d) 1 in 500

5.17. Maximum permissible gradient for station yard is

(a) 1 in 1000 (b) 1 in 500 (c) 1 in 400 (d) 1 in 300

5.18. The desirable gradient for a station yard is not to exceed

(a) 1 in 1000 (b) 1 in 500 (c) 1 in 400 (d)1 in 300

5.19. The tapered movable rail which is attached at or near end of a running rail is called

(a) Tongue rail (b) Stock rail (c) Lead rail (d) Point rail

5.20. The bent portion of rail used in front of nose of crossing which guides the train wheel in their proper route is called

(a) Splice rail (b) Wing rail (c) Check rail (d) Point rail

5.21. Obtuse angle crossing is also called

(a) V crossing (b) square crossing (c) diamond crossing (d) none of these

5.22. Frog is a

(a) Acute angle crossing (b) square crossing (c) Obtuse angle crossing (d) diamond crossing

5.23. The arrangement of track where a double line track is narrowed over a short distance is called

(a) Scissors cross over (b) Gauntlet track (c) triangle track (d) ladder track

5.24. Which of the following track arrangement can be used for changing the direction of engines?

(a) Ladder track (b) Gauntlet track (c) Scissors cross over (d) triangle track

5.25. When a number of lines are branched off from a main line in continuation of turnout, it is called

(a)Ladder track (b) Gauntlet track (c) Scissors cross over (d) triangle track

5.26. The combination of a tongue rail and stock rail is called

(a) Switch (b) crossing (c) split (d) throat

5.27. The untapered end of switch rail is called

(a) Heel of switch (b) toe of switch (c) throat of switch (d) none of these

5.28. The distance through which the toe of a tongue rail moves sideways when operated is called

(a) Heel divergence (b) throw of switch (c) flange way clearance (d) none of these

5.29. The distance between check rail and the adjacent face of a stock rail is called

(a) Heel divergence (b) flange way clearance (c)) throw of switch (d) none of these

5.30. _________ are provided to prevent the tendency of wheels of trains to climb over the crossing.

(a) Wing rails (b) lead rails (c) stock rails (d) check rails

5.31. The switch in which no tongue rail is provided is called

(a) Stub switch (b) fixed heel type split switch (c) loose heel type split switch (d) none of these

5.32. Which of the following switches has least lateral rigidity?

(a) Stub switch (b) fixed heel type split switch (c) loose heel type split switch (d) none of these

5.33. A place on the railway line at which permission to approach and authority to proceed are granted is called

(a) Block station (b) Non-block station (c) Junction station (d) Terminal station

5.34. A station where a branch line joins a main line is called

(a) Terminal station (b) block station (c) junction station (d)wayside station

5.35. The yard which provides facilities for receiving, loading and loading of goods is called

(a) Locomotive yard (b) goods yard (c) marshalling yard (d) none of these

5.36. The trains are received, sorted, new trains are formed and dispatched is called

(a) Goods yard (b) marshalling yard (c) locomotive yard (d) none of these

5.37. Hump yard is a type of

(a) Marshalling yard (b) goods yard (c) locomotive yard (d) none of these

5.38. Non-block stations are also called

(a) Class A (b) Class B (c) Class C (d) Class D

5.39. Flat yard is a type of

(a) Marshalling yard (b) goods yard (c) locomotive yard (d) none of these

5.40. The type of marshaling yard in which all sorting works are done by shunting engines is called

(a) gravity type b) hump type (c) flat type (d) none of these

5.41. The tool used to bend the rails is

(a) Rail tongs (b) crow bar (c) Jim crow (d) Tommy bar

5.42. The maintenance staff who upkeep the reports of progress of maintenance works and programs of rectification works is

(a) PWI (b) AEN (c) gang mate (d) Key man

5.43. The tool used to lift up the rails is

(a) Jim crow (b) rail tongs (c)rail gauge (d) pick axe

5.44. The tool used to align fish bolt hole to rail hole to insert bolts is

(a) Spanner (b) hammer (c) Tommy bar (d) cant board

5.45. The tool used to check the superelevation on curves is

(a) Rail gauge (b) cant board (c) rail roller (d) rail tongs

5.46. The tool used for longitudinal movement of rail panels is

(a) Rail tongs (b) Jim crow (c) Tommy bar (d) rail roller

Answers to Multiple Choice Questions

5.1 d), 5.2 b), 5.3 b), 5.4 a), 5.5 c), 5.6 a), 5.7 c), 5.8 b), 5.9 a), 5.10 a), 5.11 b), 5.12 c), 5.13 a), 5.14 c), 5.15 d), 5.16 c), 5.17 c), 5.18 a), 5.19 a), 5.20 b), 5.21 c), 5.22 a), 5.23 b), 5.24 d), 5.25 a), 5.26 a), 5.27 a), 5.28 b), 5.29 b), 5.30 d), 5.31 a), 5.32 a), 5.33 a), 5.34 c), 5.35 b), 5.36 b), 5.37 a), 5.38 d), 5.39 a), 5.40 c), 5.41 c), 5.42 a), 5.43 b) 5.44 c), 5.45 b), 5.46 d).

Short and Long Questions

Category I

5.1. What is meant by track alignment? What are the basic requirements of a good alignment?

5.2. Explain briefly various factors affecting track alignment.

5.3. Explain the necessity and significance of track alignment.

5.4. Draw a neat sketch of a double line Broad Gauge track in cutting and mark all its components.

5.5. Define gradient. What are the the purposes of providing gradient in railways?

5.6. Name different types of gradient used in railways and list the factors affecting the selection of gradient.

5.7. List the salient cross-sectional features of a permanent way along with their specifications used in Indian Railways.

5.8. What are the objects of providing transition curves?

5.9. What is meant by grade compensation? What are its specifications?

5.10. Define superelevation. What are the objects of providing superelevation on curves in railway tracks?

5.11. Derive a relationship of superelevation with gauge, speed and radius of curve.

5.12. Explain the method of providing superelevation in the field.

5.13. Define cant deficiency. What are its specifications?

5.14. Explain the term 'negative cant'.

5.15. What are the functions of points and crossings in railway track layout?

5.16. What is meant by a turnout? Enumerate its component parts and their functions.

5.17. What is a switch? What are its component parts? Discuss various types of switches.

5.18. What is meant by crossing? What are its component parts?

5.19. Sketch a diamond crossing and give its features.

5.20. Sketch a scissors crossover and a mark its parts.

5.21. Explain the purpose of providing railway stations. Discuss the various requirements of a railway station.

5.22. Describe the factors that influence the selection of site for a railway station.

5.23. How are the railway stations classified? Explain.

5.24. Explain the following with sketches: (a) Junction station (b) Terminal station.

5.25. What do you mean by a station yard? Discuss briefly different types of yards.

5.26. State the essential requirements of a goods yard.

5.27. What is a marshalling yard? What are its functions? Give its classification. Explain briefly.

5.28. What is a hump yard? Explain its functions.

5.29. Illustrate with neat sketch, the lay-out of a wayside station showing the location of necessary signals.

5.30. Differentiate the following: (a) Junction station and Terminal station (b) gravity yard and hump yard.

5.31. What are the main requirements of a locomotive yard?

5.32. Explain the necessity and significance of track maintenance.

5.33. List the important tools used in track maintenance operations and their functions.

5.34. Enumerate the duties of (a) permanent way inspector (b) gang mate and (c) Key man.

Category II

5.1. Draw a typical cross section of a single line Broad Gauge permanent way on embankment and mark all its components. Also, discuss in brief the basic functions of each component.

5.2. Explain the necessity of providing extra width of gauge at horizontal curves in railway tracks. How is it calculated?

5.3. Draw a neat sketch of right hand or left left hand turnout and show its component parts.

5.4. What are the essential requirements of a good crossing? Discuss various types of Crossings.

5.5. Draw a neat sketch showing the following components of a railway crossing: wing rail, check rail, angle of crossing, and distance block.

5.6. Sketch and state the circumstances in which the following lay-outs are used: (a) Gathering lines (b) Gauntlet track (c)Triangle.

5.7. What are the different types of track maintenance operations? Explain briefly.

5.8. Sketch and explain the organizational set-up of track maintenance.

PRACTICAL

5P1 Study on Rail fixtures and fastenings

C. Visit a nearby railway station and the track laid there. Examine by visual inspection the various fittings in the track, including different types of rail joints, fixtures at points and crossings, turnouts, track junctions and prepare a detailed report with the support of photographs.

5P2 Study on Railway stations and yards

D. Visit one or two railway stations of different classes, and also different types yards and observe how trains are operated there. Prepare a detailed report with the support of photographs.

KNOW MORE

Activity:

5.1 Visit a Marshalling yard and observe how trains are handled there and take photographs of their operations. Prepare a detailed report on it supported by photographs.

5.2 Visit a railway station and observe how the track maintenance is being done by key man and gang mate. Also, enquire those maintenance staff about the problems /issues, if any, they are facing. Discuss possible suggestions for improvement, if required, and prepare a detailed report thereon.

Some More Interesting Facts about Railways:

World's Railways

The fastest passenger train in the world:

Shanghai's Maglev (magnetic levitation) train, connecting Shanghai Pudong International Airport with Longyang Road Station in the outskirts of Pudong runs at a speed of 267mph (430km/h).

The world's slowest train:

Switzerland's Glacier Express takes eight hours to cover a distance of just 181 miles (291km), because it passes through Oberalp Pass, the highest point of the journey, and the Landwasser Viaduct, a six-arch bridge which stands at 213 feet (65m) and plunges straight into a tunnel that leads through the mountain, offers stunning views of nature.

The steepest funicular railway:

The world's steepest funicular railway is also in Switzerland, which runs from the town of Schwyz up 110m (328ft) to Alpine village of Stoos. Passengers can stay upright on the inclined floor with the help of specially constructed cylindrical carriages which would automatically adjust to the steep slope.

The longest distance to travel by train:

From Porto in Portugal to Singapore, crossing two continents, is the longest train journey, covering a distance of around 10,000 miles (16,000km), via Beijing, Vietnam, Cambodia and Thailand. The full journey would take at least 12 days to complete.

The longest direct train service:

It is the Trans-Siberian route from Moscow to Vladivostok,which covers 5,772 miles (9,289km), crosses eight time zones and *takes 166 hours or nearly a full week*. The train has 142 stops and passes through 87 cities and towns.

The busiest train station:

It is Shinjuku Station in Tokyo, Japan, with over 3.6 million passengers passing through daily (before the COVID-19 pandemic). The station has more than 200 exits and is consists of five smaller stations.

The highest railway track:

It is the Qinghai–Tibet railway, from Golmud to Lhasa, travelling at an extreme altitude. Only five pairs of passenger trains run along this track, as each has to be specially equipped for high elevation such as turbo charging of locomotives, oxygen supply for each passenger and a doctor's service in each train. The Tanggula Pass (16,640 feet above sea level), the highest point in the world that can be reached on a train is in this line.

The longest straight stretch of railway line:

It is in the 'Indian Pacific train service', the world's longest straight stretch of 303 miles (487 km), which runs in Australia's east–west rail corridor between Sydney on the shore of the Pacific Ocean, and Perth, on the shore of the Indian Ocean, where it passes through the scenic Blue Mountains as well as across the famous Nullarbor Plains.

The most remote train station:

It is also in the above straight stretch, called 'Cook', which is a ghost town with only four residents. The trains stop here to refuel and serve as a rest place for the drivers; but the station is 62 miles (100km) away from the nearest road and around 513 miles (826km) from the nearest city.

Ghost trains (Trains running on disused lines):

Due to complicated legal procedures required to shut a railway line in the UK, it is cheaper to simply run empty 'ghost trains' in and out of London on disused lines, that don't stop or take on passengers. Eg: Chiltern to West Ealing, Overground to Battersea Park, Overground toEnfield via Stratford, and Southeastern to Beckenham.

The longest train station name:

It is *Llanfairpwllgwyngyllgogerychwyrndrobwllllantysiliogogogoch*' with 58 letters which is in Wales in the UK. The station serves the village of Llanfairpwllgwyngyll.

The highest railway bridge:

It is a steel and concrete arch bridge between Bakkal and Kauri in the Reasi district of Jammu and Kashmir, India, over the Chenab river.It is 35 m higher than the iconic Eiffel Tower in Paris.The bridge has a total length of 473.25 m, the viaduct is 120 m, and it is supported by 96 cables. The overall weight of the arch is 10,619 MT.

A station without an entrance or an exit:

It is Seiryu-Miharashi station in Nishikigawa Seiryu line in Southern Japan where the passengers could get off the train and enjoy for 10 minutes, the stunning landscape of Nishiki River and the surrounding forest from the platform provided on the river bank.

Secret station hidden under the ground:

A secret station named 'Track 61' hidden deep below New York's Grand Central Station and the Waldorf Astoria, the city's first skyscraper hotel, was supposed to transport VIPs including President Franklin D. Roosevelt.

The longest railway platform:

The platform form no. 1 of Hubli Junction (SSS Hubballi Junction) in Karnataka having a length of 1505m, making it the longest railway platform in the world as of March 2021.

- More than 20 countries are there without any railway network, due to one or other reasons. Eg: Oman, Qatar, Kuwait, San Marino, Tonga, Malta, Cyprus, Iceland, etc.
- The total length of railway tracks on Earth is approximately 807,783 miles (1.3 million km), which is about 3.5 times its distance to Moon.

Indian Railways

Two Different Stations at the Same Location:

Indian Railways has two stations Srirampur and Belapur in Ahmednagar, located at the same spot but on opposite sides of the track.

Junction with maximum number of emerging routes:

Mathura Junction railway station, because of its religious value and vast rail connectivity to different cities, 7 railway lines emerge, the maximum railway routes from a single location.

Diamond Crossing of Indian Railways:

In Nagpur, two railway tracks going towards North-South and another two lines going towards East-West make a square shaped lay-out called 'diamond crossing', which is a widely used crossing where railway staff need to be attentive to operate it.

India's Longest Rail Tunnel:

It is Pir Pranjal, located in the Pir Pranjal range of the middle Himalayas in Jammu Kashmir, which is 11.25 kmlong and is in the Jammu- Baramulla railway line.

India's busiest Railway Station:

It is Howrah Junction having 23 platforms handling over 1 million passengers daily. Also, Howrah is also the oldest railway station in India.

India's longest and shortest station names:

The erstwhile Chennai Central railway station, renamed after the legendary actor-turned politician Dr. M.G. Ramachandran 'Puratchi Thalaivar Dr. M.G. Ramachandran Central Railway Station' (57 letters) is the longest railway station name in India.

'Od', on the Anand–Godhra section of Western Railway zone (Gujarat) and 'Ib', near Jharsuguda (Odisha) are the shortest station names in India.

REFERENCES AND SUGGESTED READINGS

1. *Arora N.* L., 'Transportation Engineering', New India Pub., 1977.
2. *Subramanian K.* P., 'Transportation Engineering', Scitech Publications, Chennai, 2015.
3. Saxena S. C. and Arora S. P., 'A Text Book of Railway Engineering', Dhanpat Rai Publications, New Delhi.
4. Rangwala, 'Railway Engineering', Charotar Publishing house Pvt.Ltd., Anand, Gujarat, 2017.
5. Birdi, Ahuja, 'Roads, Railways, Bridges and Tunnel Engineering', Standard Book House, New Delhi.
6. Bindra S.P. and Bindra K.,'Elements of Bridges, Tunnel and Railway Engineering', Dhanpat Rai Publications, New Delhi.
7. Antia K. F.,'Railway track', The New Book Co.Pvt. Ltd., Bombay, 1960.
8. Mundrey J. S., 'Railway Track Engineering', Mc Graw Hill India, New Delhi, 2017.
9. https://nptel.ac.in/courses/105107123
10. https://www.smartzworld.com/notes/transportation-engineering-pdf-notes-te-pdf-notes/
11. https://jntukucen.ac.in/ebook_files/166.pdf

APPENDICES

APPENDIX-A: Suggestive Template for Practicals

Aim

Explain briefly the aim of the experiment.

Relevance

Explain the industrial relevance of the experiment in your own words.

Requirements

List out all the required apparatus along with their proper specifications.

Procedure, Observations and **Inference**

Explain the step-wise procedure of the experiment and note the observations properly. On the basis of observations certain inference is to be made. You may use a table similar to that given below:

Step No.	Procedure	Observation	Inference
1			
2			
3			

Video / Animation

If possible, you can go through some video/animation to visualize the steps physically.

Calculations

Calculate properly all the required physical quantities essential for your experiment.

Result and Discussion

Obtain the final result and present it in proper units, and discuss about it considering the errors which might be introduced during your experiment, as well as the standards required/acceptable limits for the test results.

Conclusions

Finally give your conclusion based on the obtained results.

Validation of the result in the experiment

Try to validate the result of the experiment in real life scenario.

Use of ICT

You can also study the experiment using the available online resources. They are useful as there is no time constraint at all. Some of which are listed (not limited to) below:

https://swayam.gov.in

https://nptel.ac.in

https://www.swayamprabha.gov.in

Note for Instructor and Lab-Technicians:

Some general and specific instructions are listed separately [see Annexure V] for laboratory preparation, maintenance, safety aspects, etc. Laboratory Instructor and Lab-Technicians can follow those instructions properly to run the laboratory smoothly without any hazard.

APPENDIX-B: Indicative Evaluation Guidelines for Practicals / Projects / Activities in Group

Process Related Skills

Criteria and Level	Developing	Competent	Proficient
Handling the Set-up			
Recording of Data			
Time management			
Team Work			
Individual Work			
Safety Precautions			

Product Related Skills

Criteria and Level	Developing	Competent	Proficient
Content			
Research/Survey			
Use of latest Technology			
Stays on Topic			
Preparedness			
Confidence of Presentation			
ICT usage including presentation-making skill			
Time Management			
Group Efforts			
Individual Efforts			

APPENDIX-C: Assessments Aligned to Bloom's Level

Bloom's Taxonomy — It has been coupled into the following two categories for development of Questions in the Exercises of every unit in this book as given below:

Category I Questions	Category II Questions *(Higher order thinking skills)*
Bloom's Level 1: *Remember* Bloom's Level 2: *Understand* Bloom's Level 3: *Apply*	Bloom's Level 4: *Analyse* Bloom's Level 5: *Evaluate* Bloom's Level 6: *Create*

APPENDIX-D: Records for Practicals

Sl. No.	Page No.	Name of the Experiment	Date			Marks	Signature
			Actual	Repeat	Remarks		
1		Design of Geometrics of highway					
2		Combined flakiness and elongation index (CI) of aggregates					
3		Angularity Number Test					
4		Aggregate Impact Test					
5		Los Angeles Abrasion Test					
6		Aggregate Crushing Test					
7		Penetration Test on Bitumen					
8		Ductility Test					
9		Softening point test					
10		Flash point and Fire point test					
11		Study on distress in road pavements and remedial measures					
12		Study on features of Hill Roads					
13		Study on features of drainage system of Roads					
14		Study on Rail fixtures and fastenings					
15		Study on Railway stations and yards					

ANNEXURES

Annexure-I: Some general and specific instructions for working in the laboratory

General Instructions:

1. In the laboratory, work quietly and cautiously. Remember the main purpose of doing any experiment is to make faithful measurements.
2. Always share equally all the steps of the work with your partner.
3. Presentations of data in tabular form, graphs and calculations should be done correctly, legibly and sincerely.
4. Be always honest at the time of recording and presenting the experimental data.
5. It is very important to keep in mind that never make up readings or doctor them to get a better fit of the graph as per theory. If any reading appears incorrect, you have to repeat the measurement again and again to find the source of error.
6. At the time of drawing the graph all the data obtained from experiment are to be properly plotted.
7. Remember that the experiments are designed properly for the objective of learning the topic and also for the verification of the knowledge that you have gathered.
8. By doing the experiment at your own interest only, it is possible to be familiar with all the fine points and to expose you to the equipment.
9. Always perform the experiment with an attitude of learning and with your interest to verify the theoretical knowledge that you have gathered.
10. Be very particular to arrive in time in the laboratory and always with proper preparation with a clear knowledge about the experiment.

Specific Instructions:

5.35. While doing the experiment, it is important to note down all the observations neatly and legibly in the observation book.

5.36. The recorded data entered in the observation book are to be confirmed by your instructor before leaving the laboratory.

5.37. All the students doing the same experiment have to maintain individual copy of the recorded data. The laboratory notebook / observation book is required to bring in the laboratory regularly when you come for doing the experiment.

5.38. Graphs, if any, are to be drawn properly at the end of each experiment. For this you need to know how to optimize on usage of graph paper. Remember all the repeated data are to be accommodated on a single graph sheet, if possible. Graphs are to be labeled properly along with the axes showing the corresponding units.

5.39. The laboratory hours should be utilized fully, and should not leave the laboratory before the completion of the working hours. If you finish the experiment early, you may spend the remaining time to complete the calculations and necessary graphs for which you are supposed to come equipped with calculators, pencils and scale.

REFERENCES FOR FURTHER LEARNING

1. Garber, N. J., and Hoel, L. A., 'Traffic and Highway Engineering", PWS Publishing Co., New York, 1999.
2. Bateman J. H., 'Introduction to Highway engineering'. John Wiley & Sons Inc.
3. Ritter, L. J., Paquettte, R. J., 'Highway engineering', The Ronald Press Co.
4. IRC, 'Geometric Design standards for Rural (Non-urban) Highways', IRC:73-1980, Indian Roads Congress, New Delhi, 1980.
5. *Oglesby C.H.,* 'Highway Engineering', John Wiley & Sons, New York.
6. *IRC,* 'Guidelines for the design and construction of Cement concrete pavements for Rural Roads', IRC: Sp: 62-2004, Indian Roads Congress, New Delhi.
7. *IRC,* 'Guidelines for the design of Flexible pavements for Low volume Roads', IRC: SP: 72-2007, Indian Roads Congress, New Delhi.
8. *IRC,* 'Guidelines for Wet Mix Macadam',, IRC: 109-1997, Indian Roads Congress, New Delhi.
9. *IRC,* 'Standard Specifications and Code of practice for Water bound Macadam', IRC: 19-2005, Indian Roads Congress, New Delhi.
10. *IRC,* 'Specifications for Bituminous Macadam', IRC: 27-2007, Indian Roads Congress, New Delhi.
11. *IRC,* 'Standard Specifications and Code of practice for construction of concrete roads', IRC: 15-2011, Indian Roads Congress, New Delhi.
12. *MORTH, 'Specifications for Road and Bridge Works',* Indian Roads Congress, New Delhi, 2016.
13. https://nptel.ac.in/courses/105101087
14. https://www.smartzworld.com/notes/transportation-engineering-pdf-notes-te-pdf-notes/
15. https://jntukucen.ac.in/ebook_files/166.pdf
16. https://knowledge4civil.wordpress.com/2016/12/12/highway-alignment-and-survey/

CO AND PO ATTAINMENT TABLE

Course outcomes (COs) for this course can be mapped with the programme outcomes (POs) after the completion of the course and a correlation can be made for the attainment of POs to analyze the gap. After proper analysis of the gap in the attainment of POs necessary measures can be taken to overcome the gaps.

Table for CO and PO attainment

Course Outcomes	Attainment of Programme Outcomes (1- Weak Correlation; 2- Medium correlation; 3- Strong Correlation)						
	PO1	PO2	PO3	PO4	PO5	PO6	PO7
CO1							
CO2							
CO3							
CO4							
CO5							

The data filled in the above table can be used for gap analysis.

INDEX